★ NANNY STATE ★

NANNY STATE

How Food Fascists, Teetotaling Do-Gooders, Priggish Moralists, and Other Boneheaded Bureaucrats Are Turning America into a Nation of Children

DAVID HARSANYI

BROADWAY BOOKS
NEW YORK

PUBLISHED BY BROADWAY BOOKS

Published in the United States by Broadway Books, an imprint of
The Doubleday Broadway Publishing Group, a division of
Random House, Inc., New York.
www.broadwaybooks.com

Book design by Diane Hobbing of Snap-Haus Graphics

Library of Congress Cataloging-in-Publication Data
Harsanyi, David.
Nanny state : how food fascists, teetotaling do-gooders, priggish moralists, and other boneheaded bureaucrats are turning America into a nation of children / David Harsanyi. — 1st ed.
p. cm.
Includes bibliographical references and index.
1. Social control—United States. 2. Civil rights—United States. I. Title.
HM661H37 2007
303.3'60973—dc22
2007012239

ISBN 978-0-7679-2432-0

PRINTED IN THE UNITED STATES OF AMERICA

10 9 8 7 6 5 4 3 2 1

First Edition

For Carla

Of all tyrannies a tyranny sincerely exercised for the good of its victims may be the most oppressive. It may be better to live under robber barons than under omnipotent moral busybodies. The robber baron's cruelty may sometimes sleep, his cupidity may at some point be satiated; but those who torment us for our own good will torment us without end, for they do so with the approval of their own conscience.

—C. S. Lewis

Can any of you seriously say the Bill of Rights could get through Congress today? It wouldn't even get out of committee.

—F. Lee Bailey

CONTENTS

★ NANNY STATE ★

★ INTRODUCTION ★

TYRANNY OF THE BUSYBODY

The free man owns himself. He can damage himself with either eating or drinking; he can ruin himself with gambling. If he does he is certainly a damn fool, and he might possibly be a damned soul; but if he may not, he is not a free man any more than a dog.

—C. K. CHESTERTON

Too many people want to save the world.

—CHEAP TRICK

★

WELL-CARED-FOR SLAVES

In 2006, the New York City Council was working overtime to protect its constituents from the myriad of dangers inherent in urban life.

No, I'm not referring to overcrowding, crime, or failing schools. The city council had more imperative items on their agenda. The council's wide-ranging plan included proposed bans on trans fats, aluminum baseball bats, tobacco purchases by adults between the ages of eighteen and twenty, foie gras, pedicabs in parks, new fast-food restaurants in poor neighborhoods, cell phones in upscale restaurants, mail order pharmaceutical plans, candy-flavored cigarettes, gas-station operators adjusting prices more than once daily, and Ringling Bros. and Barnum & Bailey circus operating in Madison Square Garden.

Send in the clowns. Because that same year, city officials in San Francisco decreed that cookie-scented strips promoting milk be removed from bus shelters. The council had already instituted "backyard laws," which, among other things, regulated the amount of water in dog bowls, gave building specs for doghouses, and legally changed the official title of a pet owner to "pet guardian." The California state legislature took up a bill that would have prohibited the sale of all light bulbs other than the compact fluorescent kind by the year 2012. Yet another proposal would have transformed the longstanding parental tool of child spanking—even a swat on the rear of a child three or under—to an act punishable by up to a year in jail.

Chicago, once the personification of blue-collar American grit, would not be outdone, as the city council mulled over a measure requiring dog owners to implant an identifying microchip under their pooches' skin. Other suggestions included requiring horses pulling carriages to wear diapers and impounding ice-cream trucks that play excessive music. According to the *Chicago Tribune,* the local council "threatened to use their legislative might to improve living standards for elephants . . . require taxi drivers to wear crisp white shirts and matching pants and socks [and] require cigarette vendors to display photos of diseased lungs prominently."

The crucial work of shielding Americans from . . . well, from everything, is not confined to our largest cities. In Omaha, Nebraska, the city council has banned sledding at popular public hills and ice-skating and ice fishing on frozen ponds and lagoons in city parks. In Colorado, legislators looked into banning loud music in cars and alcohol vapor. In the California towns of Calabasas and Dublin, smoking is now banned—outside.

As you read this, countless do-gooders across the nation are rolling up their sleeves to do the vital work of getting your life straightened out for you. The leaders of this movement affix a higher value to safety, fairness, equality, sobriety, health, pets, other people's children—just about any quixotic thought that you could conjure up—than they do to free will and liberty.

The fact that politicians, bureaucrats, and activists long to be our parents is not new. What is inexplicable, though, is the swiftness with which Americans have allowed these worrywarts to take on the job. It's a dramatic about-face from our traditional attitudes toward overreaching government. Some Americans (still too few) are beginning to wonder: When exactly did we lose our right to be unhealthy, unsafe, immoral, and politically incorrect? What if I *want* to be fat, drunk, immoral, and intolerably foolish?

Silly as such questions may seem, they are legitimate. These days our self-bequeathed nannies have built a low-grade, feel-good tyranny that has downgraded freedom to a mere annoyance, an impediment standing in the way of salubrious living and a morally vigorous lifestyle. To these meddlers, utopia is a smokeless, transfatless world, where alcohol is sipped only in moderation, McDonald's sells Tofu McNuggets with low-fat Marionberry Dipping Sauce, and a pop star's bared nipple is worthy of congressional hearings and mass hysteria.

If you've been paying the least bit of attention the past few years, you've seen these types of laws proliferate at a frightening pace. On a low-grade level, it can mean anything from prohibiting your teenager from using a tanning bed, to outlawing "for sale" signs in your car window (urban blight), to banning low-rider jeans ("coarsening" of society). In this nanny state, you may have to pay a $100 fine for sitting on an upended milk crate or a $25-a-day penalty for failing to clean your home or yard properly. Slackers beware.

In the nanny state, a farmer can be forbidden from selling "unattractive" tomatoes, and for an aquarium owner it can mean getting rid of a genetically modified pet fish. If you're a trick-or-treater, you may soon have to obtain a permit before making your rounds, and if you're handing out candy, get ready to pay an extra tax on those unhealthy sweets. If you're building a new house, you may be mandated to install a toilet that uses 1.6 gallons of water per flush—not 1.7—so get out your measuring cups. If you're flying on a commercial airline, there's a "peanut-free buffer zone" for you to sit in courtesy of Uncle Sam. There are antiobesity initiatives that scrutinize our license plates, fines for "offensive odors," and junior high schools where students are compensated for ratting out their friends.

New York City is home to perhaps the nation's greatest nanny: Democratic assemblyman Felix Ortiz. A *Forbes* magazine profile penned by libertarian journalist Radley Balko revealed that in 2004 Ortiz introduced a law that would require every car sold in New York to come equipped with an ignition interlock device and mandate motorists to blow into a tube and pass an alcohol breath test before the car would start, then perform the test again every twenty to forty minutes.

In the first four months of 2005 Ortiz also introduced laws to prohibit cell-phone use while driving (including hands-free models); ban all pornography from newsstands; force consumers to produce two forms of identification when using a credit card; test all public-school children for diabetes; ban expiration dates on retail gift certificates; forbid alcohol billboard advertisements within a mile of every school and day-care center; require nutritional labeling on restaurant menus; measure the fat of every public-school student; and impose a "fat tax," not just on junk food but also on "videogames, commercials and movies."

But Ortiz would be outdone soon enough. In early 2007, a New York State senator from Brooklyn planned to introduce a bill banning talking on a cell phone, listening to an MP3 player, or using a BlackBerry or any electronic device while crossing the street in New York City. "While people are tuning into their iPods and cell phones, they're tuning out the world around them," Senator Carl Kruger explained.

Yes. That's the point.

In New York, once a monsoon of cultural diversity, quality-of-life campaigns have overtaken the spontaneity and once irrepressible spirit of the city. The leader of this movement is Mayor Michael Bloomberg, a nominal Republican whose only discernible ideological affiliation is nannyism. Bloomberg embraces almost every freedom-busting, micromanagement machinate one could conjure up, from putting extra lights on cars that go off when exceeding the speed limit, to instructing cops to ticket people for talking too loudly (Operation Silent Night), to making New York the first city to ban trans fats and passing one of the most restrictive smoking bans in the nation.

The mayor's nosy ways were the topic of a well-known *Vanity Fair* piece. Editor in chief Graydon Carter decided to get Bloomberg's goat by commissioning an article in 2004 by noted contrarian journalist Christopher Hitchens. The feature was to detail a nanny-busting crime spree across the city. "I Fought the Law in Bloomberg's New York" was an amusing and telling investigation into New York's vapid nannyism. Hitchens breaks as many laws as possible in Bloomberg's New York, which he moans has become the domain of a "mediocre bureaucrat."

> So there are laws that are defensible and unenforceable. And there are laws impossible to infringe. But in the New York of Mayor Bloomberg, there are laws that are not possible to obey, and that nobody can respect and that are enforced by arbitrary power. The essence of tyranny is not iron law. It is capricious law. Tyrants can be petty. And petty is not just Bloomberg's middle name. It is his name.

In flagrant violation of the law, Hitchens lights up a cigarette in a bar and in a luxury car. He feeds pigeons. He sits on an upended milk crate in broad daylight. He places a bag next to him on a subway seat. He attempted to put a plastic frame around his license plate. He rides a bike without placing his feet on the peddles. All of these actions had earned city dwellers summonses in the preceding months.

At first glance, the bills Ortiz and Bloomberg proposed might seem innocuous and well-intentioned, regulations intended to gentrify and morally sanitize a city in need of help. Many times the unintended consequences overshadow any perceived good the regulations had intended in the first place. Inevitably, they rob citizens of free will and create an unhealthy dependency.

SPREADING THE BLAME

The first recorded use of the term "nanny state," it seems, was made by Iain Macleod, who on December 3, 1965, wrote about "what I like to call the nanny state . . ." in his *Spectator* column "Quoodle." What exactly does the term mean to us? Well, unmistakably the nanny state is a place where government takes a hyperinterest in micromanaging the welfare of its citizens, shielding us from our own injurious and irrational behavior. Sadly, the new babysitter state has transcended that definition.

The nanny state is a nation plagued by cowardly elected officials—men and women who refuse to protect my autonomy and my right to be unwholesome, degenerate, or offensive. And while legislators deserve a great deal of the blame, so do government appointees like the surgeon general, the secretary of transportation, and the folks at the Centers for Disease Control, all of whom have expanded their mission from cautioning us about the dangers of "oversized" candy and love handles, to proselytizing, peddling politically motivated studies, and advocating laws that force us to comply with their wishes.

Enter the complicit media—always searching for exhilarating copy involving death, pestilence, and the afflicted—that eats up every word and regurgitates it as overwrought news and terrifying headlines.

All of the above organizations are inordinately influenced by an explosion of private-interest organizations, "concerned" citizen groups, and "family values" activists that have pumped hundreds of millions of dollars into marketing campaigns which consistently inflame public opinion and scare the holy crap out of us.

These are the high priests and safety fetishists of the nanny state. Veterans like Michael Jacobson, executive director of the Center for Science in the Public Interest (where neither science nor public interest is relied upon); Kelly Brownell, director of the Rudd Center for Food Policy and Obesity at Yale, one of the leading lights of food control; and John Banzhaf, who has, through litigation, made us submit to his own priggish predilections for four decades.

In an ideal world, karma would decree that these irritating and dangerous activists be taken behind the woodshed by a dozen minutemen reenactors for a momentous ass-kicking—with a post-beating lecture on the Founding Fathers, of course. But the world is far from perfect. Instead, these wardens of well-being are endlessly trotted out on morning and cable news programs, issuing distraught statements about the societal catastrophes that are ice cream and Girl Scout Cookies.

THE REVOLUTION THAT NEVER WAS

In his 1996 State of the Union address, President Bill Clinton felt the need to let Americans know the era of big government had ended. This curious assertion was meant to allay the growing concerns of Americans, who had begun to see government as stepping over the bounds of its charge.

Clinton's words rang hollow. In many respects, the big government was simply refocusing, consolidating, and beginning to cast its eye toward regulating private matters that had previously been out of bounds. "Big" intrusive government was now also in the hands of local city councils, which could often put the big boys to shame.

Though Republican Speaker of the House Newt Gingrich started getting crabby about the nanny state in the mid-1990s, by the time

George W. Bush, a Republican—purportedly the party of less intrusive government—was elected to his second term in 2004, the new and improved nanny state was only expanding its authority. "We have a responsibility that, when somebody hurts, government has got to move," explained President Bush on Labor Day 2003. Twenty years ago, this kind of brazen promotion of the state would have been unheard of coming from the lips of any respectable Republican—and barely any Democrats would have dared to give voice to it.

In 1997, vice president and future presidential candidate Al Gore explained that government was "like grandparents in the sense that grandparents perform a nurturing role." The word "nurturing" was perhaps too delicate for conservative Andrew Card, George Bush's chief of staff during the 2004 presidential election, who framed the idea in a more red-state, family-friendly lingo, explaining that the president "sees America as we think about a ten-year-old child." This was an evolution of sorts from Bush's fairly restrained proclamation in the 2000 race that "government must be carefully limited, but strong and active."

Today, politicians of both parties brazenly endorse nanny policies in response to the slightest anxiety or unsettling development. Many Americans have felt the government's evolution from strong and active to smothering grandparent. In 1995, a Gallup Poll found that 39 percent of Americans believed that "the federal government has become so large and powerful that it poses an immediate threat to the rights and choices of ordinary citizens." When the word "immediate" was removed from the question, 52 percent of Americans agreed. By late 2006, a CNN poll found that an overwhelming majority of Americans believe that the size and cost of government is intrusive. When asked about their views on the role of government, 54 percent of respondents said that "it was trying to do too many things that should be left to individuals and businesses." Only 37 percent believed that government should do more.

Who could be surprised by the results? The index for the Code of Federal Regulations alone is more than a thousand pages, spanning some fifty separate volumes and growing. Americans can hardly pay their taxes, not only because they are overtaxed (which they often are) but because it is becoming progressively more difficult to figure out how without hiring a professional. The United States tax code is more than 7.5 million words, runs 38,000 pages, and is unintelligible to the common human being. The entire United States Constitution and Bill of Rights, on the other hand, are less than ten pages long combined.

After reading those few venerable pages, it is not a stretch to conclude that the Founding Fathers had absolutely no intention of permitting the state to claw its way into the most private aspects of its citizens' lives. Incontrovertibly, the founders would have regarded bans on silicone breast enhancement and children's tag as beyond the realm of government participation. The framers appreciated the hazards of an overreaching state and left us with a functional set of rules that protect us from government and one another.

Happiness, or at any rate the pursuit of it, was tethered to the pillars of liberty and responsibility. One could not work without the other. And from those concepts comes our extraordinary right to be wrong, dumb, and irresponsible.

At least, it used to be so.

The questions we are forced to ask ourselves now are: What happens next year? Where do we go next legislative session? Can we reverse the current trend and regain a semblance of rational government? Or has our traditional understanding of government's role changed forever?

In the United Kingdom, according to a recent survey, three-quarters of the population desire more government intervention to discourage people from unhealthy habits—ideas we're starting to see at home: bans on junk-food advertising; laws to limit amounts of salt, sugar, and fat in foods; bans on happy hours and ladies' nights. In Ireland, Italy, Scotland, and many other European nations, countrywide smoking bans have been enacted. Across Europe, thousands of nannyistic laws, most of which make U.S.-style paternalism seem like lawless abandon, are enacted each year.

There can be serious repercussions in such a state. The Asian nation of Singapore is known as the world's leading nanny state. Lee Kuan Yew, the celebrated former prime minster of that nation, wrote in his memoirs: "We would have been a grosser, ruder, cruder society had we not made these efforts to persuade people to change their ways," and later, "If this is a 'nanny state,' I am proud to have fostered one."

Yew may have been proud—and certainly he was successful, as Singapore is one of the most prosperous nations in the world—but at what price? In 1999, *The Economist* dubbed Singapore the "world execution capital." For years, media coverage in the nation was stifled, opposition political leaders jailed, and endless draconian nanny rules imposed on the population, from penalties for infractions like spitting or chewing gum to detention without a trial for nonviolent acts against the government. "Freedom of the press . . . must be subordinated to the overriding needs of Singapore," Yew told the International Press Institute's assembly in 1971.

This book will illustrate that, while we're still a long way from Singapore's access, nannyism is a growing problem and a dangerous slippery slope. The more government feels comfortable subverting our right to live as we wish—while not hurting others—simply to create a more agreeable society, the state will feel increasingly comfortable sabotaging our rights on all fronts.

★ ★ ★

I often hear: What are you, one of those antigovernment extremists? We need laws, you anarchist. We need to protect children. We need to promote a healthy and safe society.

True. And one of the difficulties in exposing the nanny state is accurately defining a nanny law. There is some unavoidable flexibility in this regard. After all, a social conservative may deem smoking bans a shameful betrayal of property rights and personal freedom, but then call a local radio talk show and demand that the Pussycat Parlor strip club be boarded up immediately for the common good. Similarly, a progressive environmentalist may campaign for the immediate banning of all paper bags in supermarkets, but then laugh heartily at the absurdity of a dildo ban in Alabama.

Many have heard Supreme Court Justice Potter Stewart's thoughts on a case involving a theater showing a French motion picture called *The Lovers.* The film featured a brief, albeit, for its day, titillating sex scene. Stewart concurred with the majority in overturning the original obscenity conviction of the theater, reasoning that the film wasn't pornography and was therefore protected speech under the First Amendment. Yet even with the sureness of his opinion, Stewart had a surprisingly difficult time nailing down the definition of pornography. Until, that is, he distinguished himself forever with a brilliant epiphany of intuitive reasoning, proclaiming: "I know it when I see it."

Stewart's explanation of pornography should not be construed as an evasive answer. It is, actually, the standard we apply to all abstract notions. It's called common sense. And though tragically underutilized, common sense is as valuable as any cerebral skill. It is also one of the better devices—though not the only one—for sniffing out a nanny law: you know it when you see it. Political satirist P. J. O'Rourke once described the basic tenets of governance in a free society as: "Mind your own business. Keep your hands to yourself."

The intrusions discussed in this book are neither cloaked in partisan ideology or very tricky to ferret out. For those Americans who don't hold an inflexible libertarian political viewpoint—and judging from every election, that includes an overwhelming majority of you—we accepted that certain vices like prostitution and illicit drugs are distasteful and immoral enough that government should intercede on our behalf. Though I may personally disagree with the foundation and argue the consequences of such regulations, *Nanny State* will not assert that government bans and strict regulations are in and of themselves a nannyistic endeavor. Prejudices against prostitution and drugs have grown organically over hundreds of years of cultural, religious, and communal debate.

Nanny State will make a case that nanny laws—which began in earnest with seat-belt regulations and compulsory helmet wearing in the 1980s—exist because government, with the help of an infinitesimal minority of busybodies, has twisted the public's arm into obedience. *Nanny State* will argue that there is no excuse for government to protect a mentally stable citizen from making his or her own choices and that words and ideas like "freedom" and "responsibility" must again be injected into any conversation or debate about laws that affect personal behavior.

This book will argue that the populace—more educated and informed than ever before—are also more than able to make decisions about how they live their own lives. It will argue that protecting the right to make those decisions is not, at the end of the day, ideological but rather what most Americans would call common sense.

The question is: Why are we allowing it to happen?

★ ★ ★

There is good news. In the United States, our historical propensity to question authority is far greater than the need to control and homogenize society. This is why nannyism can't work here. The notion is anathema to the spirit of the American people. And *Nanny State* will spend considerable space documenting a disparate group of colorful and peculiar characters that is fighting this growing threat.

Americans are beginning to realize that this incremental loss of liberty is damaging and no longer simply an inconvenience. The phrase "nanny state" is becoming commonplace in the American political and cultural vernacular for that very reason. Mainstream news organizations have (tepidly) picked up the coverage of these battles over meddling legislation. The trouble is, the media seldom frame nannyism as what it is: a concerted movement. Without understanding it in that context we won't appreciate the full implications of a nanny state. Nannyism is a dogma. The nanny state is a collective that may not share a single driving political purpose, but its proponents do share a belief that sticking their nose into your business is the fastest way to build a superior society.

Nanny State will detail many, though far from all, of the most unambiguous and mature nanny infringements, intrusions into what we eat, what we drink, where we smoke, how we raise our children, our morality and business lives. By assembling so many of these incursion in one book, I hope those who read it will begin to see nannyism as a concerted movement and have a better understanding of how dangerous these laws are to our freedom.

Finally, this book is not a manifesto of indifference (because certainly we must help the least fortunate among us) or an endorsement of indulgence (because only a fool would deny that smoking leads to all kinds of miserable diseases, obesity is a wretchedly unhealthy state, and drinking . . . well, drinking is almost always fun—

but don't drive!) but a book about freedom, personal responsibility, and free will. It isn't about ignoring the hazardous decisions we make, it's about being able to exercise our right to make those decisions in the first place.

While we still can.

★ CHAPTER ONE ★

TWINKIE FASCISTS

The proverb warns that "you should not bite the hand that feeds you." But maybe you should. If it prevents you from feeding yourself.

—THOMAS SZASZ

Never trust a dog to watch your food.

—UNKNOWN

★

GUARDIANS OF YOUR GULLET

The fashionable eastside neighborhood of Oakhurst in Decatur, Georgia, is the last place you would imagine that an establishment like Mulligan's could survive. The area, once teeming with drug dealers and home to some of the highest crime rates in the area, has undergone an astonishing gentrification the past few years. Today, Oakhurst is home to countless upwardly mobile couples inhabiting refurbished Craftsman bungalows with luxurious baby joggers sitting unattended on front lawns.

Mulligan's, located at the end of a nondescript parking lot, is a restaurant, sports bar—and counterrevolutionary enterprise. Here, I imagine, patrons would be capable of coalescing into an armed insurgency should some squeamish busybody suggest mandating smaller food portions. Mulligan's is perhaps best known for its glorious Luther Burger—purportedly named after a favorite midnight nibble of the late R&B crooner Luther Vandross. The Luther Burger is your standard bacon cheeseburger with a Krispy Kreme doughnut substituting for the traditional bun.

What's not to like?

But there's more. A lot more. Mulligan's ratchets up the fun quotient by serving a nutritionist's nightmare known as the Hamdog. This treat begins as a hot dog, sure, but then that sucker is wrapped in a beef patty, which is then, for good measure, deep fried and covered with cheese, chili, onions, a fried egg, and a heaping portion of fries. If you want a side of deep-fried Twinkies and a large soda, go for it.

Mulligan's fame—or perhaps you could call it infamy—has spread far beyond the confines of this neighborhood. During a *Tonight Show* monologue, Jay Leno described the particulars of the notorious Luther Burger, eliciting big laughs. The Krispy Kreme corporation has joined the fun, teaming up with an Illinois minor league team called the Gateway Grizzlies to create "Baseball's Best Burger," a thousand-calorie cheeseburger sandwiched between a sliced glazed doughnut.

★ ★ ★

Why am I hanging out here? To make a point. A free citizen exercising my right to eat the most sinfully unwholesome foods I could find in this great nation. Because, you know, not everyone finds the Hamdog as entertaining or as tempting as I do. Which is their prerogative, of course. But there are growing numbers of officious activists who would like to deny me the self-determination and pleasure of eating a Hamdog or Luther Burger.

This group of finger-wagging activists advocate enhanced government control over choice. Many folks call this particular breed of militant nanny the food police. Legendary radio personality Paul Harvey once referred to them as "the guardians of your gullet." I like to call them Twinkie Fascists—among other less polite monikers. And though this movement is still in its infancy, the Twinkie Fascists are gaining momentum and influence at a startling pace.

As with all realms of nannyism, this attack on freedom and choice is fueled by good intentions. Nannies will do whatever they can to stop us from eating via city, state, or federal regulations. They'll use litigation to limit our choices and engage in government-sponsored scaremongering, penalizing food manufacturers, restaurants, or consumers with specialized taxes.

With that in mind, I decide to go all out. I order a Hamdog. It's perfect. Huge. Greasy. Impudently harmful to my health. Nicholas Lang, a professor of surgery at the University of Arkansas for Medical Sciences, once told the Associated Press if "you choke that [Hamdog] down, you might as well find a heart surgeon because you are going to need one." But what does he know? Nannies are always so melodramatic. And sure enough, after that first bite my heart doesn't explode.

Yet the truth is that despite the scrumptiousness of the Hamdog, I could only finish half. As a human being, it seems that I possess a certain level of self-control. I gather that if I, a dreadfully weak and easily seduced man, can control myself, most Americans can do even better. Most can still find pleasure in eating and reward in self-control. Two concepts that nannies, it seems, can't wrap their minds around.

PLUMP FICTION

The Centers for Disease Control and Prevention (CDC) offices are, as luck would have it, only a short drive from Mulligan's. The offices are more like a compound. This place is busy. When the CDC began as a single-floor operation more than forty years ago, it was responsible for investigating malaria and related maladies, but these days the organization deals with virtually all facets of public health, from preventing and controlling infectious and chronic diseases, to workplace hazards, to disabilities and other environmental health threats.

The CDC has a new agenda: the peculiar job not only of discouraging folks from engaging in avoidable habits but of becoming part of a propaganda war that shocks Americans. That's what happened when the CDC held a well-publicized news conference in March of 2004 to announce a new troubling study that alleged overeating was responsible for an extraordinary death toll: 400,000

Americans in 2000—a 33 percent jump from 1990. According to the report obesity was well on its way to surpassing smoking as the nation's top preventable cause of death. "Our worst fears were confirmed," claimed Dr. Julie Gerberding, the CDC's director and an author of the study.

The significance of the study was bolstered by the presence of then-secretary of the Department of Health and Human Services Tommy Thompson. "Americans need to understand," he grimly noted, "that overweight [*sic*] and obesity are literally killing us." As a matter of fact, the federal government promised to lend a helping hand to stop the madness to the tune of $400 million in research.

Imagine what sort of good that $400 million might have done in research on, say, cancer. Instead, the CDC had taken the first step toward creating an environment where intrusive public policy thrives. They vowed to revise food labels and to launch a public-awareness and education campaign to stop the mess—but that was only the beginning. Food was "literally" killing us by the hundreds of thousands each year, which called for more action.

To help perpetuate an atmosphere of panic, doom-and-gloom headlines blared across newspapers nationwide. (Leave it to the histrionic New York tabloids to excel at jolting the public: "Digging Graves with Our Teeth: Obesity Rivals Smoking as Killer" read the New York *Daily News*, and "Dying to Eat—Weight Woe Nears Cigs as Top Killer" countered the *New York Post*.) Journalists detailed the catastrophe french fry by french fry. The report sparked hundreds of opinion pieces that examined various ways the government—federal, state, and city—could step in and rescue us from this eruption of fat.

The problem was that the report wasn't exactly true. And although Americans hear distraught commentary from pundits, nutritionists, and nannies, there were many scientists and statisticians who were more skeptical about the CDC's extraordinary claims. Soon enough, these intellectually honest men and women began jabbing holes in the report.

The first salvo came in May 2004, in the pages of *Science* magazine. The investigative piece claimed that some researchers, including a few at the CDC itself, dismissed the report's prediction, maintaining that the underlying data of the report were quite unconvincing. One detractor within the CDC characterized the core data in the report as "loosey-goosey." Critics largely objected to the addition to the obesity category of deaths attributed to poor nutrition. It was a stat that, considering the vagaries of life, was impossible to quantify.

Even within the walls of the CDC, a source told *Science*, internal discussions could get contentious. Several epidemiologists at the CDC and the National Institutes of Health also had concerns about the numbers, yet before the publication of the report, some within the agency felt that the conclusions weren't debatable because of organizational pressure. One apprehensive CDC staff member went as far as to allege that he wouldn't speak out truthfully for fear of losing his job—not exactly the dynamic and transparent environment that scientific discovery thrives in. But then again, sometimes getting the right answer trumps discerning the prickly truth.

The second blow came, and it was even more damning. *The Wall Street Journal* published a front-page story in November of 2004, running a litany of errors that swamped the dramatic death number. The paper noted that the study had "inflated the impact of obesity on the annual death toll by tens of thousands due to statistical errors." In a follow-up story, the *Journal* reported that due to additional troubles with methodology the actual number of obesity-related deaths might be less than half of the 400,000 originally estimated in the CDC study.

But that didn't stop many nannies from brandishing the dubious numbers until the CDC was finally forced to disclose their gross miscalculation. With a different team of CDC scientists and more recent data, they revised their numbers to 112,000 deaths a year. In April 2005, *The Journal of the American Medical Association* put the CDC out of its misery, publishing its own study on the impact of obesity, which revealed a radically revised estimation. It concluded that obesity actually was responsible for around 25,000 American deaths each year. In other words, 375,000 fewer deaths than the CDC had originally maintained.

Oops.

Most news outlets had little to say on the revised numbers. The obesity "epidemic" was a great story, a jumping-off point to a nation under siege from corporate burger peddlers. The CDC, hoping to distract from their gross over-calculation, dispatched a disease detective to states like West Virginia to get the lowdown on the epidemic.

Getting people worried was precisely the point. That's step one. The next step was to figure out how to save people from themselves. Could they close down all the fast-food restaurants? Tax them heavily enough to convince people not to enter the golden archways? Could they coerce residents into morning calisthenics? Impose dietary restrictions or portion restriction at restaurants? Ban cookies? Ban commercials? Why not?

OUR PANIC DU JOUR

Chandler Goff once claimed that there was no practical way he could calculate the fat or caloric content of Mulligan's delectable dishes.

I believe him. And I'm thankful.

As a public service, however, Goff affixes a note at the bottom of each menu that advises diners to "have the sense to realize that although delicious, we do not recommend eating fried foods every day." Goff also urges his patrons to exercise regularly and get an annual physical. "These [dishes] are great pleasures," according to Goff. "You don't want to eat this every day." Goff's message is considerate, but unnecessary. One imagines the majority of Mulligan's customers—as well as the greater part of the nation—do not plan on persisting on a diet of Hamdogs and deep-fried Twinkies.

Unlike other spheres of nannyism—alcohol and tobacco, for instance—every one of us partakes of food. Even the healthiest among us eats insalubrious treats on occasion. Likewise, most of us have turned down that second Boston cream doughnut or pushed aside those last few curly fries. We realize the consequences. And once we recognize that it's possible to turn away food, hit the treadmill, or eat salad instead of steak, we appreciate that it's within the capacity of the other humans to follow suit.

Americans are paying more attention to nutrition. According to a 2006 Associated Press poll, nearly 80 percent of Americans claim they inspect labels on food they buy at grocery stores. The study goes on to state that of Americans between the ages of eighteen and twenty-nine, an age group that has less caloric worries, 39 percent check out the calories on the product first. That doesn't mean that these folks don't buy the product if they discover that it's unhealthy. It only means that they're not being fooled.

Yet even with the heightened understanding of nutrition, nannies will attempt to dismiss personal responsibility. Margo Wootan of the Center for Science in the Public Interest (CSPI), for instance, argues that Americans have "got to move beyond personal responsibility." The CSPI also asserts that obesity "is not merely a matter of individual responsibility. Such suggestions are naïve and simplistic."

Let's pause momentarily to be suitably disgusted by this comment. The idea that we should "get past" personal responsibility is as ludicrous as it is un-American. It cuts to the heart of what freedom is about: choices. Right *and* wrong.

Marion Nestle is another veteran of the food-police movement that has claimed that expecting individuals to practice free will was akin to "blaming the victim." Nestle, a New York University nutritionist and author of *Food Politics: How the Food Industry Influences Nutrition and Health,* has frequently equated what food manufacturers do to the actions of Big (bad) Tobacco, insinuating that both industries are pushers of hazardous addictions on children. To many nannies, a nicotine addiction (which leads to cancer) and a sugar "addiction" (which most often leads to scrumptious treats) are morally analogous. And if it were true, Häagen-Dazs and Breyers would be as complicit in harming Americans as R. J. Reynolds.

That's what Nestle would have you believe. And she's not above throwing around controversial CDC numbers to make her point: "The combination of poor diet, sedentary lifestyle and excessive alcohol consumption contributes to about 400,000 of the two million or so annual deaths in the U.S., about the same number and proportion affected by cigarette smoking." Thus Nestle wonders why sellers "of food products do not attract the same kind of attention as purveyors of drugs or tobacco. They should."

Notwithstanding the unfiltered noise coming from these corners, free will is still a popular idea with the average American. In a recent poll conducted by Dutko Worldwide, callers asked "who bears the greatest responsibility for obesity in the United States—individuals, parents, doctors, schools, restaurants, food companies or nutrition educators." An unambiguous majority of repondents (63 percent) said that "individuals themselves" bear the greatest responsibility for what they put in their mouths. This was followed by parents (22 percent). A minute number blamed corporate food providers (4 percent) or restaurants (2 percent) or even schools (1 percent). These numbers tell us that food nannies have a long road ahead in convincing the typical American that free will is a simplistic idea that needs to be overcome.

★ ★ ★

The fact that many Americans eat their food outside of the home is another point of consternation for nannies. In June 2006, a 136-page report prepared by the Keystone Center, an education and public group based in Keystone, Colorado, found that Americans consume one-third of their daily calories outside their homes. The accelerating pace of everyday life, our growing prosperity, and ever-improving choices means that Americans are more inclined to eat out.

The report, funded by the Food and Drug Administration, was in part a means to search for the most prudent way to "help" consumers manage their intake at the nearly 900,000 restaurants and food establishments in the United States. "We must take a serious look at the impact these foods are having on our waistlines," explained Penelope Slade Royall, assistant secretary for disease prevention and health promotion at the Department of Health and Human Services. The report encourages restaurants to shift the emphasis of their marketing to "lower-calorie choices" and to include more such options on menus. In addition, restaurants were encouraged to cut down on portion sizes.

In an impassioned 2005 letter to the *Chicago Tribune,* Dr. Francine Palma-Long offered up a solution that had been bandied as a possible cure to the gut-busting initiative. Why not just have the state mandate that portion sizes be cut in half at restaurants to fight obesity?

> Cutting portions in fast-food places and restaurants is the only solution. I know it is a novel idea, but we have to do something radical soon to reverse this trend. Many Americans eat at

> least two meals a day outside the home. Studies have shown that people eat more when more is served to them . . .
>
> I implore the surgeon general to demonstrate some leadership and work with the restaurant and fast-food industry to cut portion sizes by one-half to two-thirds in the interest of effectively addressing the obesity epidemic and protecting the health of the American people.

Did we really need a study to show us that people eat more when more food is served to them? What size portions would be acceptable to *The Dallas Morning News*—a newspaper which once warned its readerships that restaurants "are notorious for serving too much food"—or to Dr. Palma-Long or the FDA? And how would mom-and-pop restaurants break down every dish on their menu to live up to these expectations? The Keystone report notes that a laboratory would charge anywhere from $11,000 to $46,000 to analyze an entire menu properly. This is impractical and cost prohibitive for private restaurants prone to alter their menus all the time—unless, of course, these businesses pass the price on to consumers.

Higher prices. Smaller portions. What's not to like?

In 2006, the Chicago City Council did begin debating the pros and cons of regulating portion sizes in restaurants as legislation. An irate Mayor Richard Daley (himself a supporter of a multitude of nanny initiatives) insisted that restaurants suffered smoking and foie gras bans that year and should just be left alone by the city council.

"I'm getting ready for Christmas," he said. "You'd better believe I'm going to eat and drink. You think my family is going to prepare my calorie count at home? . . . How far should government go? Do we have to have a calorie count? Do we put it on you as an employee? Will you be walking around 24 hours a day in restaurants?

How much can we demand from the restaurant industry? Let's take our own responsibility . . . When I go out, I want to enjoy my meal . . . You know what you're going to eat—whether it's a salad, a main meal or a dessert. You know what you're going to have. There's no guilt in that. I don't want people to feel guilty."

★ ★ ★

Besides trying to guilt-trip us, it's also worth mentioning that blanket condemnation of what we eat is shortsighted in numerous other ways. There is some—not overwhelming—instability in what is and isn't considered healthy at any given moment. Not long ago, serving milk to children was an obligation of every American parent . . . well, before it could kill them. The same thing goes for red meat. And eggs. And wine. The dangers of allowing a few self-selected groups and individuals to dictate which products we can or can't ingest is not only dangerous, it's myopic.

Admittedly, as time goes on science gives us a more precise understanding of what is and isn't harmful to our bodies. So feel free to protect yours with some good old-fashioned self-control. And if you believe that the food industry is bent on slathering all things in delicious chocolate—and, certainly, there are worse crimes—you can feel at ease. They're not. All they're interested in is turning a profit. The industry goes about this greedy endeavor by offering goods that consumers are interested in purchasing—you know, like ice cream, cheese, and, yes, even cheeseburgers.

FOOD PORN

What is more red, white, and blue than cheeseburgers? Big business.

In 2005, after years of financial losses and eroding market share,

Hardee's restaurant chain decided to revamp its image. It took a counterintuitive approach, beginning its business revival by tapping into decadent food and targeting the unhealthy twentysomething red-state male.

Hardee's understood that food porn was the ideal vehicle to reignite sales. With a good deal of fanfare, the company introduced the new Monster Thickburger, a progression—or regression, depending on how you look at it—from the original, caloric monstrosity called the Thickburger. Hardee's gave the impression that it was not only consciously trying to serve up an unhealthy dish but eagerly anticipated the coming confrontation with the food police. Hardee's called their new burger a "monument to decadence." The Monster Thickburger, you see, was "assembled" not prepared. It contained 1,420 calories and 107 grams of fat and consisted of two one-third-pound "slabs of prime Angus beef, four strips of bacon, three slices of cheese, mayonnaise on a bun."

Buttered.

According to frustrated CSPI executive director Michael Jacobson, "if the old Thickburger was Food Porn, the new Monster Thickburger is the fast-food equivalent of a snuff film." Hardee's, he went on "seems not only oblivious to America's obesity epidemic, but also to the trend toward healthier fast food."

A "snuff film" is a bit severe, don't you think?

Hardee's chief executive, Andrew Puzder, refused to salute the forces of darkness. Instead, he offered a refreshing retort, letting the world know his product was "not a burger for tree-huggers." As a matter of fact, he went on to say that it was "a burger for young hungry guys who want a really big, delicious, juicy, decadent burger. I hope our competitors keep promoting those healthy products, and we will keep promoting our big, juicy, delicious burgers . . . If you're the romaine lettuce and raspberry vinaigrette crowd, this is not your burger."

Such blatant disregard for "epidemics" did not sit well with the opinion makers on *The New York Times* editorial board, who claimed that Hardee's new Monster Thickburger was "quite possibly one of the most lethal pieces of food out there." Nicholas von Hoffman, a columnist for *The Nation,* wrote that "There is profit in poisoning the population, and lethal food peddling, unlike lethal drug peddling, is legal." (Why corporations would want to poison their customers is still a mystery. It appears to be a counterproductive business model.)

The CSPI, it seems, has a habit of utilizing the word "lethal" to identify perfectly harmless foods. Some brands of chili, according to the CSPI, are not only "oddly spiced" but contain a "borderline lethal dose of sodium." When you top your bagel off with ham, egg, and cheese, you may be happy, but the CSPI states that you are adding "potentially lethal weapons."

Looking past the potential lethality of the Monster Thickburger we are exposed to a startling dishonesty among food nannies. Ostensibly, one of the justifications for imposing regulations on food choices revolves around the notion that irresponsible food providers are not completely forthcoming about the ingredients and health consequences of their products. Hardee's couldn't have been any more forthcoming, actually.

★ ★ ★

Nannies understand the necessity to compartmentalize their grievances by targeting specific ingredients rather than specific brands of food. Creating alarm over trans fats, for example, is far easier than convincing consumers to eat less french fries—an American staple. Trans fats are typically found in partially hydrogenated oils. Trans fats are unhealthy. Yes. Michael Jacobson claims that trans fats are responsible for the death of 30,000 Americans each year.

Unlikely. But the hysteria surrounding trans fats is so out of proportion that it has sent health activists into convulsions and, of course, brought about silly legislation.

"I call it the panic du jour," Dr. David Kritchevsky, a dietary fat and cholesterol researcher at the Wistar Institute, an independent nonprofit research center in Philadelphia, explained to *The New York Times*. Trans fat, he said, "is an easy whipping boy."

In New York this alarm meant that health officials could propose regulations that over a period of time would eliminate all trans fats in cooking oils and margarines everywhere in the city. Everyone, from high-priced bistros to street vendors to fast-food restaurants, would have to switch to "healthier" oils or face a fine of $2,000.

Since New York instituted the ban there has been an explosion of interest in banning trans fats, from Chicago to Massachusetts—to a town near you.

If we can ban one unhealthy ingredient, what stops government from banning many or all of them? The arguments for trans-fat bans are so illogical that once deconstructed you slowly realize that no amount of reason can stop the tidal wave of nannyism. Take Claudia Zapata, a columnist for the *San Antonio Express-News*, who maintained that trans fats were not a "freedom" to protect. "Trans fat is not a liberty. A liberty is a right and a privilege. Trans fat is a wrong that doesn't merit protests or protection."

Dear Lord. Unsaturated fat is now a "wrong"? Can one imagine the subjective, arbitrary, and wide-ranging legislation waiting to sprout? If the pretext for legislation and bans are justified for the "wrong" product, whoever happens to be running the show has a free hand. Isn't alcohol wrong? Is sugar wrong? Pornography? SUVs?

Zapata's right in one sense: trans fat is not a liberty. Taking care of yourself is a liberty—though incrementally it's being stolen by the state. *Choice* is a liberty. Government probing and guarding you from every morsel and polyunsaturated fat you consume is called "dependency."

If you believe trans fats are "a wrong," it's up to you as a consumer to boycott the establishments that use them. A good number of corporations have already seen the economic consequences of carrying food with trans fats and are switching to alternatives.

Not that it is necessarily a positive step.

Kelly Brownell of the Rudd Center for Food Policy and Obesity at Yale University says that the trans-fat ban "represents bold, courageous action by a forward-thinking health commissioner." New York City "deserves a medal," chimed in Jacobson. "The evidence really indicates that there is nothing worse. Switching to butter, palm oil, anything else would be an improvement."

The funny thing is that almost twenty years ago, the CSPI was insisting restaurants switch to partially hydrogenated oil instead of the more unhealthy oils they were using. A CSPI newsletter at the time stated that the hysteria *against* trans fat "just [doesn't] hold up. And by extension, hydrogenated oils seem relatively innocent."

Who can keep up?

The American Heart Association, for one, opposed the New York ban on trans fat. It was concerned that there was no market for healthier alternative oils and that the prohibition would force cooks to substitute partially hydrogenated vegetable oils and shortening with oils high in saturated fat, such as palm and coconut oil—in long run, probably no healthier than trans fats and the reason cooks switched to partially hydrogenated oils in the first place.

THE MARVELOUS MCDIET: LOSE TEN POUNDS IN THIRTY DAYS!

Food nannies face another daunting task when propagating the myth that consumers aren't being provided sufficient alternatives to junk food. These days there are countless magazines *(Health, Men's Health, Women's Health, Organic Family, Fitness, Cooking Light,* to name a few) and television programs (in truth, whole cable networks) devoted to advising and providing healthy alternatives. Consumers have regional and national supermarket chains (Whole Foods, Wild Oats, Earth Fare, Rainbow Blossom Natural Food Markets, to name a very few) where there are healthy alternatives in abundance. Wal-Mart, the world's largest retailer, has begun to carry high-fiber foods, healthy brands, and organic products.

Owning to market pressures and Americans' interest in finding more nutritious and varied foods, nearly every major restaurant chain in America offers some type of healthy alternative on its menu. The best polling we could ever do on attitudes about nutritious food is to watch the market. Healthier selections at chains like Chipotle, Au Bon Pain, Einstein Bros. Bagels, and Subway, along with Thai food, wraps, sushi, and salad bars have all emerged as viable alternatives to traditional fast-food fare. It's no accident. Even the most conventional fast-food operations have begun to modify their menus, offering veggie burgers, skimpy chicken sandwiches, and various salads for those who want to avoid unwholesome fare.

Mulligan's recent menu additions include a mahi-mahi sandwich and fish tacos. "We have to have something for the more anti-fried-meat people," Goff explained.

In fairness, it needs to be pointed out that many of these gourmet markets, like Whole Foods, are typically situated in areas that are either geographically or financially beyond the means of many lower-income Americans. But conventional supermarkets also carry healthy choices, from fruits, beans, and vegetables to low-fat foods of every stripe.

With that said, no one can deny that fast food, like any other industry, has had its share of ugly history. Through his absorbing and detailed investigative book (and movie), *Fast Food Nation,* Eric Schlosser unfurled most of this unpleasant past—the treacherous working conditions in meatpacking plants, hidden health dangers of fast food. (It's when Schlosser's investigation veers off into social criticism that he lapses into platitudes about the evils of corporate America, forgetting the fact that Ronald McDonald doesn't force parents to purchase Happy Meals at the end of a shotgun.)

Yet for every serious critic of fast food, there have been countless reckless and disingenuous ones. Take, as an illustration, Morgan Spurlock's popular junk-science documentary, *Super Size Me.*

Through his documentary, Spurlock persuaded a huge audience that the only possible outcome of venturing into a McDonald's was walking out a slovenly blimp. *The New York Times* found the film not only "entertaining" but "historically significant" and *The Hollywood Reporter* thought it was a "brilliantly subversive" film.

Spurlock was a master at extracting an ounce of truth from a pound of beef. During the filming of *Super Size Me,* Spurlock's achievement was gaining thirty pounds by eating more than 5,000 calories a day at McDonald's, allowing his health to deteriorate precipitously. He complains of headaches, vomiting, and depression.

Is there any alternative to gaining thirty pounds? Well, to find out what happens when a consumer practices a modicum of self-control, even eating full-time at McDonald's, we can turn to Soso

Whaley. A New Hampshire animal trainer, Whaley decided to self-finance a documentary of her experiences, re-creating Spurlock's parameters and challenging his thesis. Her month as an exclusive diner at McDonald's resulted in a completely different conclusion.

Whaley also only ate meals that the fast-food giant offered over the counter. But throughout the filming, Whaley maintained a semi-healthy lifestyle by making discriminating decisions regarding the food she consumed. She also engaged in occasional physical activity. During the making of *Me & Mickey D,* Whaley didn't gain any weight. Actually, she lost ten pounds and lowered her cholesterol.

For cynics who point out that Whaley's physiology may have lent itself to everlasting thinness (and surely, the same then could be said of Spurlock's propensity to expand), there's the case of Merab Morgan. This North Carolina woman lost thirty-seven pounds eating at McDonald's for three months straight. "The average American [Spurlock] was writing that for doesn't have the common sense to realize it is how much you eat that makes you gain weight," she said. Morgan, a construction worker and mother of two, proved that with prudent personal choices we can survive the McDonald's experience.

Did Whaley and Morgan prove that eating at McDonald's was a healthy undertaking? Should we eat anywhere all the time? Not if you care about your body. What they did establish beyond a doubt was that with a measure of self-control, physical activity, and discerning taste, eating at McDonald's 24/7 doesn't mean you need to lose all self-control. Even in a fast-food joint there are plenty of choices.

TAXING BY THE POUND

There are other prickly and annoying avenues one could take to influence the intake of food. And the most invasive is penalizing the consumer.

In April 2006, *Esquire* featured a lengthy article detailing the plans of Irwin Leba, a Texas millionaire who was proposing a federal tax based on people's body weight. I wasn't surprised to find the article, "The More You Weigh, the More You Pay," laying out in detail the incredible plans of a reclusive Texan to "balance the budget by taxing the obese."

The reader might have been amused to discover that Leba himself loved all kinds of food. "You ever had a deep-fried Twinkie?" he asked. "If you condensed all the goodness of Jesus Christ into one of those plastic wrappers, you'd have something that would be almost—but not quite—as divine as a deep-fried Twinkie." As a matter of fact, the article's author convinced Leba to meet him at a Texas McDonald's not far from his home outside Plainview. "It was a cheap journalist's ruse, really," writes Joshua Foer. "I knew full well that the parade of Big Mac gluttons was bound to get him riled." Leba accepted the invitation and went on to make fun of the "fat asses" in the McDonald's before clarifying his strategy:

> If Leba has his way, sometime between January 1 and April 15, every American will have to visit a government-sponsored weigh station and step on a scale. You'll leave with a notarized certificate attesting to your body-mass index (BMI). If that number is 25.5 or higher—24.9 is officially the upper limit of normal—you'll have to pay Uncle Sam a little something extra, corresponding to how overweight you are and scaled to your income.

> "Let's say you're five foot eight and you weigh 215 pounds—I'm just pulling these numbers out of the air," says Leba . . . "You'd have a BMI of 32.7, which is disgustingly overweight. Now let's say you're in the highest tax bracket and you pulled in roughly $2 million last year. Under my plan, you'd be looking at a $70,000 fat tax."
>
> Last year he founded a nonprofit think tank, the Institute for a Healthy America (IHA), with the sole objective of trying to make the fat tax a reality. He says he has already spent $5 million of his own money promoting the idea . . . "Fair taxation for a cellulite nation—that's what this is about."

★ ★ ★

Now, if you believe the story of Leba and the fat tax you're not alone. I did. And so did *Esquire*'s fact-checkers, almost all of *Esquire*'s readership, and most of the media.

It took nearly three weeks before *The Washington Post* revealed that the whole feature was a hoax. According to Brendan Vaughan, the magazine's articles editor, while a few *Esquire* readers recognized this as a ruse, some actually wrote in to praise the idea. The majority of the angry e-mails, however, came from buff readers, whose muscular frames gave them BMI tax burdens that would soon surpass their salaries.

"A lot of these guys clearly did not get the joke," says Vaughan. "They'd write in, saying, 'I appreciate your story and I agree that fat people are costing us money, but I go to the gym five times a week and I have a thirty-two-inch waist and I'd owe $6,000 in fat tax."

The reason so many people believed the story was that we are faced with similar, though less entertaining strategies that closely mirror Leba's.

In his 1996 book, *The Pleasure Police,* David Shaw, the late *Los Angeles Times* media critic, asked a facetious question after witnessing the antics of the ever-increasing number of antismoking nannies. If society had the right to stop you from fatally polluting your own lungs, did society then have the right to stop you from fatally clogging your arteries? "Are we going to outlaw butter?" Shaw asked. "Require warnings on ice cream labels? Impose high taxes on steaks?"

Shaw may not have been aware that in 1996 the idea of taxing unhealthy food had already been broached. Actually, it was prominently ranked among the sixteen "smart ideas to fix the world" offered by *U.S. News & World Report.* A proposal for a "Twinkie tax" was a perfect cure for the "fattest people."

And a decade later, Shaw's query was answered with a categorical "Hell, yes." Taxing steak, or the concept, often referred to as the Twinkie tax, was gaining momentum in numerous states and municipalities across the nation. What seemed utterly absurd less than a decade ago, and what was a parody in *Esquire,* was now enthusiastically promoted by medical writers like Suzanne Leigh of *USA Today,* the country's best-selling paper, with an article entitled "Twinkie Tax Worth a Try in Fight Against Obesity."

In June of 2006, those attending the powerful American Medical Association's annual conference came up with the idea of taxing sweeteners that are used in soft drinks. The money would then be used to fund an expansive public-health education campaign. A punitive tax would, theoretically, discourage poor eating habits. And as a fortuitous bonus the state could raise additional revenue to subsidize nutritious eating programs and other initiatives to assist Americans in staying trim.

CSPI director Jacobson concurred, saying, "We could envision taxes on butter, potato chips, whole milk, cheeses, [and] meat." You see, according to Jacobson, the CSPI "is proud about finding something wrong with practically everything." And a visit to the CSPI Web site quickly illustrates that he wasn't joking.

But the real mastermind behind this scheme was Kelly Brownell, director of the Rudd Center for Food Policy and Obesity at Yale. He proposed that revenue from this national tax should subsidize healthful foods and fund public-awareness campaigns to assist in curbing obesity. In his initial version of the plan, revenue would be generated from taxes of one cent per pound on candy and snack foods.

According to Brownell, "Congress and state legislatures could shift the focus to the environment by taxing foods with little nutritional value. Fatty foods would be judged on their nutritive value per calorie or gram of fat and the least healthy would be given the highest tax rate. Consumption of high-fat food would drop." A Twinkie tax, he went on to declare, would "hit junk-food junkies where it hurts: in their wallets." Since levying a tax on low-nutrition foods is one step that society hasn't tested, there's no reason government shouldn't give it a whirl.

Even if you agree that Congress should be in the business of targeting citizens who engage in unacceptable levels of poor eating, fat taxes are fundamentally unfair to everyone. A triathlete who coughs up a couple of bucks for an impressive Starbucks Banana Coconut Frappuccino Blended Coffee (410 calories) should not be penalized for enjoying himself. Unquestionably, overindulgence in virtually anything can be destructive, but will it now be government's job to defend us from watching too much television, playing too many video games, or blogging all day? If deficient eating habits are reason enough for castigatory measures then this is a slippery slope of a never-ending variety. As it turns out, taxing food based on its nutritional content is not only intrusive—and unjustly inclusive, as it punishes fit consumers who sporadically eat unwholesome food—but also extraordinarily tough to figure out.

Brownell, for instance, had concocted a convoluted calorie-to-nutrient index, with low-calorie fruits and vegetables residing at one end of the scale, while low-nutrient fatty fast food sat at the other end. Taxing a Luther Burger could get complicated. It could be taxed as a single entity, or the bacon, the greasy hamburger, the Krispy Kreme doughnut bun, and every other delicious piece of the puzzle could be taxed separately.

Moreover, who would decipher these snafus? How many pointy-headed health bureaucrats would now be added to the federal payroll? Who else would grapple with every single product's ingredients? Who would enforce this tax? The Department of Healthy Eating and Exercise?

There's always some unimaginative public servant who'll put a ludicrous theory into practice. In this case, one of the first public officials to attempt to convert this scheme into pubic policy was Detroit mayor Kwame Kilpatrick—though many municipalities have followed.

Kilpatrick—named, perhaps not coincidentally, the nation's worst big-city mayor by *Time* magazine in 2005—asked Detroit voters to support a 2 percent fast-food tax to help them slim down. The tax would be affixed to an existing 6 percent consumer tax for restaurant meals. At the time, well-known über-nanny New York assemblyman Felix Ortiz had already proposed a similar 1 percent tax on junk food—not to mention a levy on video games and commercials—to fund antiobesity programs in his hometown. But the Detroit tax would have been the country's first tax to specifically target fast-food outlets.

As we've discussed, with such a wide-ranging tax numerous feasibility problems emerge. What's most ironic, however, is that even if the Twinkie tax works in the capacity that nannies envision, it fails in the long run.

Kilpatrick may have been troubled by Detroiters' expanding

waistlines, but he was also concerned about a $300 million budget hole that had appeared during his tenure. As in many cases, Mayor Kilpatrick anticipated that folks in the already heavily taxed city wouldn't mind another one, or, at the very least, wouldn't notice the extra few cents they were shelling out on their Big Macs.

But in a deteriorating, money-strapped city like Detroit, it was the poor and working class of the inner city that would be injured most by this tax. Fast-food restaurants, which provide thousands of jobs, also hire many young people just starting out. Business would pay the price, as would, likely, overall tax revenue.

More likely, though, poor folks would pay the few cents more to eat the same food. A study by the USDA's Food Safety and Inspection Service found that taxes of this nature impact low-income consumers the hardest because they spend a greater percentage of their income on food. The study also found that imposing such costs yields virtually no benefits.

SUE THE BASTARDS

A good number of Americans haven't bought into the idea of taxation as a tool of the babysitting state. But there are other ways to circumvent popular opinion and get the job done. One such apparatus is litigation.

Jazlyn Bradley was only nineteen years old when she joined a class action suit against McDonald's restaurants. At the time, Jazlyn stood five foot six and weighed approximately 270 pounds. Her weight would later peak at an extraordinary 290 pounds.

Her immensity only helped compound what was an already troubled childhood. As a younger teenager, Jazlyn, and many of her ten siblings, were relegated to life in a homeless shelter after their mother abandoned them. The family finally settled in a two-bedroom dilapidated apartment in the Bronx, complete with "holes in the walls and lead paint dust flaking from the window frames."

For meals, Jazlyn regularly walked through the doors of the local McDonald's, where she consumed chicken nuggets, fried-fish sandwiches, Big Macs, french fries, ice-cream shakes, Egg McMuffins, and cokes. By her own admission, Jazlyn devoured a meal at McDonald's five times a week while growing up.

Believe it or not, her father, Israel, claimed that he was oblivious to the damage a consistent diet of fast food could inflict on a human body. "I always believed McDonald's was healthy for my children," he once explained, later telling *People* magazine, "If you had told me the food was unhealthy, I wouldn't have believed you."

With all we know about diet—or even the relatively little the average citizen *needs* to know about diet—no one could fault the average reader for being slightly skeptical regarding Israel's assertion. In this case, such skepticism was well-founded. Israel had already admitted (in a media interview regarding an obesity lawsuit that had never come to fruition) that he would typically consume a pound of french fries each week. But in 1993, Israel passed out and had to be rushed to the emergency room because of the medical ills caused by his diet.

As the saying goes, you can't legislate against stupid.

Quite predictably, like her father, Jazlyn now suffers from diabetes, hypertension, and dangerously high cholesterol levels. Other diseases and health maladies are likely on the horizon for her. As a victim of poor genetics, as well as circumstance and gravely indifferent parents, Jazlyn's two sisters were handed an equivalent fate: both eighteen-year-old Shakimah and fourteen-year-old Naisia are also obese. When asked who bore the responsibility for her tremendous weight, Jazlyn answered, "I'll take some of the blame, but they [McDonald's] should too."

Now who could have told Jazlyn such a silly thing?

Samuel Hirsch, Jazlyn's ambitious personal injury lawyer, by his own account, was merely attempting to liberate vulnerable Americans from the omnipotent and overpowering menace of Big Food.

"You don't need nicotine or an illegal drug to create an addiction. You're creating a craving," Hirsch once explained. But more important for the justification of his case, the lawyer maintained "that the fast-food industry has not been totally up front with the consumers." Thus Hirsch was trying to coerce fast-food companies into offering "a larger variety to the consumers, including non-meat vegetarian, less grams of fat," and a reduction in meal size.

Hirsch also demanded that federal legislation require warning labels on fast food similar to those on tobacco products. As many fast-food companies have begun to provide detailed labels of all nutritional content, this truly was grandstanding. But even if you're inclined to believe Hirsch's intentions were unsullied by the dollar—and this would be a massive leap of faith—what we have on our hands is a full-blown nanny.

In the early stages of Jazlyn's suit, the press had a field day. The always cheeky *New York Post* ran an entertaining piece accusing Hirsch of being almost "singularly responsible for making attorneys the most hated briefcase carriers in the world." Law professor Donald Garner opined in *The Washington Post* that obesity lawsuits portray "Americans as the most pathetic, pitiable people in the world, that we are incapable of limiting what we eat." Even the usually composed and regal television anchorwoman Diane Sawyer was impelled to ask Hirsch, "Do you realize the whole world is laughing at you?"

No big deal. The world had laughed before. The thick-skinned Hirsch's first crack at litigating the fast-food industry into low-fat submission utilized a highly suspect and completely disingenuous plaintiff named Caesar Barber. A maintenance supervisor in his mid-fifties, Barber claimed that he ate at fast-food restaurants four or five times a week and, until recently, had no idea that his diet was slowly killing him. Unlike Jazlyn, Barber didn't have his parents to blame, only himself . . . oh, and every fast-food joint in New York City.

Turns out, when Barber attributed his obesity, diabetes, high blood pressure, and cholesterol to a fatty diet, he was making a pinpoint medical diagnosis. Since Barber had survived not one but two heart attacks, his ascription wasn't exactly the work of a cunning detective. "I trace it all back to the high fat, grease and salt, all back to McDonald's, Wendy's, Burger King—there was no fast food I didn't eat, and I ate it more often than not because I was single, it was quick and I'm not a very good cook." Barber went on to explain: "It was a necessity, and I think it was killing me, my doctor said it was killing me, and I don't want to die."

However unfortunate his story was, as you can imagine, the Caesar Barber case didn't get very far. With a disagreeable plaintiff armed with an implausible story it simply wasn't going to sell to a jury or a judge. Hirsch, however, had learned a valuable lesson: use children.

★ ★ ★

The idea of shifting eating trends through litigation was embraced by every heavyweight nanny. In his book *Food Fight,* our friend Kelly Brownell, the ubiquitous finger-wagging architect of the Twinkie tax, set aside his expertise on eating disorders and punitive levies to tackle the dilemma of litigation. He employed a fairly forthright logic to this task: discouraging insalubrious food is too important to let market forces handle it. "When legislation and regulation occur too slowly and public opinion alone is not enough to change institutions like schools, litigation may be necessary."

Michael Jacobson of the CSPI agreed, even endorsing the idea of using children as props. He maintained that cases involving youngsters contained "an attractive element" in obesity lawsuits and could apparently inspire courtroom juries to award huge payouts. "These will help stop food companies from practicing deceptive advertising that is pulling the wool over the eyes of adults as well as kids."

Though Brownell and Jacobson are leading figures in the food-policing movement, the ideological and spiritual point man for the expressed purpose of social change through litigation is George Washington University Law School professor John Banzhaf. One of the most shameless nannies in America, Banzhaf made his name litigating tobacco companies into submission and winning huge settlements, and became a hero to many trial lawyers. His extraordinary success in this arena also has won him plenty of fawning praise from the press.

Banzhaf isn't shy about flaunting his intrusive achievements. People have made favorable comparisons between this nanny and Ralph Nader. Banzhaf's vanity license plate reads SUE BAST—shorthand for "sue the bastards." His philosophy on communal change through litigation is absolute, and judging from his comments, Banzhaf believes trial lawyers have not only the right but the responsibility to save humanity from the Big Mac.

In a CBS television interview, Banzhaf described his philosophy of the food industry by saying, "we're going to sue them and sue them and sue them." Banzhaf also once admitted that "the lawyers have definitely smelled blood in the water." On his Web site, there were links to an editorial titled "Using Legal Action to Fight Obesity." And he lists himself as an "informal" adviser on numerous lawsuits involving the notion that "discouraging" those who eat too much through law—in essence leapfrogging policy and pesky voters—was in our best interest.

One of the core justifications for legal action by intrusive food police goes something like this: The nation is in the midst of a debilitating obesity epidemic. This outbreak imposes an immense cost on the whole of society by a small, but individually portly, minority. "Why should I be forced to subsidize other people's bad habits?" Banzhaf once asked.

Another bad habit the public is forced to subsidize? Frivolous lawsuits.

We subsidize everyone's bad habits, unless society can pick and choose. If we don't allow people to eat what they want, how can we allow them to engage in any mildly risky activity—skiing, driving, suntanning?

It seems that while it is immoral for food companies to chase a "profit," it's a perfectly acceptable tact for nannies. Banzhaf acknowledges that money, as well as political consensus, is a must. "What we are seeing is a large number of groups that might not previously have had a great deal in common, coming together—vegans, Muslims, Hindus, conservative Jews, scientists, physicians, animal-rights groups, children's rights groups, sports organizations, and so on," he imagined. "Once they start joining forces, lawyers are going to smell the money, and legal action will gain its own momentum."

Momentum will only bring together vegans, Muslims, Hindus, conservative Jews, scientists, and physicians if all those folks happen to be ruthless lawyers.

SWEET JUSTICE

Thankfully, a judge with clarity and common sense—and an apt name—Robert W. Sweet, of the United States District Court for the Southern District of New York, didn't buy Samuel Hirsch's argument. He dismissed the original frivolous lawsuit that sought to hold McDonald's liable. The judge understood firsthand the problems of the nanny state when he asked, "Where should the line be drawn between an individual's own responsibility to take care of herself and society's responsibility to ensure that others shield her?"

Common sense. And a reasonable question. Still, Banzhaf believes that "somewhere there is going to be a judge and a jury that will."

He's likely right. Litigation is quickly becoming the most popular way to impact change. California attorney general Bill Lockyer filed or threatened to file lawsuits against McDonald's, Burger King, Wendy's, KFC, Frito-Lay, Heinz, Starbucks, and the makers of Cape Cod and Kettle brand snacks. Why? French fries and potato chips contain a chemical compound called acrylamide, which sounds really scary. Until you learn that this chemical is present whenever starchy foods are cooked at high temperature. The trouble was that studies published in the *British Journal of Cancer* and *The Journal of the American Medical Association* showed no added risk of cancer from acrylamide at the levels commonly found in food.

Jacobson wondered why the "FDA has been strangely silent about acrylamide" when, actually, the hyper-cautious FDA had warned Lockyer that he was "misleading" taxpayers with his suit based on no scientific evidence. According to the Center for Consumer Freedom, a group funded by the restaurant industry, using published data from the Environmental Protection Agency, "a person of average weight would have to eat over 62 pounds of potato chips or 182 pounds of French fries—every day, for his or her entire life—in order to have the weight-adjusted cancer risk found in lab rats."

The acrylamide affair bears some resemblance to the hysteria that surrounded the sugar substitute saccharin. There is another illuminating example of how alarmism devoid of sound science can be detrimental to those whom nannies purport to help.

In 1977, Canadian scientists issued a report that claimed to have demonstrated that saccharin caused bladder tumors in male rats. Though the cancer claims may have been true, the only hitch was that your average human would have to ingest a couple of hundred pounds of the stuff every day for years. If we use this template, things like water and air are poisonous.

In the end, the study led to bans and chilling warning labels that I still occasionally see at 7-Elevens around the country. Saccharin turned out to be basically harmless. Unless you consider the fact that millions of consumers may have been better off—perhaps even shed some weight—with the help of a nontoxic sugar substitute.

THE WAR ON COOKIES

When the late anchor Peter Jennings brought the vital subject of Girl Scout Cookies to the country's attention in a *World News Tonight* segment titled "Cookie Controversy," we finally understood the link between obesity and pigtailed cookie pushers. Jennings spoke with ABC medical correspondent John McKenzie, who conducted an investigative report that featured a host of nannies calling for severe curbs on peddling Girl Scout Cookies. The question of the segment was: Are Girl Scouts pushing junk food? The answer, of course, is yes. The next question is: So what?

Nannies rely on anxiety-prone parents to propagate their message. Children are fortuitous targets on numerous levels, perfect fodder for the media. But typically the public is uninterested, distracted, or simply unable to thoroughly examine the intricate claims made about the dangers its children are subjected to.

In 1997, the CSPI had already been targeting the evils of Girl Scout Cookies. "Thin Mints and Samoas" they state are some of the "worst cookies you can buy." Jacobson once said that "ideally the Girl Scouts would be selling products that don't undermine their customers' health." *The New York Times* fanned the fire of the Girl Scout Cookie controversy with an article titled "So Much for Squeaky Clean Cookies."

To temper the criticism levied against their shadowy organization by a vocal and strident minority, the research arm of the Girl Scouts issued a 35-page health report, "Weighing In: Helping Girls Be Healthy Today, Healthy Tomorrow." Cookies, thankfully, were not mentioned. Can you imagine a cute Girl Scout knocking at the door ready to sell you some high-fiber, whole-wheat snacks? The Girl Scouts—who have had a pretty strong run since 1912, growing their membership to 3.6 million—would be out of business before you can say, "I'll take the Lemon Coolers."

Girl Scouts of America former chief executive officer Kathy Cloninger asserted that "balanced, healthy living is not about denial," and if "occasionally a girl wants to have a treat or our public wants to have a treat, we believe that the Girl Scout Cookie is one of the most delicious." This, of course, is the common sense of moderation. Nearly all parents in America employ this secret weapon.

★ ★ ★

They use the same approach when it comes to ice cream.

After weeks of exhaustive investigation, I was unable to unearth a single instance of death attributable to ice cream in the entire United States—ever. There were no deaths brought on by Chocolate Chip Cookie Dough or Cherry Garcia, not even an overdose of plain old French vanilla. Nonetheless, according to the nation's foremost advocate of food control, ingesting the creamy substance means certain death.

In an appearance on *Good Morning America* to promote a report condemning ice cream, CSPI director Jacobson explained to viewers—without a doubt this included thousands of young children—that when you indulge in ice cream "just know that you're going to kill yourself."

Jacobson should have waited until Halloween. Frightening little children with their demise by way of ice cream could be forgiven if it had been an off-the-cuff remark thrown around in the heat of a contentious debate over ice cream—should such a thing exist. But it turned out this "war on ice cream" was part of a concerted effort by many nannies to frighten kids and parents.

In July of 2003, Jacobson, along with Banzhaf, sent a letter cautioning all the top ice-cream makers in the nation that lawsuits may result from their refusal to "list the calorie (and, ideally, saturated fat) content of each item" on menu boards. Now, all ice-cream brands differ to some extent, but none are what you'd call a nutritionally complete food. Pick up any ice-cream container and you will observe the calories listed on the back—and, often, saturated fat numbers and any other pertinent information.

The CSPI alert on ice cream highlights a report released—on National Ice Cream Day, for full effect—that also included the health risks involved in other treats, such as pizza, popcorn, and other assorted goodies that a number of Americans occasionally enjoy. "We know consumers don't assume that ice cream is a diet food, but most probably aren't aware how much stuff is in one portion," Banzhaf explained. Apparently it's not enough to know something is unhealthy, it's now the job of Baskin-Robbins to scare you away.

Think of it: If ice cream is a killer, what do you make of a Good Humor man? This merchant of death prowls the streets targeting children exclusively. Do you know how many calories a Fudgsicle bar contains? Try 270. A Strawberry Shortcake Bar clocks in at an even 300 calories.

★ ★ ★

It can be Girl Scout Cookies. It can be ice cream. And sometimes it's Mom's homemade birthday cupcakes.

One of the first proposed bills aimed to curtail cookie and cake sales was in Massachusetts elementary and high schools. It was not a hit. "Kids don't want to buy carrots; they want to buy cake," explained an extraordinarily sensible seventeen-year-old student named Atayvia Sowers at Amherst Regional High School after a ban on unhealthy foods in school went into effect. This bill would have prevented any student group from selling unhealthy sweets on school grounds until at least thirty minutes after the end of classes. The bill also required schools to reduce portion sizes and replace high-fat, high-sugar snacks in school vending machines and lunchrooms with low-fat milk, juice, and fresh fruits and vegetables.

The school's principal, Mark Jackson, was already having a difficult time digging up funds to subsidize after-school clubs. Bake sales were essential in his pursuit. Consequently, Jackson explained that bake sales would be effectively eliminated if they could not begin until thirty minutes after classes ended. "Prime time is at the end of the day," Jackson explained to a local paper. "I want to encourage kids to eat responsibly, [but] on the other hand, they should be able to enjoy cookies."

Since the Massachusetts edict, countless similar bills, both local and state, have passed. On the federal level, the Child Nutrition Promotion and School Lunch Protection Act of 2006—which called for updated definitions of "minimal nutritional value" of foods served in schools, including those sold in vending machines and at fund-raisers—will do the trick.

In 2006, after his son was served a "peanut butter and Marshmallow Fluff" sandwich, Massachusetts state senator Jarrett T. Barrios affixed an amendment to an already comprehensive junk-food bill that must have caused Sam Adams and hundreds of other

Boston patriots to do a double flip in their graves. Barrios wanted to ban all marshmallow spreads in school-lunch programs. "A Fluff sandwich as the main course of a nutritious lunch just doesn't fly in 2006," Barrios explained.

Fluffernutter (the official name of this most excellent sandwich) has been a staple of New England cuisine for decades. Marshmallow Fluff was invented by a Massachusetts man before World War I. "I've been eating Fluff nearly my entire life," Don Durkee, the son of the inventor, told *The Boston Globe.* At eighty years old, the president of Durkee-Mower, Inc. seemed to be pretty healthy and spoiling for a fight.

Even Alicia Moag-Stahlberg, the executive director of Action for Healthy Kids, found the amendment a "little odd" for her taste. "There is no need to call out specific foods, like Fluff, as the school lunch program of Massachusetts already meets strong nutrition standards. As part of the school meal program, maybe Fluff is just fine. Maybe kids are having it instead of jelly."

★ ★ ★

Massachusetts's meddling was something, but a couple of years ago California was the first state in the nation to exclusively ban the sale of soft drinks in middle and elementary schools. No tangible results in the reduction of obesity just yet. In New Jersey, lawmakers passed one of the nation's more meddling and sweeping laws banning the sale of candy, soda, and fatty, sugary foods in schools statewide, mandating that any food item with sugar as its first or primary ingredient will not be permitted for sale at any school cafeteria.

A school in the Raleigh, North Carolina, area adopted a "wellness" program that governs not only exercise and lunches but any treats—PTA candy, bake-sale products, hot dogs, and even school birthday party confections. Once upon a time schools would work these things out with teachers and promote healthy eating through education. Treva Fitts, a science specialist for the Durham County Schools and a "self-described health fanatic," said students could learn more about moderation if they were provided choices. "Teaching kids to make good choices is part of what we do," Fitts explained. "But cake is a part of birthday celebrations. It's cultural."

The Florida House of Representatives considered a law that would ban high-fructose corn syrup from the state's public schools. Not only is the sweetener found in soft drinks and cupcakes, it is also used in granola bars and breakfast cereals.

Oh, and in mustard.

* * *

But in conservative Texas, agriculture commissioner Susan Combs put them all to shame with her assiduous plan of attack. "Stop. Step away from the junk food and listen carefully. We Americans are overweight, and it's because we eat too much of the wrong stuff," Combs opined in a press release. And Combs was serious. She went out and banned all foods of "minimal nutritional value" at schools. Food and beverages like "carbonated drinks, frozen flavored ices (sicles), chewing gum, and candies (including hard candy, jellies and gums, marshmallow, fondants, licorice, spun candy, and candy coated popcorn)."

To undo some of the damage, the Texas legislature attempted to pass a law that allowed cupcakes just for birthday parties. "We have an opportunity to really make the children happy here," said Representative Jim Dunnam, whose school-age daughter, Lauren, had asked him if he could make cupcakes legal again. Soon enough, Combs relented, offering a "cupcake clarification" to allow cakes at school birthday parties. But just as Combs was relaxing some of the restrictions in one area, she was tightening them in another. She took the rather unique step of fining public schools more than $8,000 for failing to adhere to policy. Some of the violations:

- La Villa Middle School was fined for offering Frito chips, Pop-Tarts, and pretzel bags that were too big for Combs's liking
- Carlisle School paid $1,039 because it served food of "minimal nutritional value"—Crystal Lite drink was being sold
- Malone Elementary School anted up $474.34 because they served fried-potato products three times a week
- Tejas School of Choice High School was fined $354.45 for providing access to food with "minimal nutritional value" where reimbursable meals were served or eaten, and it was not following portion-size guidelines on candy and chips
- Cooper Elementary School was cited because a parent gave his child's friend a Dairy Queen soda

THE REAL STATE

Is this type of overbearing paternalism necessary? When I spoke to Leo Lesh, the executive director of food and nutrition services for Denver Public Schools, he was too tactful to condemn lawmakers directly, but he considers laws that regulate food in schools to be worthless. "Three years ago, our first step was replacing the regular chips with the healthy chips and that sort of thing," Lesh explains. "The following year we eliminated all the candy bars. We started doing that as a matter of course, because we thought it was the best thing for kids."

Parents pressure schools, who in turn change the way they do business. But the fact is, it might not matter as much as some would have us think. In a recent study, six Harvard doctors studied more than 14,000 American children and found that evidence "did not offer support for the hypothesis that snacking promotes weight gain." Another study run in the *Journal of Human Nutrition and Dietetics* a couple of years back found that contrary to the group's "expectations," snacks did not have an effect on body mass index. Surely this is not a surprise to parents who are paying attention.

With all the hand-wringing over exaggerated statistics regarding food, some parents may be surprised to learn that their children are no worse off now than in the days Cookie Monster actually lived up to his name (cookies are now only a "sometimes treat" for that blue puppet). Although too many children are overweight from inactivity and poor diets, according to a report released by the Federal Interagency Forum on Child and Family Statistics in 2005, children are healthier than ever. Furthermore, a little over 83 percent were reported by their parents to be in "very good" or "excellent" health. Kids were eating more soy and more health-packed fruit juices than they were soda and other junk.

Dr. Edward Sondik, director of the National Center for Health Statistics, contends that fewer children are dying. The report compiled by the Federal Interagency Forum on Child and Family Statistics found that "in 2002, there were 31 deaths for every 100,000 children in this age group, down from 33 deaths per 100,000 in 2001." This was the best ever. And the death rates of children continues to go down whether from cancer, motor vehicle accidents, poisoning, or drowning. Stephen Moore and Julian Simon, in their book *It's Getting Better All the Time: 100 Greatest Trends of the Last 100 Years*, point out just how dramatically life has improved.

This good news doesn't mean that obesity isn't a problem. But when government and hyperactive advocacy groups overstate the problem and create "epidemics" and "infectious diseases" that don't exist, we lose. Typically, the nutritionists or trial lawyers promulgate one-size-fits-all public policy that discounts independence and personal responsibility, and mercilessly crushes common sense.

At this point society has not taken food nannies seriously, giving Twinkie Fascists the collective "yes, dear" and backing away slowly. Until they have something useful to say, whenever I get the chance, I'll be heading to Mulligan's.

★ CHAPTER TWO ★

DAYS OF WHINE

You can't seriously want to ban alcohol. It tastes great, makes women appear more attractive, and makes a person virtually invulnerable to criticism.

—MAYOR JOE QUIMBY, *THE SIMPSONS*

Men are nicotine-soaked, beer-besmirched, whiskey-greased, red-eyed devils.

—CARRY NATION

★

THE BEST TIME YOU'LL NEVER REMEMBER

Denver's Democratic mayor John Hickenlooper—once voted one of the top-five big-city mayors in America by *Time* magazine—is occasionally referred to as "Mayor Brewpub." It has nothing to do with his propensity to indulge in hooch, but rather with the fact that this former geologist-turned-real-estate-mogul-turned-politician happens to own several establishments that serve liquor, including Denver's very first brewpub, the Wynkoop Brewing Company—the place that helped make Hickenlooper a millionaire.

To the west of the Mile High City, nestled in foothills of the Rocky Mountains, is the city of Golden. Though the town still radiates a level of Old West charm, including a few Western-style saloons, it has long melted into the car-infused Denver suburbs. It is best known for being home to the Coors Brewery headquarters. The Coors family is one of the leading financial supporters of politically conservative causes, lending generous support to the nation's leading think tank the Heritage Foundation, among others.

Fortunately, alcohol holds no particular political affiliation. So a few miles north of Denver in the neo-hippie enclave of Boulder, where it's safe to say, in large part, that folks hold a political outlook diametrically opposed to the Coors family, there are an estimated 250 establishments that sell alcohol within a five-minute drive of the University of Colorado at Boulder. It's a great town.

With this booze-drenched cultural schema in place, locals couldn't have been stunned when in 2004, *Men's Health* magazine published its most "intoxicated" city list with Denver perched on top. The study examined 101 big cities, comparing their number of drunken-driving arrests, alcohol-related driving deaths, and deaths due to diseases that may be caused by alcohol.

Being named "drunkest city" in the nation did bring Denver some interesting attention. Jay Leno's writing team, for instance, got hold of the study. Leno interviewed William J. Fredricks, the fictional under assistant lieutenant secretary of Denver, played by a supposedly inebriated Fred Willard. "It's been reported that Denver is the drunkest city in the United States," Leno says. "That's true, Jay," Willard answers. "The numbers, just like the people of Denver, are staggering."

Another character who enhances its reputation as a tippler's paradise—not to mention adding some much-needed levity—is Frank Kelly Rich, champion of functioning alcoholics everywhere and proprietor and editor of the refreshingly ill-mannered *Modern Drunkard*. The Denver-based publication declares a circulation of anywhere from 35,000 to 50,000 and is crammed with articles celebrating the brighter side of drinking, each issue a brazen collection of personal stories ("The Booze and I: A Love Story"), historical essays ("Ladies Thirst: In the First of a Three-Part Series Rich English Explores History's Greatest Female Drunkards"), and detailed instruction on how to be a respectable drunkard.

Take the first-ever Modern Drunkard Convention held in Las Vegas in 2004, which attracted more than five hundred serious drinkers. The 2005 convention held in Denver was billed as "The Best Time You'll Never Remember." We suspect few did. The 2006 convention, again held in Vegas, featured the tagline: "Say It Loud, Say It Plowed." Naturally, the participants drank. They partied. They listened to lectures—or "soused seminars" as they were called. They drank some more. One eager couple even got married within an hour of meeting in real life—after some drinking, undoubtedly.

As a result of his unabashed promotion of drunken fun, Rich

has also become a leading voice in opposition to the creeping nannyism of alcohol prohibition. "The government [is] getting deeper and deeper into the bars and controlling stuff. We printed a propaganda poster concerning that: 'First, they're going to come for your cigarettes. Then they're going to come for your happy hours. Then they're going to come for your booze,' " Rich once told the *National Review.* "They're doing the 'drop by drop' prohibition approach. Instead of shoving [it] down our throats all at once, they're just going to slowly take it away, piece-by-piece."

Even in the purportedly alcohol-soaked Mile High City, "the pendulum of societal norms has swung in favor of sobriety," explained Peter Adler, a professor of sociology at the University of Denver. He maintains that views are changing on when and how people can feel good about drinking. And if one believes that Rich—a self-proclaimed and celebrated liquor lover—is overstating the predicament we tipplers face, you'd be dead wrong. Neo-prohibition, like all nannyism, is steeped in good intentions. It is in its nascent stages but growing. Neo-prohibitionists—and their handmaidens in the media, academic circles, and legislatures across the country—question the decency of drinking alcohol under any circumstance at any time in any place.

Unacceptable.

IF WINE WAS GOOD ENOUGH FOR JESUS, WINE IS GOOD ENOUGH FOR ME

Let's for a moment imagine what patriot Sam Adams would make of price controls on beer, sin taxes, bans on happy hours, a twenty-one-year-old drinking age law, compulsory 3.2 percent beer at supermarkets, and random sobriety checks. A second American Revolution might be in the offing, I suspect. If we had half the heart, we'd be cleaning our muskets right now.

From the foundation of the Union, Americans have been adamant about liberty—and this includes the liberty to tipple. Thomas Jefferson, some historians suggest, wrote the first draft of the Declaration of Independence in a Philadelphia tavern. Benjamin Franklin, a great lover of the brew, allegedly said that "there are more old drunkards than old doctors." Historically speaking, drinking may have been America's first national pastime.

The temperance movement, like copious drinking, has been with us since the first days of the Republic. Benjamin Rush, a doctor and signer of the Declaration of Independence, believed many physical and psychological health tribulations in the early Republic were attributable to alcohol consumption. Though Rush preached moderation not prohibition, his followers formed a temperance association in Connecticut in the late 1700s. Soon after, eight states followed their lead with statewide organizations, including the two largest, New York and Virginia.

When attempts to quash or curtail alcohol consumption early in the nation's history did pop up, they were met with violence. There was the Whiskey Rebellion, an uprising that had its origins in 1791 but culminated in an armed insurrection in 1794 in the Monongahela valley in Pennsylvania, pitting settlers against the federal government when it tried to place controls on alcohol. It must be pointed out that it was not solely about alcohol but also about unfair taxation and the fact that in the backwoods of America, whiskey was sometimes the only currency available.

There have been other acts of rebellion, like the lesser-known Lager Beer Riot, which took place in Chicago in 1855 after Mayor Levi Boone (great-nephew of American legend Daniel Boone) proposed an ordinance aiming to close taverns on Sundays and raise the cost of a liquor license. After tavern owners were arrested for flouting this law and selling beer on Sunday, riots ensued. Waves of angry immigrants stormed the downtown area and the mayor ordered the swing bridges opened to stop further waves of protesters from crossing the river.

In the mid-1890s, the Anti-Saloon League employed an uncompromising puritanical ethos. A leading voice of the organization later wrote that the lies he told in promoting prohibition "would fill a big book." Temperance societies often administered lifelong abstinence pledges to schoolchildren. The infamous Carry Amelia Nation was a malevolent woman who would march into bars and threaten drinkers, sometimes accompanied by a hymn-singing contingent, then smash bar fixtures with a hatchet she liked to carry around. Then there was Anthony Comstock, who in addition to being the fierce abolitionist behind the Comstock Act, which made illegal the delivery or transportation of contraceptives, was vehemently opposed to alcohol.

Then, of course, there was the big one: the most infamous and counterproductive intrusion into lifestyle choices came in 1920, with enactment of the Eighteenth Amendment to the Constitution—which along with the passage of the Volstead Act (defining the specifics of "intoxicating liquors") established Prohibition. In a spasm of righteousness after World War I, fanatical advocates of the reform persuaded an overwhelming majority of federal and state legislators to support this method of abolishing the use of intoxicants which, they insisted, would greatly uplift and vastly benefit society.

The results of this hyper-nannyism were calamitous. And though it wasn't any harder to find yourself a gin and tonic—it is estimated that by 1925 there were at least 15,000 "blind pigs" (slang for a speakeasy) in Detroit alone, and by the end of the 1920s at least 32,000 speakeasies in New York, not to mention thousands of shops nationwide that sold substandard homemade liquor for additional income—a massive illicit criminal industry was born.

In the three months preceding the Eighteenth Amendment's ratification half a million dollars of liquor was stolen from government warehouses across the country. A few months after ratification, federal courts in Chicago reported being overwhelmed with more than six hundred pending liquor violation trials. Within three years, thirty Prohibition agents were killed in the line of duty.

The year Prohibition was repealed the homicide rate had peaked to levels that would not be seen again for a half century—9.7 per 100,000 people. In fact, a multitude of severe societal ills, some of which were the very rationale behind Prohibition in the first place, grew and other unforeseen maladies emerged from this brazen act of social engineering.

Congress officially adopted the Twenty-first Amendment to the Constitution in 1933, thus ending the most destructive nannyistic intervention in American history.

★ ★ ★

Historian Paul Johnson, writing in *A History of the American People,* observed that this nation's temperance movements exhibited "both the evangelical spirit of the Pilgrim Fathers and the witch-hunting fanaticism of the Salem elders." This ideology, he writes, was infused with a "feeling that pleasure itself was enviable and sinful." When you begin probing the philosophy employed by leaders of today's temperance movement, you find similar rationalizations.

With the Eighteenth Amendment's spectacular failure and the remarkable societal impact it inflicted, it's startling to discover there are quite a number of revisionists who deem Prohibition a success. Unlike the ugly Fascist Carry Nation, today's prohibitionists do not show up at saloons with scowling mugs and hatchet in hand, rather they flash Harvard degrees, work under the banner of Columbia University, and discharge endless bloodcurdling studies to set the table for their nannyistic goals.

From the panjandrum of neo-prohibitionists, there are few with more experience than Joe Califano, head and founder of the

National Center on Addiction and Substance Abuse at Columbia University (CASA). Califano's boilerplate health and safety concerns are occasionally spiced up with puritanical prose. "For me," Califano once declared, "establishing and building CASA and committing myself to this battle against substance abuse was doing the Lord's work."

Califano, were he not a Catholic, would make Cotton Mather proud. As a Jesuit-educated lifelong civil servant, Califano has occupied the high moral ground. Though CASA does provide assistance for those who suffer from the very genuine blight of substance abuse, he also busies himself issuing blanket condemnations of alcohol. Califano says that "Availability is the mother of abuse." And CASA's motto could easily be: To use it *is* to abuse it.

For Califano, the Lord's work entails diligently avoiding peer reviews. This allows CASA to create implausible alarm regarding the menace posed by the cocktail. What are they really about? Arthur Sobey, writing in *The Wall Street Journal,* summed up Califano's win-at-all-costs approach: "Using Mr. Califano's false logic, I can prove with statistical precision that eating bread leads to a life of crime."

One such hard-hitting study asserted that more than 25 percent of women receiving welfare were either alcohol or drug abusers. Someone at CASA, it seems, forgot to check with the Department of Health and Human Services, which puts the number closer to 4.5 percent. Another study alleged that 60 percent of college women with sexually transmitted diseases were under the influence of alcohol when they contracted their ailment. The same inquiry also declared that 90 percent of campus rapes occurred when either the assailant or the victim was using alcohol. In an analysis of that study, a senior editor at *Forbes Media Critic* found that CASA had used antiquated statistics that were "not credible" or conceivably just "pulled from thin air."

How convenient.

One of the more egregious of these reports was the 2002 CASA release entitled "Teen Tipplers: America's Underage Drinking Epidemic." This report declaring that "underage drinkers account for 25 percent of all the alcohol consumed in the U.S." was explosive news which could have affected public policy.

If only it were true. The day after the release of the study, *The New York Times,* in the article "Teenage Drinking a Problem but Not in Way Study Found," reported that the percentage of alcohol consumed by underage American drinkers was less than half of CASA's published figure. Even the Substance Abuse and Mental Health Services Administration, a group with aligned ambitions, issued a news release announcing that CASA had misinterpreted its data. One critic pointed out that for minors to account for a quarter of all alcohol consumption, everyone in the twelve-to-twenty age group would have to average two cocktails a day.

True to nanny form, Califano continued to throw this discredited number around. Discussing his memoir, *Inside: A Public and Private Life,* in a 2004 television interview with NBC's Tim Russert, Califano took the time during a righteous rant against alcohol companies that "sell addiction" to assert that "20 percent of their product is consumed by underage kids."

Wobbly interpretation of facts hasn't damaged Califano's exalted stature in the media or the financial prospects of CASA. Between 1992 and 2004, CASA—a group that also supports alcohol sin taxes, draconian restrictions on the availability of alcohol, and the banning of alcohol advertising on television—raised more than $150 million.

"Califano is essentially a reincarnation of the old temperance warriors," Ethan Nadelman, director of the Lindesmith Center in New York, told *The Chronicle of Higher Education.* "It's 'demon alcohol,' 'demon cigarettes,' 'demon drugs.' It's Carry Nation and the old anti-alcohol warriors, given a gloss by his association with Columbia University and this 'sophisticated' research center."

Califano alleges that he "strongly opposes" Prohibition, but he has a funny way of showing it. In a May 1996 *Washington Post* op-ed, he helped "set the historical record straight and temper the revisionist view of legalizers" who attack Prohibition. Though ostensibly discussing illicit drugs, many of Califano's positions in this editorial were a rehash of a remarkable 1992 op-ed in *The New York Times* written by Mark Moore, a professor at Harvard University. Candidly titled "Actually, Prohibition Was a Success," Moore crunched some numbers and argued that since alcohol consumption had declined during Prohibition, it can't be considered a failure. No. In effect, it should be considered a success. He cited declining cirrhosis rates, a drop in admission to state mental hospitals for alcoholic psychosis, and a decline of 50 percent in public drunkenness and disorderly conduct arrests between 1916 and 1922. For the population as a whole, he estimated, the consumption of alcohol declined by 30 percent to 50 percent during Prohibition.

Moore's op-ed is instructive in that it helps us define terms—specifically his definition of "success"—not only because Moore deems a decline of 30 to 50 percent during an *absolute* prohibition as something to write home about, but also because he defines success entirely in terms of enhanced public health and little more. That's not the case in the real world. Take this extreme: If we eliminate all vehicular deaths via a total car ban, would that mean the prohibition is a success?

Society cannot quantify success in the way temperance activists would have us believe. Lowering the number of those who seek treatment for alcohol-induced psychosis, for instance, is certainly a positive development, but it must be measured against the debilitating social disaster on the other side of the ledger: the rise in criminal activity which in turn spurred on a growing police state and loss of civil liberties.

An important thought seems to slip the neo-prohibitionist's mind from time to time—or perhaps it holds no weight with them: our constitutional freedom does not guarantee the citizenry sobriety or perfect health, only the choice.

BOOZE CLUES

In South Dakota a couple of years ago, a bill was under consideration that would have made it felony child abuse for a pregnant woman to order a single glass of wine in a restaurant without a doctor's prescription. Thankfully it failed.

The state's alleged need to "protect children" (even in the womb) is the seed for all kinds of overreactions related to alcohol. For neo-prohibitionists, then, the 1984 National Minimum Drinking Age Act, which prevents anyone under the age of twenty-one from buying or possessing alcohol, was one of the most important moments in the movement's history.

In the early 1980s, the federal government threatened any state that failed to conform with the new prospective drinking age by withholding federal highway funds. The act not only cut off young adults from booze but it gave temperance activists the license—as we've seen witnessed with Califano—to refer to eighteen-to-twenty-year-old adults as "underage kids," "youths," or "minors."

At the time, there was a great deal of debate over the pros and cons of instituting a drinking-age limit of twenty-one. The majority of us have heard the arguments against such a regulation: nineteen-year-old young adults can sign up with the Armed Forces and die for their country; purchase pornography (heck, star in pornography); lease an apartment; run for public office; get married; file for divorce; get an abortion—without informing their parents . . .

but they can't have a beer, even with their parents' permission at a baseball game.

Alas, those arguments didn't gain a large amount of traction. In the two-plus decades since the National Minimum Drinking Age Act went into effect, it has gained broad mainstream acceptance. Polls dependably show that a substantial majority of Americans approve. Any deviation means political suicide.

In 2004, during the Colorado senatorial race, opponents of candidate Peter Coors—the scion of the famous Golden brewery family—dredged up a quote from a 1997 interview with *USA Today* wherein he flaunted convention by asking some heretical questions about the drinking age. "Maybe the answer is lowering the drinking age so that kids learn to be responsible about drinking at a younger age," Coors had said. "I'm not an advocate of trying to get people to drink, but kids are drinking now anyway. All we've done is criminalize them."

Before he knew what hit him, Coors was assailed by his own party as a peddler of depravity (it certainly didn't help that Coors beer commercials regularly featured scantily clad blonde twins) and by Democrats as a stooge for "big" corporate beer companies—namely his own. Soon enough, the opposition began running TV spots featuring still images of cars in various stages of wreckage to remind Colorado voters that Coors wanted young adults to end up in mangled ruins. Despite his superior name recognition and unlimited funding, Coors lost his bid for the Senate.

Whatever his intentions may have been, Coors asked an entirely reasonable question: Why should the state penalize young adults from engaging in behavior that is perfectly acceptable for other adults?

One of the central rationalizations behind bumping around the idea of raising the legal drinking age in the early 1980s was the fact that the age group of eighteen to twenty-one was involved in the highest percentage of vehicular accidents while intoxicated. Well, now the group with the highest vehicular accidents while intoxicated is the age bracket of twenty-one to twenty-four. Should we raise the drinking age again? In 1984, transportation secretary Elizabeth Dole argued that a national drinking age could reasonably be set at twenty-four. The injustice, she argued, was not in the age discrimination but in the difficulty that some young women—largely innocent in drunken-driving deaths—were being penalized. (Dole also likely knew that in 1976 the Supreme Court struck down an Oklahoma statute setting the drinking age for beer for men at twenty-one and for women at eighteen, creating a precedent that classifications based on sex were presumably invalid.)

It's a wonder that Dole didn't deem it significant enough to mention that *every* accountable drinker—male or female—was being punished for the transgressions of a comparatively few lawbreakers. The transportation chief believed that President Ronald Reagan had a duty to support efforts to boost the drinking age because "federal leadership" was warranted on the issue, and states, whatever their positions or situations, capitulated and criminalized mainstream behavior.

A self-proclaimed conservative, Dole could favor intimidating states into buying federal mandates by stating the relative importance of the law. Many Republicans will drop any pretenses of supporting states' rights when "federal leadership" is needed on an issue they find unusually pressing—or, you know, just politically expedient.

BINGE JUSTICE

One question we could ask nannies is: How is it that even in the face of the twenty-one-year-old drinking-age limit we are told that this young generation's drinking problems have gotten worse?

Shouldn't the situation have improved? After a recent "rash" of tragic deaths in colleges from alcohol poisoning, "binge" drinking—and by "binge," experts at the National Institute on Alcohol Abuse and Alcoholism mean four drinks at one occasion (three for women), and by "rash" they mean a handful of incidents—the need to curbing drinking on college campuses became the cause du jour for antialcohol activists.

A Harvard School of Public Health study declared binge drinking the single most pressing drug crisis on college campuses. (Thankfully, it's not meth or heroin.) How could we, as a community, tackle the affliction of booze? The answer, naturally, was to intensify prohibitionary tactics: review alcohol licensing policies for local bars, enact stricter zoning laws and code enforcement, ban beer sales at football games or to fraternities and sororities, and much, much more.

"We want people to be free, but we also want to keep them from hurting themselves," Aaron White, a research professor of psychology at Duke University told *The Christian Science Monitor.* Glynn Birch, the then–national president of Mothers Against Drunk Driving (MADD), had more thoughts on the binge-drinking epidemic. He partially blamed binge drinking on the proliferation of "drinking games" on college campuses. Now, there are literally hundreds of variations of drinking games, a large amount invented on the spot—though for the persnickety there is always the International Drinking Rules.

"When you play drinking games, you're not really in charge of how much you drink," explained Brian Borsari, a psychologist at the Center for Alcohol and Addiction Studies at Brown University. "Your drinking is at the whim of other players, which can be very dangerous, especially if you're trying to fit in."

It might be convenient to assert that the individual is not "in charge" of the amount of alcohol they consume, but there is a gaping hole in this argument. It's a lie. No one is forcing you to drink—unless your fraternity brothers have tied you to a chair and stuck a funnel down your throat. Which bring us to another convenient fact antialcohol types can't seem to digest: plenty of young adult students want to drink. They want to drink *a lot* of alcohol.

MADD's Birch, whose twenty-one-month-old son was tragically murdered by a drunk driver, doesn't see it that way. He claims that "drinking by college students, ages 18 to 24, contributes to an estimated 1,700 student deaths, 600,000 injuries, 700,000 assaults and more than 90,000 sexual assaults." Those are some big numbers with plenty of zeros to frighten parents. Surely he will forgive some parents for believing that criminals, miscreants, rapists, and thugs, not alcohol, are responsible for these crimes.

What does this alarmism beget? In Madison, Wisconsin, legislators deemed alcohol a date-rape drug. Alcohol, like date-rape drugs, can undeniably be an aggravating factor in sexual assaults. This new law means a woman who has gotten drunk during a sexual encounter can be found powerless to give consent. Under state law, having sexual contact with a person incapable of consent because they are under the influence of an intoxicant—things like a surreptitious date-rape drug or a glass of beer—is defined as second-degree sexual assault. The offense is punishable by $100,000 and a prison sentence of up to twenty-five years. This means that two adults engaging in a fun romp are risking going to jail for the most natural activity on the planet.

The local district attorney Brian Blanchard argued that the law was "long overdue." His reason was, according to the *Wisconsin State Journal*, that the message about alcohol that the law sends is "namely, that it can be just as dangerous as other drugs." The truth is that alcohol *can* be as dangerous as other drugs. But primarily, we've learned our limitations.

★ ★ ★

The Great Binge Drinking Epidemic did generate more countless, genuinely irrational—and thus remarkably popular—"solutions" among politicians.

One antidote sweeping the nation requires consumers to register beer kegs as if they were a fully automatic rifle. The process goes something like this: You head to the local beverage depot to purchase a keg for your barbecue. You're asked for identification. Then the store clerk, acting as a surrogate for the police, records your personal data, along with the keg's registration number for future use should any underage drinker be caught partaking from your keg's goodness in the future.

The specifics of keg tracking can vary depending on municipality. In the college town of Chapel Hill, North Carolina, for instance, a beer-keg proposal called for vendors to mark barrels with the buyer's name, address, and driver's license number. In 2006, North Carolina governor Mike Easley signed a law that would undercut the legal rights of defendants to challenge "illegally or incorrectly" obtained evidence by the state in regards to illegal drinking. In this state, an eighteen-year-old, who without a criminal history can easily purchase a shotgun, cannot buy a keg of beer.

In Austin, Texas, it was reported that a bill would ask alcohol buyers to "swear" they are at least twenty-one, in addition to showing an ID. New York governor George Pataki signed a statewide law requiring that all beer kegs to be registered with the state and that the deposit on a keg be increased to $75.

SO WHAT IS TO BE DONE?

Some suggest that temperance warriors have got this whole problem turned inside out. How are young adults expected to grasp the idea of drinking responsibly, to understand the consequences of alcohol abuse, when they can't even legally drink a glass of wine with their parents at a restaurant or have a beer at a family barbecue?

For the majority of young adults, the initial alcohol experience will be accompanied by peer pressure. "There is a ritual every university administrator has to fear," John Portmann, a professor at the University of Virginia, told *Psychology Today.* "Every fall, parents drop off their well-groomed freshman and within two or three days many have consumed a dangerous amount of alcohol and placed themselves in harm's way. These kids have been controlled for so long they go crazy."

In a *New York Times* op-ed piece, "What Your College President Didn't Tell You," John M. McCardell Jr., president emeritus of Middlebury College and a charter member of Presidents Against Drunk Driving, dispensed some common sense on the topic, arguing that the twenty-one-year-old drinking-age limit is bad social policy and "terrible law":

> Our latter-day prohibitionists have driven drinking behind closed doors and underground. This is the hard lesson of prohibition that each generation must relearn. No college president will say that drinking has become less of a problem in the years since the age was raised. Would we expect a student who has been denied access to oil paint to graduate with an ability to paint a portrait in oil? Colleges should be given the chance to educate students, who in all other respects are adults, in the appropriate use of alcohol, within campus boundaries and out in the open.

Dr. Morris Chafetz, founder of the National Institute on Alcohol Abuse and Alcoholism, has been involved in public health and treating alcoholism for fifty years. In his eye-opening book *Big Fat*

Liars, a study on the manipulation of science for political purposes, Chafetz recalled that during his tenure as chairman of the Education and Prevention Committee on the Presidential Commission on Drunken Driving, he regretted his failure "to act on a major societal concern: underage drinking." Chafetz claims that the commission pressured him into voting to raise the drinking age across the nation to make the decision unanimous. He relented. Now he says it was the wrong decision.

Chafetz maintains that kids who are denied something will want it more. And there is plenty of evidence to support his contention. Portugal, a nation where there is no legal drinking age, experiences one of the lowest of alcohol problems in the world. In Argentina, Spain, France, and countless other nations, there are few age limitations on alcohol, and abuse remains rare.

★ ★ ★

If you happen to be one of those insubordinate parents who have decided to ignore the law and take the responsibility of parenting back, you could land in deep trouble.

Gregg Anderson was resolute about having a senior prom party. His mom and dad consented to allowing him to have it at home—but only after learning about a potential all-night beer party at a local beach. Gregg's dad, William, ended up confiscating the keys of thirty-four potentially sauced teenagers. He supervised their actions all night. He might have saved someone's life. But when the police showed up at his house at 4:30 A.M. in response to a noise complaint, William was arrested for providing liquor to minors.

"We knew the chances we were taking," Anderson explained. "We knew the party was probably flouting the law one way or the other. But we aren't trying to make a statement. We aren't trying to take a stance. We simply said, 'We aren't just going to let our kids go out drinking and driving,' because we are the ones who will have to live with it later on—live with knowing we didn't do what we did—if somebody got hurt."

Many anti-drinking groups disagree with this strategy. "We want parents to understand that underage drinking is not just kids being kids, or a rite of passage. It is a serious—even deadly—problem," said Wendy Hamilton, then-president of MADD.

The assertion that alcohol—no matter what amount is consumed—is deadly, provides the justification for almost any intrusion. To sum up this position neatly, we can turn to a pretty amazing MADD television ad which declares that "if you think there's a difference" between heroin and alcohol, "you're dead wrong."

This, of course, is a lie. Indeed, not only is moderate alcohol consumption not as damaging as heroin, but overall, it's probably pretty good for you, as we'll discuss later.

THE HAPPY LIFE

There are other differences between heroin and alcohol. For one thing, I can only seem to purchase one of those substances in inner city parks.

To improve the life in parks a couple of years back, the Denver director of parks recommended a mild slackening of restrictions on alcohol consumption to help bring crowds back to the park for more civilized events like jazz and classical-music concerts. The idea was met with immediate resistance from many community leaders, despite strong public sentiment supporting the changes. At the time, I penned a column in *The Denver Post* detailing the predictable overreactions of do-gooders and others who'd been hoodwinked into believing that alcoholic products, not irresponsible drinkers, were the cause of lawlessness.

Treating citizens like conscientious adults was a refreshing change, I thought. Adults, after all, follow the law even when it's a dumb law. Irresponsible adults rarely adhere to the law, even when it makes sense. Hence, only accountable adults are barred from enjoying a glass of wine at a picnic with friends, or from drinking a bottle of beer while attending a public concert.

Well, this column caused a fairly hostile letter-writing campaign that took me to task. Was I freaking nuts? Was I an alcoholic? Obviously I couldn't care less about the children. I didn't care about the city. I didn't care about the parks. I didn't care about alcoholics . . .

But especially, I didn't care about the children.

So I gave this criticism some serious thought. And I was concerned about children—up to a point. As a father of two young daughters it occurred to me that one day all this carefree talk of freedom to tipple would come back and bite me. (Though I noted that if I had intended to be responsible for *everyone's* children I would have become a teacher or, better yet, a policy expert at the Center for Science in the Public Interest.)

Was it negligent to bring attention to a provocateur like Frank Kelly Rich? Someone who had the nerve to actually *celebrate* intoxication? Was it reckless of me to mock those who were taking on America's number-one drug problem? How could I possibly pass judgment on MADD?

These were *mothers* and they are *against* drunk driving.

But a journalist's job—and sometimes people forget this—isn't to write public service announcements, or even to "educate" readers about the latest scare that they transcribe from a press release. (A father's job, on the other hand, is somewhat more of a mystery.)

How can the author defend getting drunk? What helped me appreciate my own position was a 1994 op-ed article by Coleman

Andrews of the *Los Angeles Times* titled "In Defense of Getting Drunk." Andrews wasn't writing about the "falling-down/throwing-up/screaming-and-flailing-or-sniffing-and-sobbing/out-of-control drunk" but rather the kind of intoxication that almost all of us have experienced at a wedding or ball game or at home with our family.

Andrews had two young daughters at the time. His wife asked him what he would do when his one-day teenage daughter approached him and says "Dad, I'd like a glass of wine before I do my homework"? Coleman replied that he'd tell her no. He would explain that some of the good things in life you must wait for "like coffee in the morning, a driver's license and that glass of wine."

> I realize, though, that that's far from enough. I realize that I have to imbue in my daughters a sense of respect for alcohol's heady powers and a sense of responsibility in its use. I hope, too, that I can inspire in them a deep affection for the concept of conviviality, and for the almost sacramental implications of breaking bread and sharing wine with someone.
>
> But I also hope—and this is the really tricky part—that I can teach them this about getting drunk: That drinking, like life, is a matter of balance; that balance isn't always the same as moderation, though it keeps moderation at its core—and that you can't keep your balance if you can't see the edge.

Seems like a sensible way to deal with life—and a perfect lesson for how to deal with children. Nevertheless, common sense and moderation, a healthy and balanced life, seem to elude the nanny at every turn.

ZERO TOLERANCE

If you're looking for a story that defies common sense look no further than Debra Bolton. A lawyer, single mom, and resident of the Washington, D.C., suburb of Alexandria, Virginia, isn't your average criminal. This straitlaced woman probably never imagined that she'd spend a night in the tank. Yet in May of 2005, after leaving friends at the Café Milano in Georgetown, that's just what happened.

Bolton had driven only a few hundred yards before being pulled over by D.C. police for driving without the headlights on in her SUV. While being interrogated, she explained to the officer that the parking attendant had most likely turned off her vehicle's automatic-light feature. No big deal, it would seem.

The police requested that Bolton step out of the car, walk a straight line, recite the alphabet, stand on one foot and count to thirty, then the officer checked her eyes for jerkiness . . . and so it went.

Ultimately, a breath test revealed that Bolton's blood alcohol content was at .03, which equates to a single glass of wine and was well below the legal .08 limit presuming intoxication in D.C. Not low enough for the arresting officer, however. This middle-aged mother of two, who hadn't abused alcohol, who hadn't run a red light or stop sign, was handcuffed, fingerprinted, and arrested. The arresting officer, the poorly named Dennis Fair, clarified the situation: "If you get behind the wheel of a car with any measurable amount of alcohol, you will be dealt with in D.C. We have zero tolerance . . . Anything above .01, we can arrest."

Fair displayed little compassion for conscientious drinking or Bolton, and though he recognized the fact that nearly everyone in the D.C. area was unaware of the draconian policy of zero tolerance, he said, "If you don't know about it, then you're a victim of your own ignorance."

★ ★ ★

What Bolton and the vast majority of Washingtonians didn't know at the time was that according to the city code, the District of Columbia employed a "zero tolerance" policy. Bolton's apprehension at the hands of the D.C. police wasn't a unique incident or the work of a single overzealous cop. Police arrested 321 people for driving under the influence with blood alcohol levels below the legal limit of .08 in 2004. The year before, 409 people.

After the Bolton incident, James Klaunig, a toxicology expert at Indiana University's medical school, told *The Washington Post*, "There's no way possible she failed a test from impairment with a .03 blood alcohol level."

Blood alcohol content (BAC), one of the primary tools used by law enforcement to catch drunk drivers, is a measurement that determines how much alcohol is present in the bloodstream. A BAC of .08, for instance, means that your blood has a .08 percent blood alcohol content level. At that level, though you're hardly slurring your words or staggering, it is illegal to drive in a majority of states.

In 1998, the U.S. House approved a measure by a convincing 344 to 50 vote, and later the Senate gave the legislative approval 78 to 10, to lower the BAC from .10 to .08. MADD president Karolyn Nunnallee maintained at the time that a nationwide .08 law "will save nearly 600 lives every year." In 2000, President Clinton signed a federal law to lower the legal BAC, measured in percentages, from .10 to .08. States that didn't go along were threatened with—you guessed it—the loss of federal highway funds. Furthermore, Nunnallee's contention has been demonstrably false. Vehicular deaths have leveled off. Instead what we have done is corrode the fight against drunk driving by shifting our attention away from the root—serious alcohol abusers with no regard for the law—and toward accountable drinkers.

The point, of course, is to muddle the distinction between "drunk driving" and "drinking any amount of alcohol and driving." For temperance activists this logic makes all the sense in the world. California senator Barbara Boxer once stated that the law "may wind up in this country going to zero tolerance, period." Former MADD president Katherine Prescott concurred, once saying, "There is no safe blood alcohol and for that reason responsible drinking means no drinking and driving."

Technically she's correct. As a matter of fact, driving is never absolutely safe. Indisputably driving is not risk free while you're speaking on the cell phone (banned in many places across the country) or to a friend, applying lipstick, eating a sandwich, drinking coffee, turning the radio knob, singing aloud, reprimanding the kids in the backseat, or daydreaming about weekend plans. The way things are progressing in this country, I suspect it won't be long before we're facing legislation banning all those things.

Bolton, from the available evidence, looked to be a responsible social drinker. She, like many others, was experiencing the firsthand effects of the inanity of nannyism. Bolton, who sat in a jail cell for hours, was not released until 4:30 in the morning.

★ ★ ★

Though alcohol nannies support zero tolerance, it's interesting to note one dissenting voice that doesn't. "I thought the emphasis on .08 laws was not where the emphasis should have been placed," Candace Lightner, the founder of MADD, told the *Los Angeles Times* in 2002. "The majority of crashes occur with high blood-alcohol levels, the .15, .18 and .25 drinkers. Lowering the blood-alcohol concentration was not a solution to the alcohol problem."

Lightner was not someone whose word can be easily dismissed.

In 1980, her thirteen-year-old daughter, Cari, was murdered by a hit-and-run driver on a suburban street in Southern California. When the perpetrator was apprehended, he was drunk, and it turned out he had been convicted four previous times of driving while intoxicated—once, only days before the incident. Incredibly, he received a paltry two-year prison sentence—which he avoided by serving time in a work camp and a halfway house. Arrested for a sixth time for drunken driving in 1985, the man was sentenced to four years in prison by a judge who said he continued to pose a danger to the community.

The inconsequential sentence her daughter's killer received spurred Lightner to promise herself that she "would fight to make this needless homicide count for something positive in the years ahead." She did just that. When Lightner first organized Mothers Against Drunk Drivers—later tweaking the name to Mothers Against Drunk Driving—she ended up changing the world for the better by raising public awareness of the serious nature of drunken driving and promoting tough legislation against the crime.

Due to her potent grassroots work, aggressive campaigning, and popularization of the concept of designated drivers, MADD swelled rapidly in its first five years. By 1985, it boasted 364 chapters, 600,000 members, and a budget of $12.5 million.

Lightner, however, soon left, or was ousted from (depending on who you listen to), the organization she founded. Some MADD execs claimed she was making extravagant salary and budgetary demands. She maintained, on the other hand, that it was a *coup d'etat* at the organization. Since then she has come out protesting the shift from attacking drunk driving to attacking drinking in general. "I worry that the movement I helped create has lost direction. [The .08 legislation] ignores the real core of the problem," she once explained. "If we really want to save lives, let's go after the most dangerous drivers on the road." Lightner argued that MADD had developed into an organization that was far more "neo-prohibitionist" than she had ever envisioned. "I didn't start MADD to deal with alcohol. I started MADD to deal with the issue of drunk driving."

I expect that nearly every parent in the United States is deeply opposed to drunk driving. Yet I don't believe every parent in the United States would be willing to go to the lengths MADD does to stop drinking.

As for Debra Bolton's case, it backfired on neo-prohibitionists.

Soon after a noisy reaction from local citizens and national attention, the D.C. City Council voted in favor of a resolution to abandon the "zero tolerance" policy. "D.C. is once again open for business," said council member Carol Schwartz, principal author of the legislation. She said visitors "can come in and have a glass of wine and not be harassed or intimidated."

That's good news. Sadly, it's not always the case.

ROAD WORRIES

According to the National Highway Traffic Safety Administration, for the past decade, somewhere between 16,000 and 17,000 traffic-related fatalities are attributed to alcohol—which amounts to around 39 percent of total vehicular fatalities each year.

But it used to be a good deal worse. Back in 1982, a shocking 60 percent of all traffic fatalities were alcohol related. For years, nothing was done. Since then, public awareness has grown through ad campaigns and education. States have instituted stricter punishment for drunk driving and law-enforcement officials are better prepared. A lot of the credit must be given to the hard work MADD engaged in through educating the public about the menace of drinking and driving.

Almost every year saw progress and the decline in alcohol-related deaths persisted until 1997. Since then, the vehicular death toll contributable to alcohol has remained stationary at around 40 percent. This stagnation in drunk-driving deaths has initiated considerable consternation among activists and law-enforcement officials.

What can be done? Well, the next threshold of nannyism is heading off potential criminals before they can do anything wrong. The prospective criminal in this case happens to be you and me.

There are more than forty states that require convicted drunken drivers to install ignition-interlock devices in their cars. The ignition interlock prevents drivers who have alcohol in their system from starting their cars. By breathing into this device it will determine your blood alcohol concentration and if the level is measurable the vehicle simply won't start.

Considering the high recidivism rates among drunk drivers, the ignition-interlock system may be a reasonable preventive measure for those who have proven they are dangerous to society. But you, who haven't ever been arrested, perhaps you've never even had a ticket, or taken a drink . . . can you be trusted to start your own car without taking a blood test each time?

New Mexico state representative Ken Martinez introduced a bill that would have forced every driver in his state to hook up to an ignition interlock. Incredibly, the bill breezed through the state's House of Representatives by forty-five to twenty-two. "Honestly, I put forward this bill to start some dialogue," Martinez claimed. "And it became a very thought-provoking process . . . We want New Mexico to be a leader at using technology to curb some societal ills."

It always starts with some conversation. And this bill should incite dialogue, brimming with indignation and contempt for those who attack our civil liberties—and burden us with impractical obstacles. In the end, the consumer would be forced to pay an additional $1,000—at last estimate—to hook up each one of these gadgets. This does not even take into account the bureaucratic nightmare that goes along with keeping track of these devices.

The New Mexico Senate, thankfully, let the bill die. But it's not the last we've heard of this bad idea. Soon legislators in both New York and Oklahoma were making noise about using the ignition interlock. "If the public wants it and the data support it, it is literally possible that the epidemic of drunk driving could be solved where cars simply could not be operated by drunk drivers," explained Chuck Hurley, once with MADD and now with the National Safety Council. "What a great day that would be."

The quixotic notion that life would just be groovy if some magical contraptions could stop us from wrongdoing tells us a lot about the philosophy of the neo-prohibitionist. Preventative—or preemptive—measures on this scale have become a dicey proposition for those interested in civil rights.

In 2007, a bill was introduced in the Pennsylvania House of Representatives which would have mandated that every new car sold in the state be equipped with ignition interlocks by the year 2009—whether the driver has a record of drunk driving or not. But then again, Pennsylvania legislators and courts aren't always worried about the presumption of innocence.

In 2005, a Pennsylvania state appellate court rejected an appeal from a man whose driver's license was revoked after he told doctors that he knocked back more than a six-pack of beer daily. (A 1960s Pennsylvania law requires doctors to report any physical or mental impairments that could compromise a patient's driving ability.) Impressive, sure. But that doesn't mean we can snatch his rights away preemptively, does it?

Yes. A three-judge Commonwealth Court panel said the Pennsylvania Department of Transportation was justified in recalling the license of Keith Emerich. Not because he had driven intoxicated—but rather because he *might.* Emerich didn't have any DUIs. His job attendance was as exemplary, as was his driving record.

THE WOBBLY WALK

Then there are numerous law-enforcement initiatives we take for granted that are unduly invasive and ineffective. The roadblock is a case in point—a well-intentioned preventative measure that does little more than create pollution and waste our time. This form of anticipatory law enforcement intimidates social drinkers and fails to address hardcore types who simply avoid roadblocks. It targets those who aren't driving recklessly, haven't had a single drink, and have places to go.

According to numerous studies and reports dating back to 1987, the chance of getting picked up at a roadblock for being intoxicated is minuscule. One police estimate maintained that only 1 in 2,000 drunken drivers are nabbed—after which the driver is typically charged with lesser crimes. The National Highway Traffic and Safety Administration data on alcohol-related deaths for 2003 and 2004 showed that most of the states that experienced a drop were states that didn't use sobriety checkpoints.

Nonetheless, MADD is a big supporter of sobriety checkpoints. It alleges that roadblocks reduce fatal alcohol-related crashes by as much as 20 percent. The beverage lobby—granted, also with a dog in the fight—notes that nearly all the reductions in fatal crashes in 2004, for instance, occurred in states that don't use checkpoints.

By the end of 2006, MADD had convinced many in the New York Metropolitan Transportation Authority that banning alcohol from commuter trains on Metro-North and the Long Island Rail Road was a great idea. "Times have changed and drunk driving is a major concern," explained MTA board member Mitch Pally.

Times have indeed changed. Nowadays *fewer* people drink and drive than used to. Pally's proposal was based on accidents wherein commuters had fallen through the gaps between the platforms and trains and died. A well-known tragic incident involved a Minnesota teen who died on the Long Island Rail Road on her way to a concert. Her blood-alcohol level was 0.23 percent, nearly three times the legal driving limit.

★ ★ ★

During the Christmas season of 2003 in Herndon, Virginia, a suburb of Washington, D.C., and mere miles from the site of Debra Bolton's arrest, local police took preemptive law enforcement to a dubious extreme, launching a sting operation that targeted twenty local restaurants and bars.

The mission: apprehend "drunk" patrons inside local bars. Patrons who were far from their cars—or, in some cases, did not even own cars. What type of evidence did police employ to ascertain the levels of intoxication deemed appropriate enough for an arrest? According to one law-enforcement official involved in the sting, the determination as to whether you were drunk could be made from seeing unflicked cigarette ashes, an excessive amount of restroom visits, noisy cursing, or a wobbly walk. In other words, they could be after partially deaf, gimpy patrons with enlarged prostates.

Still, it was apparently a necessity for ten cops to show up in SWAT-like gear to pick on clientele and haul them outside. "They tapped one lady on the shoulder—who was on her first drink and had just eaten dinner—to take her out on the sidewalk and give her a sobriety test," according to the general manager of one of the targeted establishments. "They told her she fit the description of a woman they had complaints about, and that they heard she was dancing topless."

In one raid, of the eighteen drinkers who were tested for sobriety, nine were hauled to jail for public intoxication. When asked to make clear the reasoning for the raid, Police Chief J. Thomas Manger stated that you "can't be drunk in a bar."

Where can you be drunk?

"At home."

"Or at someone else's home."

"And stay there until you're not drunk."

★ ★ ★

If we keep this up, watching television under the influence in your own home—not far removed from the privacy of private business—will be grounds for paramilitary raids. A Super Bowl gathering, a wedding shower, or a bachelor party can feature dozens of guests, many of whom will be drinking. Why not target those people as well? They have cars.

And no one argues that public intoxication is illegal—as is jaywalking and selling water yo-yos in Illinois—but most often, law enforcement uses common sense, prioritizing their resources to protect citizens in the most efficient way possible. So it's hard to believe that the most pressing problem in all of northern Virginia was an inebriated, *allegedly* topless woman.

The immediate effect of hauling a few inebriated bar patrons down to jail is insignificant, yet the long-term influence, once the word gets out, provides exactly the publicity the nannies were hoping to garner. Although it has sporadically backfired on them. In a display of political unity, the entire city council of Herndon, Virginia, criticized the practice of targeting law-abiding businesses and drinkers. "It is the unanimous opinion of the council that police overstepped their bounds and overreacted," one city council member said, further remarking that the sting "was improper behavior."

The more pertinent question that arises is whether we will tolerate this sort of random and aggressive police activity: Is it accepted or is it an unacceptable slippery slope? Numerous states and municipalities are finding this brand of intimidation worth a shot. In 2005, the Texas Alcoholic Beverage Commission warned that it would be conducting "sales to intoxicated person stings" in various parts of the Lone Star State.

"We believe responsible adults should drink responsibly," revealed Heather Hodges, a victims advocate for MADD who was involved in the planning of this wretched policy. "A bar is not intended to be a place to get fall-down drunk." On this premise, the program went under way as planned, even with the negative reaction in Virginia. In March 2006, one of the first sting operations was conducted in a Dallas suburb where agents infiltrated thirty-six bars and arrested thirty people for public intoxication.

"It's killed our business," one Dallas bar owner told local TV news. "People are scared to come out. I don't even drink, and I'm scared to go out, and it's not right. We don't want to put drunks on the road, but we don't want people to be afraid to do something that's legal. If they don't want people drinking, they should outlaw alcohol."

BAR NONE

Bar owners and other servers of alcohol are increasingly liable if a customer becomes intoxicated on their premises and subsequently injures someone or causes property damage. A majority of states have some variety of liability laws on the books. In Texas, minors can sue a drinking establishment for their own injuries should they get their hands on enough alcohol to be intoxicated and hurt themselves. Then there are the extremes. Under an Illinois law, plaintiffs don't have to prove that the bartender was aware of the customer's inebriation at all.

In New Mexico a bill holds bar owners responsible for two hours after the sale, service, or consumption of alcohol. Such sales can be considered evidence that the person was intoxicated at the time of the sale. In other states, liability extends to serving the "habitually intoxicated," which will be a cinch to determine for all those clairvoyant bartenders.

MADD, in one of their policy positions, states that they "strongly support" the right of victims of alcohol-related traffic crashes to seek "financial recovery from establishments and servers who have irresponsibly provided alcohol to those who are intoxicated or to underage persons, or who serve past the point of intoxication individuals who then cause fatal or injurious crashes."

I'm not sure if any of these neo-prohibitionists has been to a saloon lately, but the local *Cheers*-style tavern where everyone knows your name is all but dead. In large cities, working at a bar can mean serving alcohol to hundreds, if not thousands, of patrons each night. Once we rewire servers to double as seers and human lie detectors, this law would make sense. Until then, we can have mandatory breathalyzer tests for patrons.

★ ★ ★

It's hard to imagine government forcing an industry to keep its prices higher, but this twisted logic is behind the growing idea of banning happy hour. It's certainly not a new tactic. Scotland already bans off-hour price drops. In the United States, way back in 1984, a cadre of tut-tutting prigs in the Massachusetts legislature passed a regulation banning happy hours at bars and restaurants.

The Massachusetts bill kicked off a superfluity of happy-hour limitations around the country. From Ohio, where bars were compelled to end two-for-one premiums at 9:00 P.M., to West Virginia, where even bars must have food available during happy hours, to Mississippi and Oregon, where happy hours are still allowed but cannot be advertised, the happiness is being snatched from law-abiding Americans. Dozens of other states have similar mind-numbing nonsense legislation pending or passed.

Consequently, in many places across this country, a bar and a consumer are prevented from entering into a transaction for a legal product that is accepted by both parties because somewhere a city council member thinks you're an idiot and can't handle one-dollar Buds. This type of policy not only is an assault on basic liberties but it ignores basic economics.

When a 1990 Illinois law banning happy hours hit bars, restaurants and other establishments that served alcohol came up with a creative solution, changing "happy hours" to the even better "happy days." A "happy day" for many means reduced prices on drinks for the entire day, since the price of drinks cannot be changed during any one business day.

We'll see if happy days are here again.

On their online policy page, MADD strongly supports the termination of what it calls "Practices Which Encourage Excessive Alcohol Consumption." What they're talking about here is the abolition of happy hour, ladies' night, and any fluctuations in pricing that bring in consumers during what are traditionally off-hours. The group calls upon the "hospitality industry to voluntarily end all practices associated with excessive alcohol consumption."

MADD also supports state agencies and legislatures passing clear and comprehensive guidelines that prohibit such practices in all fifty states.

This measure might be a lot of different things, but not one of them resembles anything approaching the word "voluntary."

★ ★ ★

In 1998, David Gillespie filed a complaint with the New Jersey Division on Civil Rights. Gillespie declared that it was unfair that area bars offered free admission and discounted drinks to women on ladies' night while men were stuck paying full price. The Division on Civil Rights agreed, ruling that offering free drinks or admission to women but not to men was unlawful and discriminatory. Similar cases have played out across the country.

A dozen other states, including Iowa and Wisconsin, have banned such discounts for women, calling them an unfair form of gender discrimination against men. I would argue that abolishing ladies' night is discrimination against men who now have a smaller number of women to hit on. "I think it's outrageous," said one New Jersey bar owner. "Ladies' night was never intended to discriminate against anybody. As a matter of fact, 70 percent of the patrons on ladies' night are male. They certainly don't feel discriminated against."

Obviously the force of litigation—or even the threat of litigation—can kick off some of the most preposterous policies imaginable. The commentator Christopher Hitchens, who was in his fifties at the time, related one such incident in a speech at a Southern Methodist University conference in 2005:

> I was in a bar in Kentucky the other day. I asked for a drink and the barman said that would be fine but he would need to see my ID. I was partly flattered and partly insulted. I said to him are you serious? He said I'm very serious. No ID, no drink. So I said well, you must be joking. And he said are you trying to make me look stupid? And I said no, only you can do that, but why is this? He said it was zero tolerance; everyone had to show an ID . . . He said, well, our whole chain has had to take this policy be-

> cause we were recently sued by a 70-year-old man [who] asked for a drink and wasn't asked for an ID, and he sued on the grounds of age discrimination. In other words, if he had been 18 he would have had to show an ID but if he was 70, he didn't. What could be more discriminating than that? And I said, and you are telling me that the courts upheld that suit, aren't you? He said, that's right. That's what they did.

Ludicrous and worthless conversations like these go on across America every day. And there are other inconveniences on the way. Bar crawling is common in cities like New York, Chicago, and Los Angeles. A customarily twenty-to-thirty-year-old set gets together and, for a fixed price, bars offer them a tour of unlimited drinks. Why, then, was the practice banned in New York by Governor George Pataki? It seems that the governor believes that the practice encourages "irresponsible binge-drinking." In truth, adult binge drinking (if that's even the case) is none of Pataki's business, as adults have the right to get smashed as long as they don't hurt anyone else.

Bar and nightclub owners, not surprisingly, didn't mind that Albany prevents them from engaging in expensive price wars with competitors. The pubs' chief trade group lobbied strenuously to stop the practice.

It's what we like to call nanny state synergy.

★ ★ ★

Let's imagine for a second that a sporting arena is an enormous bar, which in reality it sort of is. Then we can understand why nannies have targeted them as well. What they do is immediately grab on to any brawl or misconduct by fans and blame alcohol. Of course, at each sporting event—typically averaging around 20,000 people—you will have a handful of louts. But, as with other nannyistic ventures, this is enough evidence to treat grown men and women like children.

George Hacker of the Center for Science in the Public Interest (CSPI), a man whose tender neo-prohibitionist prodding included accusing winemakers of "hawking America's costliest and most devastating drug," had plenty of ideas—and for sports fans who enjoy a beer, one was more infuriating than the next.

- They should stop hawking in the stands . . .
- They should eliminate beer signs all over the stadium . . . every exit has a beer sign over it, so the first thing you're thinking about is having a beer.
- Police in the stands should be much more aggressively looking for people who are obviously intoxicated.
- Sell smaller quantities of beer. Turn those 16-ounce cups into 10-ouncers.
- Sell only beer with lower alcohol (3.2) content.
- Raise the price of beer sold at stadiums.
- Not only cut off beer sales before the game ends, but limit the amount of time beer is sold before the game.

What, are we in Europe? Americans, after all, are not soccer hooligans. For the minority who do misbehave, aggressive policing of alcohol consumption will make little difference, as those folks will always find a way to get their hands on alcohol. As for the majority of law-abiding drinkers, the watered-down beer will become even more expensive (as stadiums try to recoup losses). And worst of all, the honest citizen will once again be treated like a child.

Japanese baseball import Daisuke Matsuzaka signed a six-year, $52 million contract with the Boston Red Sox in 2006. Before he ever threw a major-league pitch, a Japanese commercial for Asahi Super Dry beer, featuring the pitcher innocently sipping the beer, threw hysterical nannies into a panic. He was in his civilian threads, but United States law prohibits humans from consuming beer in television advertisements. And major-league baseball—despite making millions off the product each year—does not allow players to endorse beer.

Arthur Resnick, director of public and media affairs for the Alcohol and Tobacco Tax and Trade Bureau in Washington, D.C., claimed at the time that Matsuzaka's ad might be investigated by the government despite its running in a foreign market. "Our jurisdiction runs to false and misleading ads," explained Resnick, "which depict any individual (famous athlete or otherwise) consuming or about to consume an alcoholic beverage prior to or during an athletic activity or event," or advertisements claiming that drinking alcohol "will enhance athletic prowess, performance at athletic activities or events, health or conditioning."

So continues a long history of overreaction concerning advertisements featuring alcoholic beverages. In 1936, members of the Distilled Spirits Council of the United States voluntarily banned ads promoting hard liquors like vodka and whiskey on the radio. Twelve years later, the industry extended that ban to include the new medium of television. Liquor manufacturers dutifully adhered to this self-imposed embargo until, to the howling protestations of health officials, Seagram decided to cease the practice in 1996. Good for them.

It was reported that President Bill Clinton personally requested

Edgar Bronfman Jr., the president and chief executive of Seagram, to desist from advertising liquor products on television. Fresh off his reelection win, Clinton used the first radio address of his new administration to hector the liquor industry for their decision, asking them to reconsider.

Utilizing the politically expedient "family values" rhetoric that helped him beat Republican candidate Bob Dole at his own game, Clinton charged the industry with damaging the family structure by making the parents' job of raising children even harder. Since when is it the government's job to make parenting easier? How many steps before we hand over the kids to the state at birth?

As expected, "public health" advocacy groups, government officials, and meddlesome citizen activists joined Clinton in reacting with indignant distress and worse, arguing that spirits ads would inevitably lure vulnerable children and transform them into a bunch of diminutive alcoholics.

The Federal Communications Commission (FCC), at the behest of the administration, got into the act to "investigate." That riled the Association of National Advertisers, who argued that it was the Federal Trade Commission's job to regulate national advertising, not the FCC's. The Center for Science in the Public Interest, true to form, placed a panic-stricken ad in *The New York Times* blasting the Seagram marketer's latest "predatory broadcast."

Massachusetts congressman Joseph Kennedy—grandson and namesake of patriarch Joe Kennedy, who profited in untold millions from liquor bootlegging—introduced a bill to censor hard-liquor advertisements across the board. Kennedy asserted that "the enormous impact that alcohol advertising is having on young people today—alcohol is now the number-one killer—alcohol abuse—of people under the age of 34 in the United States."

Seagram had apparently tweaked the uptight Kennedy clan by placing advertising in New Hampshire—which spills over into the

Boston market. Why? Some believed that the hard-liquor industry either wanted a full ban on television advertisement or the right to compete. One of the first questions a congressman should ask is: How does this mesh with the First Amendment? In an interview on *CBS This Morning,* Kennedy said that had nothing to do with it.

> **CBS:** Where does the First Amendment come into this, Congressman, or does it?
> **Kennedy:** I . . . I'm sorry; missed the question.
> **CBS:** I said, where does the First Amendment come into this whole controversy, or does it?
> **Kennedy:** Well, I think, of course, the First Amendment is an issue—in this particular instance, I think, when we look at the kind of action that has been taken with regard to cigarette advertising, this is an issue that the Supreme Court has already ruled on and has ruled constitutional. I think it's much the same in terms of the accuracy of advertising. You can't tell kids that they're going to be better off by having a drink and think that you're accurately reporting on the effects of alcohol.

Kennedy was confused. There has never been an advertisement for liquor that says you're going to be better off—but even if there was, it wouldn't be false advertising, as we will see, because you might be. As Kennedy mentioned, the Supreme Court had indeed ruled in 1971 that a congressional ban on cigarette advertising on television and radio was legal. This was clearly worded and had nothing to do with alcohol or the First Amendment. In 2001, the Supreme Court also upheld tobacco companies' free-speech rights to market their "poisonous products" to adults who choose to put their health at risk.

Activists may believe that alcohol is a toxic product, but the majority of Americans do not have the same belief. It's not surprising that a philosophy that can equate moderate alcohol consumption with heroin use, can quite easily put forward habits of smoking and alcohol as linked.

Clinton, Kennedy, the FCC, the CSPI, and all the other critics of free speech didn't offer any valid substantiation that alcohol advertisements increased the likelihood of underage consumption. They couldn't because no reputable link was available. The Department of Health and Human Services concluded that "research has yet to document a strong relationship between alcohol advertising and alcohol consumption." The Federal Trade Commission also found "no reliable basis to conclude that alcohol advertising significantly affects consumption, let alone abuse." And since a good number of Americans who drink, drink moderately and responsibly, there is no evidence that the public at large can be easily induced to alcoholism through trendy commercials.

SWEET 'N' LOW

The recent market explosion of syrupy alcoholic beverages like Mike's Hard Lemonade, Smirnoff Ice, Bacardi Silver, and Jack Daniel's Original Hard Cola has opened another front on the war against alcohol. Since "malternatives," as they are often called—think modish wine cooler—are technically beers, neoprohibitionists believe they can be easily and amply advertised on broadcast television.

Naturally, with stylish products come trendy ads. Hyperactive edits of scantily clad models, appropriately quaffed men ogling them with energetic music hitting hard in the background certainly appeal to the MTV demographic. This was too much for some nannies to bear. George Hacker, the director of the Alcohol Policies

Project at the CSPI, carped that ads for alcoholic beverages like these "press all of the adolescent hot buttons—sex, music, rebellion, independence."

Hacker's distress at the thought of alcohol ads was predictable, but someone should tell him that even in the thirty-to-ninety-five demographic "music," "sex," and "independence" are still hot buttons.

"They may believe they are targeting adults," alleged Hacker. "But these products disguise the taste of alcohol and make it easier to drink. They are intended as bridges to other forms of alcohol." And so the CSPI decided to petition the federal government in hopes of finding the link. But it didn't happen. A Federal Trade Commission investigation that included a "10-city retail placement survey, a review of advertising and an analysis of internal alcohol company documents, including market and consumer research records" concluded that beverages that were sweet weren't automatically targeted to minors.

The CSPI maintained that the feds have "cavalierly dismissed" the potential for malt beverages misleading consumers. "Many of them look like soft drinks, and they taste like Sprite or lemonade," Hacker says. "These are alcoholic beverages for the 'Pepsi Generation.' These are beer or liquor on training wheels."

But drinking among the young has not proliferated in spite of the supposed influence of these kiddie drinks. What we're left with is more scaremongering.

★ ★ ★

And let's not forget cartoons. Kids love cartoons. In 1995, the label of Bad Frog Beer depicted an unsightly green amphibian extending its middling finger in "a well-known human gesture of insult" accompanied by such delightful slogans such as "An amphibian with an attitude" and "He's mean, green and obscene"—oh, and barred from the market.

Eight states were outraged by the threat of an antagonistic frog and banned Bad Frog. The New York State Liquor Authority, charged with approving labels, denied Bad Frog's application twice. Tom Ridge, then-governor of Pennsylvania and later head of the Department of Homeland Security, favored banning the sale of Bad Frog Beer because, he explained, the label jumped the boundaries of good taste.

As for Bad Frog, well, the brewery argued—quite convincingly—that a frog with only four fingers couldn't possibly raise a middle one. There were some other First Amendment issues in play as well. The resulting case, *Bad Frog Brewery, Inc. v. New York State Liquor Authority*, cleared up many things, including the meaning of the middle finger:

> The gesture, also sometimes referred to as "flipping the bird," see New Dictionary of American Slang 133, 141 (1986), is acknowledged by Bad Frog to convey, among other things, the message "fuck you." The District Court found that the gesture "connotes a patently offensive suggestion," presumably a suggestion to having intercourse with one's self.

In the end, the New York court told the State Liquor Authority to, in effect, go have intercourse with itself, ruling that the potential for an image to attract a child is not reason enough to ban it from a beer bottle. The statewide ban was lifted.

Around the same time the pivotal Bad Frog Beer was being debated in a New York appeals court, in Pennsylvania the Alcohol Control Board banned the sale of an imported beer called Manneken Pis White Ale due to its label. The beer, produced by a company in Belgium, featured a likeness of the celebrated Brussels landmark Manneken Pis—which literally translates to "man who urinates"—a small bronze fountain sculpture depicting a little boy urinating into a fountain's basin. In nearby Ohio, officials called the label "offensive and in poor taste" and banned the company from shipping the beer to its state.

The company argued that Manneken Pis wasn't just a puerile stab at sales but a famous artwork that dates to at least the year 1377. The company lost its first round in appeals when the court agreed that the government can't legislate taste, but upheld the ban because Ohio law forbids any portrayal of children (even if said child happens to be a statue) on beer bottles.

In 2005, a British import called Seriously Bad Elf became the topic of great consternation. Connecticut state officials tried to ban the ale because they held that its label might entice children to drink. The label they spoke of featured an illustration of a malevolent-looking elf with a slingshot firing Christmas ornaments at Santa's sleigh dashing overhead.

Numerous states have laws prohibiting any use of Santa Claus imagery to sell alcohol. Obviously, this law is meant to quash any thoughts the two-to-seven-year-old set may have about purchasing a six-pack of overpriced microbrew. Many states have laws governing the presence of military scenes or even a depiction of an American flag in the pursuit of selling alcohol. "There are certain symbols and images that appeal more strongly to children and this regulation includes the most obvious among them," explained Connecticut attorney general Richard Blumenthal. "The state has wide discretion to regulate the sales of alcohol."

To back this up, nannies will often point to a 1996 study which showed that more kids recognized the Budweiser frogs than Tony the Tiger or Smokey the Bear. "This kind of advertising has great appeal to young people, but the line where the states and the government can restrict that speech is very squishy," Hacker once explained.

Hacker and friends are trying to firm up the squishiness a bit by asserting that simply because an adult-oriented product has the possibility of tempting a child its advertisements can be banned. They also assume that recognition alone means a child will want to partake of the product. Funny, because there are countless commercials I enjoy and I eagerly look forward to watching that advertise products I would never buy (including cars I will never be able to afford or gadgets I have no interest in owning). Often, I'm not even sure what the brand is.

BONUS: IT'S GOOD FOR YOU

As you probably all know, drinking can make life more bearable at times. So finding out that it may also extend my life is damn near a miracle. Mind you, this is science, not just wishful thinking. Researchers at Harvard Medical School and the National Institute on Aging discovered that a substance found in red wine protected mice from the damaging effects of obesity. The study also raises the prospect that someday this magical substance will be extracted and dispensed in pill form.

"We've been looking for something like this for the last 100,000 years, and maybe it's right around the corner—a molecule that could be taken in a single pill to delay the diseases of aging and keep you healthier as you grow old," David Sinclair, a Harvard molecular biologist and leader of the study, told *The New York Times.* "The potential impact would be huge."

Let's not forget the adage: People aren't mice. But, then again, this is wine. The Hebrews, the Romans, the Greeks, even Jesus—someone who I'm told knows a thing or two about immortality—thought wine was worth a miracle. Certainly, many of you remember the French paradox. The question was simple: Why are the French, even with their love of fatty food, smoking, and drinking, suffering relatively low incidences of heart disease?

According to an article published online in *Cell* by Johan Auwerx at the Institute of Genetics and Molecular and Cellular Biology in Illkirch, France, mice that were given resveratrol, a component of red wine, ran twice as far as those who weren't. Mice were finding extraordinary endurance through red wine—well, sort of.

But it's not just wine.

Dr. Abigail Zuger, a health columnist at *The New York Times*, tells us that a drink or two a day provides the "equivalent of a potent cholesterol medicine and a weak blood thinner." She also writes that alcohol raises the blood levels of HDL, the "good" cholesterol, more than 10 percent. "A drink or two a day of wine, beer, or liquor is, experts say, often the single best nonprescription way to prevent heart attacks." Yep. Better than a "low-fat diet or weight loss, better even than vigorous exercise," according to Zuger.

"The science supporting the protective role of alcohol is indisputable; no one questions it anymore," said Dr. Curtis Ellison, a professor of medicine and public health at the Boston University School of Medicine.

Were you aware that people who regularly drink moderate amounts of alcohol are less likely to be obese than those who abstain? This is what a study published in *BMC Public Health* tells us. Did you know that in 1997 researchers from Brigham and Women's Hospital and Harvard, in a journal of the American Heart Association, found that men who had two drinks a day had a 32 percent lower risk of hardening arteries in the legs?

A 2006 Italian study found that moderate drinking of any alcohol can lengthen your life. The study was based on data from thirty-four larger studies that involved more than one million people. What our friends in Italy found was that drinking moderately (four drinks per day for men and two drinks per day for women) can decrease the chance of death from any cause by approximately 18 percent.

So is drinking a prerequisite to a happy or a healthy life? Of course not. But drinking is a ritual that we've enjoyed for thousands of years. Approximately 75 percent of Americans say they drink alcohol at least occasionally. I'm not a heavy drinker, and still, I can't imagine, nor do I want to, a life without alcohol. Nor should I have to.

★ CHAPTER THREE ★

THE SMOKISTS

The movement which began on the West Coast of America among an uncompromising ragbag of New-Age nutters and radish worshippers has now gained the momentum to sweep the world. We laughed when they first started with their bleating, but laughs are now rare among the little groups of office workers huddled in the street, taking a nicotine hit with all the deep joy of a tramp swigging meths.

—PETE CLARK, BRITISH JOURNALIST

Smoking is one of the leading causes of statistics.

—FLETCHER KNEBEL

★

THE ANTI-HERO

In the classic movie *Mr. Smith Goes to Washington,* Jimmy Stewart's character says, "Lost causes are the only ones worth fighting for." From the looks of it, Washington, D.C., councilperson Carol Schwartz has embraced that sentiment wholeheartedly.

Schwartz is one the few big-city politicians who has had the guts to challenge paternalistic encroachments of government. Her distinctive legislative style has made her a colorful local celebrity. Often seen zooming around town in her red convertible, Schwartz is a pro-choice, urban-minded, witty, populist Republican who has carved out a niche for herself in a city where registered Democrats outnumber GOPers by ten to one. She has run for mayor on four occasions (1986, 1994, 1998, and 2002) and, considering the circumstances, has shown respectably each time despite losing.

When the Capitol Hill neighborhood broached the idea of placing security cameras on streetlights along a strip of Pennsylvania Avenue a few years ago, the only city leader to express opposition to the idea was Schwartz. "I am in favor of more foot patrols and bike patrols," she explained. "I really want to see the presence of officers, not the presence of cameras. It's too Big Brotherish."

In 1997, the Big Brotherish intrusions took the form of the Metropolitan Police Department targeting denizens of northwest D.C. who were drinking alcoholic beverages in front of their doorways (one embattled woman was innocuously sipping red wine while working on her garden). Schwartz promptly sponsored legislation that would allow adult residents to drink a glass of wine or a bottle of beer on the doorstep in front of their home. Similarly, when the case of Debra Bolton (the woman arrested under Washington's zero-tolerance alcohol policy discussed in Chapter Two) came to her attention, Schwartz again was at the forefront of the effort to stop this wretched nannyism, sponsoring a bill to protect drivers.

With her history of defending individual rights and choice, it was no surprise that Schwartz was also the lone councilperson to oppose the proposed Washington, D.C., smoking ban. In her two-year battle as chairman of the Committee on Public Works and the Environment, she repeatedly blocked progress on a citywide smoking ban. Her staunch resistance drove nannies—accustomed to getting their way on these things with little debate—nuts. The holdup led Citizens for Smokefree Workplaces to launch a campaign funded with a $250,000 grant from the New Jersey–based Robert Wood Johnson Foundation, the big mama/sugar daddy of all nanny organizations, to give it a bit of help.

Schwartz wouldn't budge. She whipped up so much trouble, as a matter of fact, that smoke-free advocates attempted to bypass the council altogether and take the issue directly to the ballot. To the nannies' chagrin, D.C. superior court judge Mary A. Gooden Terrell ruled that the initiative banning smoking in all workplaces in Washington was "invalid" and "improper." She then ordered the D.C. Board of Elections and Ethics to yank it from the ballot.

Alas, all good things must come to an end. And in January of 2006, Schwartz finally surrendered to a throng of nannies and fellow travelers. But not without making a worthwhile point, sponsoring a bill to ban all alcohol beverages by using the indistinguishable arguments that smoking-ban advocates employed for their cause. She delivered a tongue-in-cheek speech to the council in which she derided drinkers as irritating and unworthy of a place in our society.

> All my life I've been around people who drink, and I don't—and never have. My personal preference is to be around people who do not drink. I am tired of going to a bar or a restaurant and having these noisy and often sloppy—or worse—drinkers disturb my night out.
>
> I never thought I could ban drinking just because I didn't like it, but now I know I can. The impending smoking ban has empowered me. My personal preference can prevail. And I know many people who don't drink now, even if they did in the past. Why should they and I have to be bothered by non-sober individuals, with their often offensive behavior and smelly breath?

While Schwartz delivered her brilliantly contemptuous speech, many of her compatriots rolled their eyes and giggled dismissively. For them the joke was a rogue councilperson stubbornly fighting for free will and property rights. As Schwartz said, "I like freedom of choice about abortion and nude dancing—consenting adults should have choices."

When Schwartz completed her speech, council chair Linda Cropp referred the bill to committee, calling it "a very thought-provoking piece." Several hours later, Schwartz pulled the proposed legislation, explaining that she had made her point. When the smoking bill reached the council for a vote it passed twelve to one and soon after D.C. mayor Anthony Williams allowed the bill to become law. Schwartz had offered concessions like tax incentives for smoke-free businesses and mandated ventilation systems, and each of these ideas was met with derision or stiff-necked opposition. Compromise is not possible with dogmatists. And as we'll see that's precisely what nicotine nannies are.

Like nearly all nannyism, antismoking advocacy began with the ideological notion that government should be there to lend a hand. Yet at some point, public health warnings and other reasonable, justifiable help transformed into something excessive and intrusive. A perfunctory warning became a nudge then became a forceful shove, and now we have government intimidation, castigating, and laws that undermine property rights and basic freedom of choice.

NO-FUN CITY

Comprehensive antismoking education programs and policies began in 1964 with the publication of the U.S. surgeon general's special report concerning the health consequences of smoking. Cigarette warning labels were first placed on packages in 1965, after years of tobacco companies portraying their product as innocuous—sometimes as healthy and invigorating.

In 1971, Congress took what was at the time the extraordinary step of banning cigarette commercials, which were until then a staple of television advertising. For the first time in contemporary American history, a legal product was banned from advertising because the effects were deemed harmful to the individual. The decision made common sense to the majority of people: Why let children watch cigarettes ads? The ideological matter of whether the ban was a violation of our constitutional right to free speech was, in essence, ignored.

Cigarette consumption in the United States has dropped every year since 1980—long before the first smoking bans or sin taxes or other intrusive regulations were adopted—and per capita cigarette consumption has dropped every year since 1975. Most likely this occurred because more of us took the health consequences of smoking seriously and a new generation had been educated on the perils of smoking. But for the nicotine nanny this decline wasn't quick enough. And at some point along the line, well-meaning activists figured out that it was, to a great extent, simpler to coerce people than to convince them into deciding on healthy alternatives.

In 1975 *U.S. News & World Report* reported that in San Francisco—perhaps ground zero of nannyism today—authorities rejected a rather mild antismoking ordinance. One opponent even went as far as to refer to it as "another effort to legislate morality." Such a proclamation from any elected official would be a (excuse the pun) breath of fresh air today. "Indications are that antismoking forces still have a long road ahead," the article went on to portend.

★ ★ ★

Having grown up in and around New York City, it was almost impossible for me to believe that a smoking ban could take hold in the great city. But there it was. "First they cleaned up Times Square, then they said you couldn't dance in bars or drink a beer in the park. Now you can't even smoke when you go out on the town," Willie Martinez, thirty-seven, a denizen of the East Village in Manhattan told *CBS News* after the New York smoking ban was instituted. "This is like no-fun city."

By the time New York City banned smoking, approximately four hundred communities across the nation had adopted comparable measures according to the Americans for Nonsmokers' Rights Foundation. New York City, though, had passed one of the most wide-ranging bans in the entire nation, covering all workplaces, including bars, restaurants (small and large), bingo parlors, Off-Track Betting offices, and other areas the city's previous smoking laws may have missed. Those who ignored this government-imposed prohibition could be fined $400 a pop and have their business licenses suspended and eventually revoked.

As was the case everywhere else in the nation, New York's

smoking ban was politically expedient and faced scarcely any opposition. Few politicians or solid citizens would contest a ban that allegedly saves the lives of children and relegates the ugly habit of smoking to the fringes of city life.

Approximately 90 percent of the nation doesn't light up and a good number do not appreciate smoke wafting through the air in their favorite eatery. Smoking is an all-too-familiar nuisance to nonsmokers and their annoyance is understandable. Yet with enough grousing, more exclusively nonsmoking restaurants began popping up—in the neighborhood of Denver where I reside, finding an establishment to smoke indoors would have been hopeless long before a statewide smoking ban was enacted—and more were sure to follow. And most important, few polls demonstrate that Americans were terribly concerned about the issue. Demands for legislation came from select nanny groups and politicians, not from the public.

The New York ban was the handiwork of one of the nation's most energetic meddlers, Mayor Michael Bloomberg. Drawing on a self-righteousness typically reserved for crown heads, Bloomberg's pomposity was the result of a billionaire do-gooder being handed the reins of political power.

What was wrong with the man? Well, we can begin with his mendaciousness. Bloomberg incessantly lectured the public about the risks of secondhand smoke (a topic we'll soon investigate) as the pivotal justification for smoking bans. But his genuine motive, discerned from his speeches and actions, was the prohibition of *all* smoking through government directive.

"There are roughly 5 million people who are killed by tobacco in this world each year, and, unless we take urgent action this century, a billion people will die from smoking," Bloomberg said after donating $125 million to fight tobacco worldwide. "We know how to save millions of lives, and shame on us if we don't do it."

Bloomberg, like many other antismoking nannies, intertwined the goals of "protecting" nonsmokers from the nicotine addicts and of saving the lives of smokers.

When raising sin taxes on smokes—for the umpteenth time—Bloomberg claimed, "It's not a revenue source. We're trying to save the lives of our children." When his ally Christine Quinn, who chairs the city council's health committee, was asked about the smokers fleeing New York, she declared: "If someone is going to drive from Manhattan to Orange County to have a cigarette then there is really not much we can do to help that person."

The crucial questions here are: Who exactly asked for anyone's help? And what responsibility, if any, does government have to impel people to be healthy? Unquestionably, not a single person on Earth is killed *by* tobacco. No more than they are killed by fatty foods. Sure, millions of people *choose* to smoke. They may be killing themselves. And as a public-policy matter, it's none of my business. Those are the risks, rewards, and choices associated with being free. With self-determination, we have to be prepared to accept that some people will make choices that fly in the face of reason.

This is a dilemma for nannies. The answer, naturally, is to frame the smoking of tobacco as a disease, an uncontainable addiction, with victims powerless to resist. Former Centers for Disease Control director William Foege once wrote that, "Free will is not within the power of most smokers." Scott Ballin, chairman of the Coalition on Smoking OR Health, explained that "The product has no potential benefits . . . It's addictive, so people don't have the choice to smoke or not to smoke."

No choice? Conceivably Foege and Ballin somehow missed the tens of millions of Americans who have quit smoking on their own. It seems those individuals had a choice and exercised it. Or perhaps Foege and Ballin have never met any of the millions of Americans, fully aware of the health consequences linked to tobacco, who smoke because they enjoy the pleasure that smoking gives them. Some folks derive their gratification through telling others how to conduct their lives . . . others enjoy a cigarette after sex. To each his own.

The sociologist Anne Wortham, a smoker herself, best summed up this doctrinaire impulse when she remarked: "Tobacco's opponents believe that if you smoke, you are in a state of false consciousness, because you are not aware of what is in your interests. It's the refusal to acknowledge people's capacity to make choices. You just define them out of the discourse."

And this discourse did not adhere to the normal political paradigms. Though nominally Republican—former New York Democratic mayor Ed Koch once pointed out that Bloomberg was about as Republican as he was—in truth, Bloomberg engaged in little on the political or social front that wasn't colored by paternalistic intent.

In the eyes of some New Yorkers—noteworthy New Yorkers—Bloomberg was guilty of a far more egregious sin than government-sponsored health directives. He was guilty of stultifying the edge, the spirit, the life force, the chi of their beloved city.

Bloomberg's predecessor, Rudolph Giuliani, was often disparaged by locals for his uncompromising efforts to wipe all crime and pornography from the city landscape—as it took with it a large amount of the inimitability of Manhattan. In this regard, Bloomberg made Giuliani look like a crime lord by comparison. Handed a gentrified New York, scraped clean of much of the grubby criminality of the 1970s and early 1980s, Bloomberg, with little constructive cleaning up left to do, began injecting himself into the personal lives of residents.

Surprisingly, in New York the moderately small revolt against the smoking ban did not come exclusively from conservative/libertarian elements but primarily from the high-minded liberal literati. "I understand, of course, that many people find smoking objectionable," wrote the chain-smoking New York satirist Fran Lebowitz years ago in her classic essay "When Smoke Gets in Your Eyes . . . Shut Them." "That is their right. I would, I assure you, be the very last to criticize the annoyed. I myself find many—even most—things objectionable. Being offended is the natural consequence of leaving one's home. I do not like aftershave lotion, adults who roller-skate, children who speak French, or anyone who is unduly tan. I do not, however, go around enacting legislation and putting up signs."

The typically reclusive Lebowitz was so incensed by the New York City smoking ban that she went on local television and let loose a barrage of criticism against the ban and the mayor, calling it absurd, childish, peevish, pious, anti-urban, antidemocratic, hypocritical . . . and so on.

Lebowitz didn't believe that New Yorkers were wringing their hands over smoking. She believed that it was a crusade carried out by do-gooders. "If people want to go to a clean place, there are many clean places. I came to New York when I was eighteen—and not because I heard it was so clean."

According to the *New York Post,* Lebowitz's outburst persuaded city council minority leader James Oddo to fire off an e-mail to the television station, which took umbrage with Lebowitz's fiery verbiage. "Putting aside my overall disdain for Fran Lebowitz," he wrote, "listening to her last night made me sick. I cannot think . . . when you had a guest that was as misinformed on an issue and who spewed opinions not based in fact. I was waiting for [her] to come out and say nicotine is not addictive and that tobacco companies never targeted kids."

We must forgive Oddo for bringing up Big Tobacco and the defenseless children. It's a nanny reflex. After all, Lebowitz never asserted that nicotine wasn't addictive, nor had she posited that tobacco companies hadn't once targeted children. She was simply defending the right of the individual to partake in a habit of their choice on private property without the interference of the New York City government.

Lebowitz wasn't the only high-society critic of the nanny state. Nor was she the most effective. "Under current New York City law, it is acceptable to have a loaded handgun in your place of work, but not an empty ashtray," Graydon Carter, editor in chief of *Vanity Fair,* grumbled in one of his editor's letters. Carter was a vocal critic of New York's nannies, particularly incensed because he had earned three summons for having the audacity to leave an open ashtray on display at his Condé Nast office on Times Square—yes, in his own office at the magazine he runs.

Carter explained that the importance of this issue lay in "freedom and your own civil liberties, and it is about the city. This is not Denver, it is not Seattle, it is a big rough turbine that is fueled by cigarette smoke and food and liquor. People want to go out at night." Carter used *Vanity Fair* to admonish Bloomberg on a monthly basis. Deservedly so.

100 PERCENT PROPAGANDA (NOT THAT IT MATTERS)

"Fundamentally, people just don't want the guy next to them smoking," Mayor Bloomberg explained when the ban was instituted. "People will adjust very quickly and a lot of lives will be saved."

Here we have the entwining of the three motives for antismoking nannyism: it's irritating (people just don't want the guy next to them smoking); freedom of choice is no big deal (you'll adjust); and, the most critical, smoking kills (lives will be saved). It's the final argument that changes everything. It transforms smoking from an unhealthy personal habit into a murderous vice.

The argument that exposure to passive tobacco smoke is dangerous is irrelevant. If a pub owner in Manhattan or Chicago or Los Angeles elects to hang a prominent "smoking allowed" sign on the front door of his establishment, he's practicing sufficient transparency to warn potential patrons. The owner certainly isn't forcing the passersby to enter or to breathe in secondhand smoke any more than he is coercing them into drinking alcohol.

This situation places the nanny in an untenable position. To rectify the situation, they did what they always do: created a victim. Matthew Myers of Campaign for Tobacco-Free Kids explained to *USA Today* a couple of years ago, in characteristic fashion, why all states and municipalities should immediately ban smoking in the workplace: "No employee should be forced to choose between making a living and increasing the risk of heart disease and lung disease . . . No employer should be allowed to place their employees at risk."

There are four fundamental difficulties with this argument.

Not a single employee is ever "placed" at risk. Unless, of course, they've been enslaved by their employer. Like thousands of Americans, the waitstaff in restaurants and bars must make important decisions about their professional lives and their health each day. They make choices. Employees of establishments that allow tobacco smoke (or used to) are free to work elsewhere.

What if an employee isn't averse to secondhand smoke at all? Smoking bans, characteristically, do not allow for an employee to *voluntarily* work in a smoking establishment, even if they happen to be smokers themselves or have absolutely no trepidation about passive smoke. Take for instance me. I couldn't care less if other patrons smoke near me. I might even welcome the musky aroma. I'm nuts. So government allows employees to smoke voluntarily (for now), with far more serious health consequences, yet it denies the same worker the right to find employment in a place that allows smoking.

Millions of workers in today's workforce engage in occupations that hold potentially precarious health consequences. Certainly some are far beyond those purportedly triggered by secondhand smoke even if we're to believe the fairy tales of government. A toll booth operator sits for hours in exhaust fumes; a cabdriver in Manhattan does the same, as well as facing the considerably increased risk of accidents or robbery; a stockbroker lives much of his life under tremendous stress due to the unpredictability of the market—stress, in fact, is one of the leading causes of early heart disease and far surpasses anything allegedly caused by the inhalation of secondhand smoke. Firemen and the police put themselves in mortal danger on a daily basis.

We're persistently led to believe that sniffing from a rogue plume of cigar smoke can lead to instantaneous heart disease and a trip to the hospital. Mark Wernimont, proprietor of the Web site Clearing the Air, pointed out in his research that the Occupational Safety and Health Administration (OSHA) allows airborne chemicals at levels far above those found in passive tobacco smoke. When Wernimont took a closer look, he found that in certain areas of New York State air-quality results measured secondhand smoke at levels ranging from fifteen to five hundred times safer than OSHA regulations allow in other areas of work. Other states, it seems, have similar regulations in place. Why are those who work around tobacco smoke a special case?

The campaign to transform the trivial dangers of secondhand smoke into a national trauma has been a concerted government mission for more than a decade. This crusade came to a crescendo in June of 2006, when the surgeon general of the United States dropped the tendentious 700-page study, *The Health Consequences of Involuntary Exposure to Tobacco Smoke.* The report warned of the invasive and all-encompassing hazards of secondhand smoke.

Even the title of the report is misleading: "involuntary" exposure to tobacco smoke is almost nonexistent in society. Living with a smoker is voluntary. Spending any time indoors with a smoker is voluntary. Frequenting an establishment that allows smoking is voluntary. Many people argue that when you allow smoking in establishments you rob others of their freedom of choice not to smell smoke. Such an argument makes little sense. No one is forcing you to enter such an establishment in the first place.

Yet the most deceitful feature of the study was that it purports to end all discussion on the matter. "The debate is over," claimed Surgeon General Richard Carmona. "The science is clear. Secondhand smoke is not a mere annoyance but a serious health hazard." Carmona went on to state that there was "massive and conclusive scientific evidence" of the "alarming" public health threat posed by secondhand smoke and finds smoking bans are the only way to protect nonsmokers. "Even brief exposure to secondhand smoke," Carmona went on to declare, could kill you. And scores of antismoking groups now claim that more than 50,000 people die each year due to secondhand smoke.

It is laudable to want to decrease smoking, but it isn't laudable to lie. Gio Batta Gori, an epidemiologist and toxicologist, who is a fellow at the Health Policy Center and the former deputy director of the National Cancer Institute's Division of Cancer Cause and Prevention, wrote in a January 2007 op-ed in *The Washington Post* that long-term evaluations on secondhand smoke are bad science—and worse, politically motivated science.

> Lung cancer and cardiovascular diseases develop at advancing ages. Estimating the risk of those diseases posed by second-

> hand smoke requires knowing the sum of momentary secondhand smoke doses that nonsmokers have internalized over their lifetimes. Such lifetime summations of instant doses are obviously impossible, because concentrations of secondhand smoke in the air, individual rates of inhalation, and metabolic transformations vary from moment to moment, year after year, location to location.

Gori goes on to dismantle many of the surgeon general's assertions about secondhand smoke but makes the more vital point about how this governmental agency has quashed rational debate and substituted alarmism. "Presumably, we are grown-up people, with a civilized sense of fair play, and dedicated to disciplined and rational discourse. We are fortunate enough to live in a free country that is respectful of individual choices and rights, including the right to honest public policies."

That presumption is false. Few scientists or statisticians have the time, funding, or inclination to disprove secondhand-smoke fears. Let's hope they have better things to do. But all a layperson is required to understand is that the report presented absolutely no new evidence or science to back up Carmona's extraordinary claim that brief exposure to secondhand smoke causes heart disease or lung cancer. And to this point, the only studies that have linked passive smoke to lung cancer or heart disease are typically after long-term exposure to smokers.

When Michael Siegel, a physician who specialized in preventive medicine and public health and is also a professor in the Social and Behavioral Sciences Department at Boston University School of Public Health, heard about the surgeon general's report he was immediately skeptical. Siegel—a *proponent* of smoking control who runs a blog called The Rest of the Story, which takes a closer look at the claims and science used by antismoking proponents—had this to say about the conclusions of the surgeon general:

> So how could it possibly be that for an active smoker, heart disease takes 25 years of exposure to tobacco smoke to develop, but for a passive smoker, it only takes a single, transient, brief exposure?
>
> It is also quite misleading to tell the public that a brief exposure to secondhand smoke increases the risk of lung cancer. There is certainly no evidence for this and the Surgeon General's report itself draws no such conclusion. In fact, the report makes it clear that most of the studies linking secondhand smoke and lung cancer studied nonsmokers with many years of intense exposure.

This type of exaggeration is not new for the antismoking nanny. In 1992, a study released by the Environmental Protection Agency (EPA) announced that secondhand smoke was the cause of three thousand lung-cancer deaths each year. Consequently, the EPA classified environmental tobacco smoke as a "Group A" carcinogen, a substance that causes cancer in humans. Nannies' hearts were aflutter. This meant new intrusive legislation would be easier to pass.

Once skeptics began to take a closer look, however, holes started to emerge. The study had been based on the combined analyses of eleven other short-term studies. Soon after the report was issued, critics began pointing out that the study used faulty methodology and what looked suspiciously like the EPA working backward from a politically predetermined decision.

In 1998, the classification of tobacco smoke as a carcinogen based on the EPA study was declared void by a federal district court. The judge found that the EPA had manipulated the agency's "standard scientific methodology" and acted in "complete disregard of statutory procedure." In addition, they had cherry-picked data, evaded review by outside experts, and altered the methodology during the course of the study. The judge "denied" that the EPA scientifically proved that secondhand smoke caused lung cancer by ruling that "the EPA disregarded information and made findings on selective information; did not disseminate significant epidemiologic."

The EPA could have saved themselves quite a bit of time and effort had they only listened to New York University professor Mort Lippmann. The then-chairman of the Science Advisory Board of the EPA's Committee on Indoor Air Quality was quoted in 1991 as saying that the risk in secondhand smoke was so small that it was "probably much less than you took to get [to the EPA building] through Washington traffic."

To this point, the few long-term studies that have been conducted on the matter of passive smoke demonstrate a risk so small as to be just about statistically insignificant. In May of 2003, Dr. James Enstrom from the School of Public Health at the University of California at Los Angeles and Dr. Geoffrey Kabat from the Department of Preventative Health at the State University of New York released a thirty-nine-year survey of more than 35,000 nonsmoking residents of California—selected by the American Cancer Society in 1959.

The researchers of the study concluded that the "results do not support a causal relation between environmental tobacco smoke and tobacco-related mortality" and that the association between "exposure to environmental tobacco smoke and coronary heart disease and lung cancer may be considerably weaker than generally believed."

A long-term study released in 1998 by the World Health Organization (WHO) on passive smoke had the dramatic headline "Don't Let Them Fool You: Passive Smoking Does Cause Cancer."

But anyone who actually bothered to read the content of the report found nothing of the sort. After tracking two thousand people in six European countries, WHO concluded, in truth, that "there's a good chance that there's no association whatsoever" between passive smoke and cancer. For an organization that crusades against smoking, the headline "Secondhand Smoke Is Scientifically Meaningless" would have wasted millions of dollars of propaganda.

Michael Gough, a program manager at the now-defunct congressional Office of Technology Assessment, which advised committees on scientific policy, told *Investor's Business Daily* after reading the report that "there's a good chance that there's no association [between secondhand smoke and cancer] whatsoever."

As Gough was the director of the Office of Technology Assessment when they released a milestone study that found smoking the cause of 30 percent of cancer cases in the United States, he's a hard man to dismiss as a lackey for Big Tobacco.

★ ★ ★

The surgeon general's 700-page bombshell is what some skeptics like to call "press conference science." And with only a small group of journalists and experts willing to take this issue on, nannies are left to make assertions that often defy common sense. The most notable example of this ensued when the citizens of Helena, Montana, voted in June 2002 to ban smoking in all public buildings, including restaurants, bars, and casinos. After six months the ban was rescinded. In the meantime, a couple of local doctors claimed that they had noticed a marked decrease in heart attacks during the ban.

Richard Sargent and Robert Shepard were the two Montana physicians who announced that the smoking ban in Helena led to a jaw-dropping 60 percent decrease in heart attacks in the six months after it took effect. By the time the doctors' study was published in the April 2004 issue of *British Medical Journal,* the percentage had dropped to 40 percent, but even that was an incredible number.

It wasn't long after the Helena study was published online in January 2006 that it was comprehensively debunked. Its sample was tiny and failed to take into consideration numerous other reasons that might have attributed to the heart-attack drop in the area. Brad Rodu, of the University of Kentucky, and Philip Cole, of the University of Alabama, both doctors, reviewed the history of Helena's heart attacks from 1990 to 2003. The research revealed other variations in heart attacks in a similar time frame in the 40 percent range. Their conclusion: the Helena ban saw a 40 percent drop in heart attacks by dumb luck. Later, Missouri chemist David W. Kuneman studied government statistics from California, New York, Florida, and Oregon—all states with widespread smoking bans—and couldn't find any drop at all in heart attacks after the bans were enacted. Obviously, antitobacco crusaders had cherry-picked a couple of cities so they could make a case.

To illustrate the damage this species of hit-and-run science can do we need only turn to a glowing *New York Times* op-ed piece that ran in October of 2003. Headlined "Miracle in Helena," the editorial gave credence to this glorified study as another reason to legislate smoke-free businesses. Naturally, there was no editorial to correct the mistake once the Helena myth was exposed.

THE NEXT-BEST STEP

When panic, junk science, and paternalism manifests in public policy, you usually end up in California. In this case, we begin in Calabasas, a well-to-do Southern California community of twenty thousand. Rather than fooling around with piecemeal solutions and partial bans in restaurants, bars, parks, and offices, town leaders took the next logical step and outlawed smoking almost altogether.

California, as we've noted, has long been on the forefront of limiting liberty for smokers. The state passed a statewide ban on smoking in restaurants and workplaces by the mid-1990s, and many California cities took the initiative to pass citywide bans in restaurants and bars. Since 2003, Southern California hasn't allowed any smoking on beaches or piers.

In February 2006, the Calabasas City Council took it a bit further, and unanimously voted to ban smoking on sidewalks, at bus stops, in parks, at outdoor seating of restaurants (the inside had long been banned), and on apartment balconies. They became the first city in the nation to, for all intents and purposes, ban smoking in public. The only exceptions in Calabasas were allotted and desolate "smoker outposts"—outlying areas, like corners of parking lots, where nicotine addicts could huddle together while salubrious parents safely ensconced in SUVs could point out a curious and ostracized tribe to their healthy children.

After the prohibition was passed in Calabasas, there was near-universal praise from nannies around the nation. Many held up Calabasas as the model for all American cities to follow. A spokesperson for the American Cancer Society in nearby Sacramento said, "We salute Calabasas for raising the bar. Smoke regulations can play a very important role in reducing public exposure to harmful secondhand smoke."

Before we salute the ban, let's take a closer look at three of the rationalizations given for the legislative prohibition by city leaders, each taking us farther down the slippery slope toward full prohibition.

The ban will "protect children" from secondhand smoke. As we've noted, the hazards of short-term secondhand inhalation indoors are suspicious at best. Nonetheless, now it appears that we're supposed to believe that brief *outdoor* exposure to secondhand smoke is reason enough to pass legislation. (We eagerly anticipate the study that establishes out-of-doors cigarette smoke as particularly dangerous for others.)

If this is the road we're on, why not ban smoking in the houses where children reside? If a private business and outdoor sidewalk is within the reach of law enforcement, crafting legislation that bars smoking in front of a child anywhere within city limits would be far more effective. As it is, there is always the possibility that some uncivilized, politically incorrect clod might light up a Marlboro at a backyard birthday bash, putting the lives of his offspring in jeopardy. Relying on individuals to regulate their own activity is taking a chance.

The ban defends children from the risk of confusing smoking and tobacco with a "healthy lifestyle." Let's assume children are confused about smoking and believe it's a "healthy lifestyle." This, again, puts us on the never-ending road of state-sponsored paternalism. Sorry, but only an idiot could possibly teach their kids that smoking is anything but unhealthy. So please forgive parents if they were under the impression that lessons on what is and isn't healthy was their domain. Utilizing this rationalization, the city of Calabasas could just as easily ban McDonald's, liquor stores, and the sale of bacon at supermarkets.

The ban will promote a "family-friendly atmosphere." Let's talk about the malleability of the term "family friendly." There are some, unambiguous, family-friendly zoning laws that allow citizens to preserve a level of cohesion and order in their community. But at some point, government must let people live their lives. After all, there are more socially conservative cities wherein a family-friendly atmosphere could necessitate dress codes barring salacious outfits (they exist). Public kissing could be outlawed in other towns—an act unfriendly to a genteel family environment. Planned Parenthood offices could be boarded up, certain books and magazines could be put to flames. Does that sound like a place where you'd like to raise your family?

According to George Washington University law professor John Banzhaf—a leading nanny trial lawyer (see Chapter One) and a combatant in the war against personal liberty—claims that banning habits he deems uncouth is perfectly legal. "Every court which has ever addressed the issue has held that there is no legal right to smoke, regardless of the location," said the professor.

He's right. And Action on Smoking and Health (ASH), an influential antismoking group that Banzhaf runs, has been upping the ante, pushing legal action to ban smoking in condominiums and apartment buildings. As a matter of fact, the ASH Web site declares: "If you can smell it, it may be killing you!" Banzhaf has been sanctioning the "civility" and "murder" angles for years. Not long ago he even compared smoking to public masturbation.

But has the nanny finally gone too far? Even abroad, some have come to their senses. The British Action on Smoking and Health (ASH-UK) questioned the necessity for outdoor bans in places where nonsmokers can avoid exposure to secondhand smoke, suggesting that perhaps the Calabasas ordinance is a bit much. "OK, but let us briefly adopt the Californian position. What if someone sparks up on their balcony, there's a big gust of wind and some hapless person 50 yards away is hit by a diluted puff of smoke? You may as well put in a call to the undertakers there and then, eh? 'You've got to get this issue down to what's reasonable and sensible,' [Deborah] Arnott of ASH-UK explained. 'That's an extreme, fundamentalist position. And I don't think we're that kind of country, are we?' "

If the prim and proper tut-tutters of England find this brand of contravention beyond the pale of good or fair government—"an extreme, fundamentalist position," if you will—then why are nannies here at home rejoicing?

There are ways around these awkward questions. In Dublin, California, a bedroom community near San Francisco, the city council approved an ordinance that leapfrogged justifications by declaring secondhand tobacco smoke a "public nuisance." Councilwoman Kasie Hildenbrand put it this way: "We have to legislate civility at times."

Now some may contend that a noble way to start legislating civility would be to legislate every city council out of existence. But to Hildenbrand and her cohorts civility meant adding secondhand smoke to the list of nuisances like loud music, garbage, and public urination. Citizens could now go to small claims court and seek up to $7,500 in damages if their neighbors annoyed them by smoking. Dublin already outlaws smoking within fifteen feet of public playgrounds (you know, for the children), at ATMs, and at bus stops, as well as in the outdoor seating areas of restaurants and taverns, and the enclosed common areas of condominiums, nursing homes, and retirement communities.

Then there is Belmont, California, where in late 2006, the city took that final step and made history by becoming the first in the nation to ban smoking on its streets and in all condos and apartments. The Belmont City Council voted unanimously to pass a law prohibiting smoking anywhere in the city—except for single-family detached residences. No smoking on the street or in the parks, or even in your own car.

"We have a tremendous opportunity here. We need to pass as stringent a law as we can, I would like to make it illegal," said Councilman Dave Warden. "What if every city did this, imagine how many lives would be saved? If we can do one little thing here at this level it will matter." He's right. Others will surely follow his lead.

In late 2006, a Colorado district judge ruled that a couple in the town of Golden could no longer smoke in their own home. The judge had compared the "smoke and/or smoke smell" to "extremely loud noise" that "constitutes a nuisance." Under the condo declarations, the judge noted, "no nuisance shall be allowed . . . which is a source of annoyance to residents." Though it said nothing about smoking specifically, the couple now had to walk outside to the corner of the parking lot to light up.

"This is my home, and I worked for it," Colleen Sauve, one of the smokers, said. "I can't relax and have a cigarette in my own home. If I do, I'll get fined."

SMOKE-EASIES

Sauve and other smokers will soon create their own spaces to engage in what is still a legal habit. In Chicago, R. J. Reynolds Tobacco tried its hand at skirting the city's iniquitous smoking ban by bankrolling a new establishment in the Wicker Park neighborhood that provides a secluded environment for smoking residents. Marshall McGearty Tobacco Lounge serves alcohol but its business license classifies it as a "tobacco retailer"—meaning 65 percent of all sales are for tobacco or tobacco-related items. This designation allows Marshall McGearty exemption from the smoking ban that hits all bars in 2008 in Chicago. "We looked around at other categories like beer, cigars and chocolates and saw super premium brands which arrived in the last 10 or 15 years were doing very well," said Brian Stebbins, a marketing director at R. J. Reynolds.

"This is just a slimy trick by Big Tobacco to circumvent the system," an upset Annie Tegen, program manager for Americans for Nonsmokers' Rights, claimed. R. J. Reynolds's grandson Patrick

Reynolds, now with the Foundation for a Smokefree America, claimed that following the law was some sort of rebellion: "It's a rebellion on the part of R. J. Reynolds. It really is an in-your-face effort to say, 'Hey, here's a bar where we found a loophole, where you can still smoke.' "

Actually, Marshall McGearty is the exact opposite of in-your-face. It is a place where smokers can stay out of your face. The slippery reasoning of antismoking activists always fits the crime at hand. Secondhand smoke interfering with (even killing) innocent bystanders was the problem. Now that smokers congregate in a room together, it's a slimy trick. But because of these sorts of establishments antismoking advocates have vowed to shut down these loopholes in future legislation. One might think that an establishment like Marshall McGearty would be the perfect antidote to allow law-abiding Americans the choice to continue to smoke while "protecting" nonsmokers from the wafting toxicity of secondhand smoke. But it's not.

In Astoria, Queens—home to a large immigrant community across the East River from Manhattan—an exemption like the one Chicago enjoys does not exist. And in this part of the borough, business owners and consumers have simply contravened the law. Astoria was one of the biggest violators of the city's smoking ban. In 2006, the Health Department issued more than six hundred violations citywide to "smoke-easies" for permitting smoking during spot inspections; 232 of them were issued to businesses in Queens.

A *New York Post* reporter scoped out this nefarious underworld and found one establishment in particular that flouted the law. In Café Scorpio, thirteen of approximately fifteen people present were reported smoking. "The sleek, dimly lit bar was lined up with packs of cigarettes and cigarette lighters. People also smoked at lounge tables or while playing billiards, watching ballgames or viewing the Croatian news channel."

In Seattle, a similar underground has begun to sprout. Smokers find out the locations of smoke-easies by word of mouth, which normally involves "a swearing of secrecy." One eyewitness account claimed that five smoke-easies had popped up in neighborhoods across Seattle, "making the transformation from law-abiding bar to subversive smoking habitat in the wee hours of the night."

SMOKER'S DELIGHT

Sin taxes are another nannyistic economic tool that manufactures criminal behavior. "Nobody likes taxes," Mayor Bloomberg intoned after raising taxes once again. "But cigarette taxes are something different." Bloomberg's justification for raising taxes was indeed more than revenue. It was to inflate prices high enough to dissuade smokers. Bloomberg has stated that "we all know that smoking kills. And increasing the cigarette tax saves lives." The New York mayor raised taxes by more than 1,500 percent on cigarettes to help save lives. Though if sin taxes are a moral question, why not raise taxes further to induce others to quit, why not $100 per pack? Or $1,000?

The fact is, even according to Bloomberg's ideologically allied Centers for Disease Control, large tax hikes on cigarettes haven't led to a significant decline in the number of smokers in New York. The number of adult smokers in the state has dipped only slightly during the past decade, from 24.4 percent in 1991 to 23.2 percent in 2001. This mirrored the national average. The same can be said of New York City, where rates fell from 21.7 percent in 1993 to 20.7 percent in 2001. This modest waning occurred in spite of nearly doubling the real cigarette tax rate in the state during the period.

At some point, if sin taxes keep piling on, prices will become prohibitive and cigarettes will become unaffordable. And it's then that criminals have their incentive to engage in illegal behavior. To some extent we've always had a black market for cigarettes, and it's only going to get worse. A New York Health Department study showed that 70 percent of smokers bought cigarettes from low- or no-tax sellers at least once in 2004, while 34 percent to 42 percent relied on those sellers "all the time" or "sometimes."

The cigarette bootlegging (which includes no-tax smokes), which sounds like small-time stuff, is used by local crooks, the Mob, and, yes, terrorists. According to Patrick Fleenor, former senior economist at the Joint Economic Committee of Congress, "While investigators have not found any connection between cigarette smuggling and those responsible for the September 11, 2001, attacks, a wide range of terrorist groups are known to use the proceeds from cigarette smuggling to fund their operations." The federal Bureau of Alcohol, Tobacco, Firearms and Explosives had more than three hundred open cases of illicit cigarette trafficking in a five-year span. Why is it dangerous to create yet another prohibition?

- Mohamad Hammoud was found guilty of providing support to the Lebanese terror group Hezbollah. His cell raised money by smuggling cigarettes.
- Counterfeit cigarette tax stamps were found in an apartment of the Egyptian Islamic jihad cell that carried out the 1993 bombing of the World Trade Center.
- Those accused of being part of the al-Qaeda sleeper cell busted near Buffalo had a criminal history that involved cigarette bootlegging.

Black market cigarette sales are nothing new—the business of bootlegging tobacco has been ongoing since the Western discovery of smoking. Nannies shouldn't be accused of serving terrorists or mobsters, but they can be criticized for creating an exorbitantly high price on a *legal* product—one that amounts to nothing more than a prohibition for poorer Americans. We must expect these exorbitant taxes to lead to illegal behavior because, after all, there isn't a prohibition on Earth that doesn't lead to a surge in criminality.

MAGIC, OR SOMETHING LIKE IT

A few years ago smoking scenes in classic Tom and Jerry cartoons were banned in Great Britain following a single parent's grievance to the government agency that polices the airwaves on these matters. One particularly egregious episode featured the irascible cartoon cat Tom toking hard on a hand-rolled cigarette in an attempt to impress a fetching young female cat.

The children's TV channel Boomerang agreed to edit out scenes deemed to glamorize or condone smoking. "We note that, in 'Tom and Jerry', smoking usually appears in a stylized manner and is frequently not condoned," explained the station. "However, while we appreciate the historic integrity of the animation, the level of editorial justification required for the inclusion of smoking in such cartoons is necessarily high."

Nannies here at home have already begun to rewrite many unsightly historical truths. All it takes is a puritanical urge and some rudimentary comprehension of Adobe Photoshop and you're on your way.

One of the more notorious recastings of a smoker revolved around the children's classic *Goodnight Moon,* authored by Margaret Wise Brown. If you happen to have been an American parent or child in the past sixty years, it's likely you're acquainted with the tale of a rabbit avoiding his slumber. When the revised edition of the book was released in 2006, the publisher HarperCollins retroactively impelled illustrator Clement Hurd to quit smoking. The original photograph on the trade hardcover edition of *Goodnight Moon* for the past fifty years, which featured Hurd with a cigarette in hand, was digitally altered to eradicate the protruding transgression. HarperCollins claimed that it made the change to avoid the appearance of "encouraging" smoking.

Soon enough a Web site and grassroots effort emerged challenging this transgression. One site, Goodbye Reality, displayed two photographs—one with cigarette in hand, one without—of Hurd. "In a single stroke, HarperCollins has changed our collective history, and created an alternate reality in which Clement Hurd does not smoke. It calls to mind a censorship tactic most famously associated with Joseph Stalin, who falsified the archival record of the Soviet Union by literally removing images of his political enemies from photographs in an effort to re-create history in his own image."

Perhaps invoking the name of Joseph Stalin can be chalked up to a bit of hyperbole (and who among us isn't guilty of making an inappropriate analogy?), but the digital sleight of hand seems, even to some less prone to protest about such intrusions, overbearing. "Excellent start, HarperCollins, but why stop there?" retorted Karen Karbo, in a hilarious *New York Times* op-ed. She pointed out that *Goodnight Moon* was replete with messages potentially harmful to young readers:

> Tell me this rug is not made of the skin of a Siberian tiger. Suggested change: Digitally remove to avoid appearance of condoning hunting of planet's endangered species.
>
> A fire blazing in the fireplace while Bunny sleeps? Suggested change: Get rid of it. At the very least, digitally add a fire extinguisher to the wall. And hello? Where are the smoke detectors?
>
> Clearly the bookshelf is unanchored to the wall. If an earth-

quake hit, Bunny could get squashed flat. Suggested change: Digitally remove. We can't see the titles on the spines of the books anyway, which might convey to children it's all right to pick up any old book and read it.

But it's not only impressionable children that nannies are shielding. Teenagers, discovering the joys of classic rock for the first time, will soon be at the will of salubrious editors. The Beatles, for instance, had a considerable smoking habit. Yet as EMI shipped out a new version of the LP *Capitol Albums Volume 2,* there was a subtle difference on the picture from the 1964 version. Originally, John, Paul, and Ringo had cigarettes in hand. Now politically correct executives made sure they kicked the habit on the rerelease by digitally altering the picture.

One of the most famous album covers of all time is the Beatles' *Abbey Road,* which features Paul McCartney holding a cigarette as he walks across the famous crosswalk. Needless to say, many fans were surprised when they purchased the new poster edition of the cover and found the small cigarette had been removed.

A spokesman for the Beatles-founded label Apple Records told the BBC: "We have never agreed to anything like this. It seems these poster companies got a little carried away. They shouldn't have done what they have, but there isn't a good deal we can do about it now." Luckily for Beatles fans the group didn't go with the original name or they might not be able to listen to the album at all. "At some point the album was going to be titled *Everest,* after the brand of cigarettes I used to smoke," recalls Geoff Emerick, the engineer for *Abbey Road.*

I'll be quite curious to see what kind of supernatural trick these worrywarts pull to clean up Keith Richards and Jerry Garcia up for the next generation. Will musical historians be allowed to explain how Jim Morrison, Jimi Hendrix, and Janis Joplin met their tragic ends? Clue: It wasn't the cigarettes. Then again, youth may be relegated to listening to the Dave Clark Five and the Monkees if this conspiracy is allowed to evolve.

Just a warning.

Then we come to more serious matters of high culture. Thornton Wilder, the playwright and author of the American literary classic *Our Town*, was like many men of his time a prodigious smoker. Yet in the artwork depicting him on the Literary Arts series postage stamp, someone had removed the cigarette from his portrait.

The United States Postal Service worked a similar magic on a stamp featuring Jackson Pollock, the famous abstract impressionist who would paint with a smoke dangling from his mouth. Pollack probably smoked while sleeping yet the stamp rendered him cigaretteless. The mint pulled another stunt with the paintings of blues singer Robert Johnson and James Dean. The stamps used familiar photographs of the subjects, but with a twist: in the originals, the men are smoking; on the stamps, the cigarettes are missing.

★ ★ ★

Attorney generals of thirty-two states requested that movie studios add antismoking messages, much like the ones found on packs of cigarettes, to DVD releases for movies. Maryland attorney general J. Joseph Curran Jr. got the ball rolling with a complaint to all the major film studios—and no, they aren't located in Maryland—asking that home versions of their films include an antismoking public service announcement. (Baltimore, incidentally, consistently ranks as one of the more unsafe cities in America. And it's not because of the smoking.) "This is consistent with the state's long-running commitment to reduce underage teen smoking," said

Janelle Guthrie, spokesperson for Washington State attorney general Rob McKenna.

Dr. Stanton Glantz, a professor of medicine at the University of California at San Francisco's School of Medicine and one of the leading antitobacco activists in the nation, suggested during testimony in California on the issue of smoking in movies, that two proposals could put into play to end it: end brand identification and give an "R" rating to movies with smoking scenes. Referring to the "R" rating of movies containing curse words, Glantz explained to the panel that "We should treat smoking like we do the f-word."

That gives me a great idea for how to use the f-word.

•

"SMOKING IS HEALTHIER THAN FASCISM"

I read the above axiom a couple of years ago on a T-shirt in a Washington, D.C., bar. And the thought sums up my basic feelings toward smoking. Many people will ask me how I could so flippantly correlate something as inoffensive, even constructive, as antismoking laws with an ideology as insidious as Fascism. Prodding smokers to quit isn't a bad thing, is it? Shielding us from irritating secondhand smoke—dangerous or not—makes our world more pleasing and healthy. Unquestionably advocates are only trying to protect children and save lives. That's not tyranny. That's liberty.

And while antismoking legislation is often driven by the tyranny of the majority—which John Stuart Mill warned us "was at first, and is still vulgarly, held in dread, chiefly as operating through the acts of the public authorities"—these meddling laws are often colored by experience and the personal predilections of those in power.

Take Governor Mike Huckabee of Arkansas, who often and quite erroneously describes himself as a small-government conservative. As it happens, Huckabee subscribes to big-government intervention into lifestyle choices. His agenda is self-involved and driven heavily by his own achievements. As *The New York Times* reported, in the three years leading up to the article Huckabee had shed more than one hundred pounds and become a health enthusiast and exercise nut.

We salute his conversion to wholesome living. What we should not salute is his contention that everyone must now live as he does. Huckabee started this crusade with the Healthy Arkansas initiative, which began with a fairly mundane coercion of elementary and high schools to take on stricter rules regarding snacks. Soon Arkansas restaurants offering healthy alternatives and nutritional information were given special government stickers of approval. Neither of these issues, incidentally, are any of his business.

Then Huckabee became involved in eradicating smoking through government mandate. Like many, he successfully passed a strict smoking ban. It was Huckabee's frankness regarding the objectives of the movement that are particularly worthwhile. "I think the day will come when we probably won't sell cigarettes," Huckabee said on his radio show. "If cigarettes were introduced to the marketplace today, they wouldn't be sold. They'd never make it because what we didn't know when they were first created, sold and marketed is just how deadly harmful they were."

He's absolutely right. And this isn't a positive development. Just because something is a "harmful product" doesn't automatically mean it's a useless product. Cigars, pipes, and chewing tobacco are all harmful, yet millions of Americans enjoy them each day. We have full knowledge of the dangers of smoking and some Americans still choose to partake. This might be frustrating for health officials. It may seem unreasonable or even suicidal. But that doesn't mean government has the right to babysit adults.

And babysitting is just the beginning. Antismoking nannyism, the most evolved form of this philosophy, has gone further. There was the case of Ron Teck, a conservative Republican in the Colorado legislature, whose stepfather had died from lung cancer. This tragedy brought on a bright idea. Why not deny Medicaid benefits to Americans who smoke? Teck decided that those eligible for Medicaid who started smoking before 1975 would get full benefits, while those who started after would get none. He saw little difficulty in dictating behavior through government intimidation. But someone else's stepfather may have died from fatty foods. Or lack of exercise.

Teck's plan first came to my attention through an op-ed in *Investor's Business Daily,* appropriately titled "Health Bigotry." And bigotry is a pretty good description of the policies practiced against smokers. Soft bigotry, perhaps. Bigotry fueled by good intentions, sometimes. But bigotry nonetheless. Former *National Review* columnist Florence King said it best in her 1990 essay "I'd Rather Smoke Than Kiss": "A misanthrope is someone who hates people. Hatred of smokers is the most popular form of closet misanthropy in America today. Smokists don't hate the sin, they hate the sinner, and they don't care who knows it."

In 2006, when an intrepid reporter for the alternative paper *Seattle Weekly* decided to investigate the growing nannyism in his city, he sought out the director of tobacco prevention for Public Health–Seattle and King County for comment. What he found was not only a meddlesome bureaucrat enforcing Seattle-area smoking laws but a power-happy public servant handing out lessons on how to corrupt the Constitution.

"Americans think they have a lot of rights they really don't have," he told the reporter. "Smoking is one of those things where people think they have the right to smoke, but you don't . . . You have no right to smoke. It's an addiction. It's something you should see a doctor about."

You have no right to smoke. See a doctor, you sickos.

If you're too stupid to figure out that smoking is harmful, or you're too weak to really care, then we'll make that decision for you through legislation or litigation. Sure, at the same time we're robbing citizens of their free will. Granted, that's a small price to pay for a smoke-free utopia.

★ CHAPTER FOUR ★

THE PLAYGROUND DESPOTS

The whole aim of practical politics is to keep the populace alarmed (and hence clamorous to be led to safety) by menacing it with an endless series of hobgoblins, all of them imaginary.

—H. L. MENCKEN

Prop 10 is about children. Vote yes on Prop 10, or else you hate children. You don't . . . hate children . . . do you?

—"GNOMES," *SOUTH PARK*

★

NO RUNNING—OR MUCH ELSE

A few years back, I began a job in Denver, a bustling, liberal, modern, tech-savvy city. My wife and I decided to move our two kids into a newly constructed, trendy, mixed-use urban neighborhood. And like any responsible parents, one of our first jaunts outside the home was to the local playground.

To refer to the abstract sculpture garden before me as a "playground" would have been an affront to all the playgrounds I had ever visited in my life. The only clue to its intended purpose was the high concentration of children roaming aimlessly around the cordoned area. My kids ran to the preposterous contraptions—they knew no better—hoping to climb, or perhaps glide or maybe even hang. No such luck. I watched neighborhood children straddle equipment anticipating some form of gratification. They wandered sporadically over to what looked like an enormous abacus and stared. Metal slides—or teeter-totters, or jungle gyms, or anything resembling a rigid surface, for that matter—were nowhere to be found.

This was nothing like the playgrounds I so fondly remember: towering jungle gyms with blacktop floors; sky-high slides that would burn your skin as you slid down; swings (without restraints) that swung so high you felt like you might go all the way around; seemingly endless concrete mazes in which you could hide from mom and dad. It's a wonder I survived.

According to the U.S. Public Interest Research Groups, approximately seventeen American children die each year from injuries on playgrounds. And 170,000 kids are hurt badly enough to hasten a visit to the emergency room. These numbers would be bone-chilling were it not for the fact that tens of millions of children use playgrounds every day.

There are those activists, nevertheless, who won't just sit around and wait for tragedy. One morning, parents and children in the upscale suburb of Plano, Texas, woke up to find that the swing sets at all forty elementary schools had vanished—ripped out by officials over "safety concerns." An exasperated Plano father lodged complaints with the district, claiming that most parents he'd spoken to believed the changes were absurd. His attempts to bring back swings were to no avail.

Preposterous playground safety regulations have been creeping up on children for a decade now. The twin engines that drive this form of nannyism are a small number of hyper-litigious parents and a small number of administrators with cloyingly good intentions. A lethal mix.

The Dallas-area nannies exhibit a finicky obsession with creating a mind-numbingly risk-free atmosphere. Diving in the public pool, for instance, may be an activity of distant memory. When local pools opened Memorial Day weekend in 2006, the high dive was gone in accordance with Section L of Chapter 265 of the Texas Administrative Code, which prescribes, in detail, the constraints of diving boards, water depth, and "slopes of pool bottoms."

A similar scene played out in Portland, Oregon, as all swings from elementary-school playgrounds were yanked out without a great deal of consultation with parents. The school district also discarded precarious equipment like merry-go-rounds, tube slides, track rides, and teeter-totters. "The rationale behind it is ludicrous," a father said of the Plano swing-set ban. "Kids swing. They've swung for a millennium . . . It's a good, healthy childhood exer-

else." From now on, he said, his kids will have to swing at the city park where swings were still legal.

In Broward County, Florida, a painfully detailed, fun-nullifying sign awaited children as they entered a local park. Among a multitude of rules and regulations to ensure that kids would leave without a scrape—or without having any fun—there were these incredible directives:

- Do Not Use Equipment When Wet
- No Bare Feet, Wear Proper Footwear
- Do Not Use Equipment Unless Designed for Your Age
- No Bike Riding or Skate Boarding

And another warning for the children read: "No Running . . ." But other than those rules, kids, have fun!

YOU'LL SHOOT YOUR EYE OUT

Aren't all our treasured toddlers, our accident-prone preschoolers, and our impressionable teenagers worth shielding from harm by *any* means at our collective disposal? It depends, of course, on who is doing the parenting. Generally, there is already a super-scrupulous nanny devising an endless number of personalized regulations for children. Kids typically refer to these despots as "Mom" and/or "Dad." The question this chapter asks is: How much help do parents require from government when it comes to parenting?

Libertarian author Charles Murray poses the question this way: "Suppose that a regulation does produce a net good, such as saving some number of children's lives. Is this enough to justify the regulation?" Murray contends that those who answer yes without first considering the costs and benefits associated with the excessive safety regulation embark on a "never-ending road." And the off-ramp onto that unbounded road begins with the notion that government can shelter consumers and their children from every scrape and bruised feeling out there.

This mission creep had its beginnings in 1972 when Congress enacted the Consumer Product Safety Act, establishing the U.S. Consumer Product Safety Commission (CPSC) as an independent federal regulatory agency. The CPSC was bestowed with expansive powers in the hopes that it could guard consumers from defective and dangerous products. Regulations originating from this department have almost certainly saved many Americans from hidden dangers.

The problem is that expectations of consumer safety—especially when it comes to children—have morphed from rational safeguards against concealed hazards to the unrealistic notion that government can safeguard children from *all* threats. The CPSC brought this on itself by ignoring consumer markets or common sense, proclaiming mandatory safety standards for any product at any time for any reason it saw fit. The commission also ignores the fact that any product is hazardous in the wrong hands. Here is a perfect illustration of the necessity to have some common sense.

During the domineering reign of CPSC commissioner Ann Brown (1994–2001), common sense, it seems, was misplaced and a wide swath of products became fair game for regulation. Generally heralded by the media for her progressive stands on product safety, Brown demonstrated an acute gift for sniffing out consumer peril everywhere—sometimes genuine, often imagined—and cosseting us from as many products as possible. Think bunk beds, upholstered furniture, and all types of allegedly perfidious toys.

Not long before stepping down from her post, Brown secured her legacy by engineering a nannyistic lawsuit against the Daisy Manufacturing Company. The company, famed for half a century as the maker of Red Ryder BB guns (who can forget Ralphie Parker's ill-fated *Christmas Story*?), was sued and forced to recall millions of air guns. The commission's staff had made an inconceivable discovery: since 1972, Daisy's Powerline Airgun was to blame, due to design defects, for "at least 15 deaths."

Are fifteen tragic deaths in more than thirty years enough to rise to the level of public hazard? Columnist Andrew Ferguson pointed out at the time that in nearly thirty years, 7.5 million Powerline guns had been sold and that given "the vagaries of life, and the unpredictability of teenagers, a layman might be surprised the number of deaths 'attributed' to the 'alleged design defects' is so low. Indeed a layman could be forgiven for assuming that since 1972 at least 15 people had broken their necks tripping over them on the basement steps."

This story had a happy ending: in 2003, after promising to plaster a warning label on the gun and pay for a $1.5 million ad campaign pointing out the "safe handling" and various other nonsensical "safety" guidelines, the Daisy Powerline was allowed to come back on the market. The majority of products do not.

If the impetus for regulation is total safety we will find all situations hopelessly hazardous. The vagaries of modern living claim lives each day. According to the CPSC, more than three hundred children under five years of age drown each year in swimming pools. There are hundreds of deaths in bathtubs every year. Around sixteen deaths are tied to amusement park rides—a majority associated with roller coasters and rides of the "whirling" variety. From 1990 to 2000 alone, the CPSC has received reports of approximately a dozen deaths relating to trampoline use. Four children—five and eleven years old, and seventeen and twenty-two months old—choked on or were aspirated by balloons in one year alone. As one of the commissioners, Mary Sheila Gall, pointed out, the average number of deaths per year associated with the use of bicycles by children aged fifteen and under is 250. Yet the government permits Schwinn and Ross to peddle their death machines.

Commissioner Gall, one of CPSC's three members, held a consistently contradictory perspective on the extent of government protection. Gall made her opinion known in a 1999 letter where she disparaged her own commission for "the procession of proclamations . . . on behalf of the federal Nanny State." In Gall's view the CPSC's duty was to certify the safety of products. It was not to tutor parents in the use of those products and it certainly wasn't to hold the manufacturers accountable any and every time a child was hurt in an accident.

This attitude landed Gall on the losing end of deliberations within the CPSC as she continued to contest the status quo. One of the more contentious debates revolved around the baby bath seat. At the time, approximately 800,000 baby bath seats were sold yearly and perhaps somewhere around 120 deaths over a period of fifteen years had been "linked" to the seat—meaning an accident had befallen the child when the seat was present. How unsound was this baby seat? It was such a serious threat that the editorial pages of the Cleveland *Plain Dealer* excoriated the CPSC for its lack of aggressiveness in the matter:

> Parents who have never used a baby bath seat to bathe their children should feel blessed. And the woefully misnamed U.S. Consumer Product Safety Commission should feel ashamed. Although the seats have been linked to more than 120 deaths since 1983, the federal commission has never banned them . . . It's time for the commission to get tough on these devices and issue an outright ban.

What *The Plain Dealer* expediently failed to mention was that one of the key justifications of the request for a baby bath seat ban was that the product *instills a false sense of security*. The product was too safe.

Damn them.

Gall argued that the death and injuries caused by inattentive parents who left their children alone in the bathtub could not, by any reasonable standard, be blamed on a chair. She could have added that somewhere in the area of 799,000 parents had the wherewithal to make sense of the product each year.

Brown came at this debate from a different angle. The nanny angle. She said, "Imagine a parent holding a soapy, squiggling baby. A parent would never leave that baby alone for a second. But even the best parent can be seduced into bad behavior if they see a child sitting upright in a little seat. But it takes only a couple of minutes for a baby to drown, and it's a silent death that can happen in three inches of water."

When President George Bush was elected in 2000, he nominated Gall to serve as Brown's replacement. Almost immediately, fierce opposition popped up. "This is a consumer protection agency," groused Senator Hillary Clinton. "It should not be too much to ask that the person who chairs it actually will protect consumers. Ms. Gall's record demonstrates that, when children die in bunk beds, baby walkers and bath seats, she enthusiastically blames the parent and defends the product."

These apprehensions become a powerful tool of the nanny. Gall had never blamed anyone "enthusiastically." She had merely pointed out a painful truth: a few parents and regrettable circumstances, not wicked corporations, were to blame for the ill-fated deaths. Awful things happen in life and we can't shut down entire industries for the sake of a few accidents. Any parent can tell you it doesn't take a village to watch a baby in a bathtub, only a single responsible mom or dad.

TOYS THAT DON'T CARE

Another government-approved mandate that is intended to aid parents wrestling with the many hazards of the real world are warning labels. During the baby bath seat controversy, for example, a label warned parents that "Children have drowned while using bath seats. ALWAYS keep baby within arm's reach."

Good advice. But let's not kid ourselves: warning labels do not exist for safety's sake alone. The fear of litigation hangs over the heads of manufacturers like a precarious mobile ("may cause dizziness") does over a defenseless newborn. The fact is that the majority of consumers pay little or no attention to labels. They ignore them for two reasons: first, the preponderance of such warnings and second, the preposterousness of such warnings.

The impulse to make sure everyone is mindful of every potential threat imaginable has been taken to an outlandish extreme in places like California, where even the fetus enjoys mandated warnings to guard it from all known and unknown carcinogens and chemicals. The columnist Debra Saunders fills us in on the warning-label state of California:

> Since California voters in 1986 approved Proposition 65—which mandates warnings when people are exposed to known carcinogens or chemicals that cause birth defects—to live in California is to be warned. Most office buildings and parking garages post Prop. 65 warnings. When you fill your gas tank, there's a warning. When you go to a department store or a restaurant, there are warnings. Ditto the grocery store, where there are warnings not just about lighter fluid, nail polish and the effects of alcohol, but for fruits and vegetables, nuts and fish.

The group Common Good undertakes the tough job of detailing the out-of-control warning culture that has enveloped us. Common Good, a bipartisan coalition "dedicated to creating policy solutions that restore rationality and common sense to American law," grew out of the work of lawyer Philip K. Howard, author of the bestseller *The Death of Common Sense.* The group's Wacky Warning Labels contest, ongoing for almost a decade, highlights some of the ridiculous and ineffectual warning labels that have become commonplace in society.

Here is a sampling of the delightful lunacy.

- A bottle of drain cleaner: "If you do not understand, or cannot read, all directions, cautions and warnings, do not use this product."
- A snow sled for children: "Beware: sled may develop high speed under certain snow conditions."
- A twelve-inch rack for storing compact disks: "Do not use as a ladder."
- A five-inch brass fishing lure with a three-pronged hook on the end: "Harmful if swallowed."
- A smoke detector: "Do not use the Silence Feature in emergency situations. It will not extinguish a fire."

Warnings are everywhere when it comes to toys. But if warnings don't work, bans are sure to follow. Like when Illinois became the first state to ban yo-yos. Governor Rod Blagojevich signed legislation in 2005 outlawing the sale of yo-yo water balls—a toy made of a liquid-filled ball and elastic cord. "If we know a toy like the yo-yo water ball is dangerous to young kids, then the responsible thing to do is take it off the market," the governor claimed.

Really? How dangerous was this particular variety of yo-yo? There are more than ten million yo-yo water balls reportedly sold in the United States and there is little evidence that suggests this spinning toy was any more perilous than a chess set. No, the governor's signature was the result of a two-year nationwide lobbying effort by a persuasive nanny named Lisa Lipin. This Skokie mother claimed that her five-year-old was nearly—yes, *nearly*—strangled by a yo-yo water ball in 2003.

⋆ ⋆ ⋆

There are the Nervous Nellies and then there are those safety fetishists who seem to issue panic-stricken warnings faster than Fisher-Price can produce new toys. The group World Against Toys Causing Harm, or W.A.T.C.H. (obviously they've done some tricky work formulating the perfect name), claims to have "fearlessly exposed potentially dangerous toys to the general public," which, with all due respect, isn't an especially demanding task, considering almost every product is *potentially* dangerous.

W.A.T.C.H.'s founder, Edward M. Swartz, is the author of two disconcerting, irrational, toy-hating tomes. These books establish once and for all that ambivalence—even when practiced by inanimate objects—can lead to murder. You see, Swartz's first book, released in 1971, was titled *Toys That Don't Care.* It was followed by the bone-chilling *Toys That Kill* in 1986. What's next? Perhaps the final installment of his trilogy will be called *Toys That Commit Genocide.*

"I have been able to force the industry to redesign and, in some cases, eliminate many offending toys," he writes. "While this is gratifying, more must be done. What is necessary is to educate the next generation of consumers about these perils." What perils, you ask? Well, killers like blocks and dolls. But what's most striking about W.A.T.C.H. and other groups like them is the vivid imaginations they display. Like a classic Stephen King novel, W.A.T.C.H.

will take the most harmless set of circumstances and extrapolate the most catastrophic consequences. It's a distinctive talent shared by nannyists across the country. One could, for instance, only marvel at the work of New York City Council Health Committee chairwoman Christine Quinn. This woman introduced a bill that would have outlawed the sale of "dangerously sized candy," such as large mint balls and jawbreakers, to children.

The candy committee came up with a precise definition of dangerously sized sweets: anything between 0.75 and 1.75 inches in diameter. Confections larger than this predetermined size were reckoned less likely to impede a child's windpipe as they need to be chewed. Why they're focusing solely on candy, though, is a mystery. By their rationale, we should stop our kids from eating cherry tomatoes, broccoli florets, and plums, among other nutritional goodies that fall within those parameters.

★ ★ ★

With the omnipotent threat of candy—both as an unhealthy snack and a choking hazard—you can imagine what many nannies must make of Halloween. In numerous Ohio municipalities, children are required to solicit licenses in order to participate in this age-old candy crawl. And that's just the start. Halloween parties are forbidden for a glut of nannyistic reasons, including the menace of hazardous costumes, classroom distractions, and, most incomprehensibly, the religious discrimination such celebrations may cause.

Schools and parents, naturally, should have the choice to protect children. In some New York schools, kids are barred from dressing up or having any classroom Halloween parties whatsoever. The edict came straight from the top. New York City school chancellor Joel Klein decreed: no costumes, no candy, no parties, and no fun. "Remind students that no costumes, masks or Halloween makeup should be worn while in school," one memo stated. "The customary Halloween tradition of Trick or Treat should never take place in schools . . . Halloween parties in school during instructional time should be prohibited and strongly discouraged for after-school hours."

The threat of sweets and candy has led administrators to institute absurd bans. Hard candy is unsafe, but let's not forget chewing gum. No, this isn't just any chewing gum, but narcotic-laced chewing gum. A middle-school student in Pennsylvania was suspended for three days for sharing a caffeinated chewing gum called Jolt with her friend. The gum was, as the school superintendent put it, "a stimulant that has no other redeeming quality." Products acting as a stimulant are prohibited and possessing them is grounds for discipline. The suspension was mainly based on the girl's decision to share the gum. "What if the gum had been given to a student with a heart condition?" the principal explained.

The school, by the way, featured well-stocked vending machines filled with liberally caffeinated soda. No worries. The nanny state will get to those soon enough.

SAFETY TAG

Dodgeball. In spite of the inherent aggressiveness of the game, generations of Americans have found a way to enjoy this playground favorite. These days it's become the well-known target of nannies.

Not long ago, the New York appellate court refused to dismiss a lawsuit that claimed a school was at fault because a girl broke her elbow while playing dodgeball. In 2001, seven-year-old Heather Lindaman decided to participate in a spontaneous game of dodgeball on a hardwood court in the school. The game included several balls and, as the Associated Press put it, "no safety or protection zone to run from the thrown balls." In a regrettable accident, young Heather became tangled with another child and fell, breaking her elbow. But was this case of a kid getting hurt dodgeball's fault? You bet. State education officials claim that what makes Heather's case unique isn't that the lawsuit faults the school for poor supervision of the child—it doesn't—but that it faults the school for allowing children to play dodgeball at all.

In 2005, a schoolyard game of dodgeball became a nightmarish legal ordeal for a twelve-year-old girl and her family. Complaints by parents of an injured student at a California school prompted authorities to charge Brittney Schneiders with battery. Five other students also accused of battery opted to take probation, but Schneiders—an honor-roll student who had received good citizenship awards—refused. "I don't think I did [commit a crime]," Brittney said. "I thought I was just playing a dodgeball game. I never thought it would come up to this level."

How did we get to this point? The crusade to outlaw dodgeball has been going on for years, and the reasons are simple. "Any time you throw an object at somebody it creates an environment of retaliation and resentment," a physical-education teacher told *The Boston Globe*. "There is nothing positive that can happen except a bully gets to beat up on little kids."

Not every game children play has an inherent positive aspect to it—that's what makes them childhood games. By the late 1990s, zero tolerance for dodgeball was infecting schools nationwide. This oppressive policy was so rigid that some schools wouldn't even allow voluntary dodgeball games or ones that utilized super-pliable, spongy, cuddly Nerf balls. To properly understand the rationale behind this mollycoddling, we can turn to a 2001 academic symposium in the *Journal of Physical Education, Recreation & Dance* titled, "Is There a Place for Dodgeball in Physical Education?"

Dennis Docheff, of the Department of Health and Human Performance at Concordia University, writes: "A person trying to record the positive attributes of dodgeball would end up with a very short list . . . In today's world, with so many things breeding violent behavior in children, there is no room for dodgeball anymore."

Using this logic, should we assume that there's little room for games like hockey or football—both featuring a considerable amount of aggressive physical interaction? Didn't these stolid academics ever have a snowball fight as children? Mindless fun can provide benefits of its own. In fact, the most edifying aspect of dodgeball is that it provides incomparable life experience.

For those who lay blame, even partially, on dodgeball as a contributor to violence in schools, they should not bother. According to a report from the Centers for Disease Control and Prevention, violent behaviors among high-school students have been markedly decreasing. The percentage of students involved in "physical fighting" dropped precipitously between 1991 and 2003. And this drop started long before anti-dodgeball fanatics got their claws into school policy.

One of the few categories that has risen in recent years has been the number of high-school students who avoided school *because of safety concerns*. It's a telling statistic. If schools have gotten safer, taking draconian lengths to ensure utopian safety conditions, should students feel less safe? Are administrators, teachers, and parents projecting their own overwrought concerns on kids who would feel completely safe had we just let them be?

Across the country, tag has become the focus of safety fanatics. In Beaverton, Oregon, at Barnes Elementary School, rules forbid the game of tag. In Salem, Oregon, an elementary-education director claimed that they "don't encourage the game of tag because it encourages fights." The principal of Willett Elementary School in Attleboro, Massachusetts, banned tag—as well as touch football and any "chasing games"—in late 2006. In 2004 a school principal in Santa Monica, California, was quoted as saying she banned tag because "little kids were coming in and saying, 'I don't like it.' Children weren't feeling good about it."

Tag?

"The idea of loosely running around and chasing each other is not safe," Long Hill, New Jersey, superintendent Arthur DiBenedetto, explained. In recent years, similar bans have been put in place at schools throughout the country, frequently because children were being hurt when they fell or were piled on by classmates. "Tag may look OK socially, but it can be a double standard because kids can use it to bully a certain student," according to Mary Beth Klotz, a psychologist with the National Association of School Psychologists, who further maintained that there is "potential for *some* victimization."

Neil Williams, a professor at Eastern Connecticut State University, wrote in the *Journal of Physical Education* in 1994: "Tag games, when structured correctly, can be great additions to a physical education curriculum . . . However, all too often, tag games are organized as classic elimination games (like Musical Chairs) in which students supposedly develop their quickness, thinking skills, and fitness." Musical chairs. The potential for victimization is as inherent in tag as it is in playing in a sandbox, hanging out by a locker, or riding a bicycle. There is no way to legislate the kid out of kids.

★ ★ ★

Happily, though, some children can learn valuable lessons from those who over-intellectualize spontaneous fun. When tag was banned in a Madison, Wisconsin, elementary school, a self-proclaimed "shy" third grader named Olivia Lichterman got "mad."

As opposed to allowing a childhood staple to be stolen from her and her friends, she organized. The kids fought to overturn the ban on tag, because, as Olivia contended, "Most kids can't focus well when they don't get exercise, and kids who don't have football, they all play tag."

Her mom shared in this reasonable approach, telling the media that the ban was out of line. "There's got to be something more going on," Nina Eliasoph explained. "You can't just be banning tag, because tag is sort of a rite of childhood." Olivia, at the tender age of seven, possessed more common sense than many of her teachers and administrators.

The sanction against playing tag was overturned after officials agreed on rules for a "safe" version of the game.

WIMPS, JOKERS, AND GEEKS

Some experts maintain that children saddled with the excessively structured regimen that nannies envision will one day struggle with independence. In a *Psychology Today* article entitled "A *Nation of Wimps*," Barbara Carlson, president and cofounder of a group called Putting Families First, explained that kids are having a difficult time playing in neighborhood pickup games because they can't figure out how to choose sides. "They've been told by their coaches where on the field to stand, told by their parents what color socks to wear, told by referees who's won and what's fair."

Keeping score is considered ugly and demeaning. "You're all winners" is a platitude parents often repeat to kids but parents never actually buy themselves. In some Massachusetts municipalities, nannies would like to take it a step further and force these unlucky kids to wear helmets while playing soccer.

Initially, all leagues, from preteen to pro squads, would have been required to wear soccer helmets. An updated measure was rewritten at the last minute to clarify that professionals would not be mandated to put on these silly apparatuses. Thus, Major League Soccer's New England Revolution would be spared the indignity (not as if anyone would have noticed).

The trend for mandatory soccer helmets is growing. In the Temecula Valley Soccer Association in Southern California, players under eight years old are required to wear some form of headgear. Peter Schilperoort, president of the association, offered that helmets prevent injuries previously suffered by his players, claiming that the equipment is "the best thing since sliced bread."

Now if the soccer helmet had the ability to cut off circulation to the brain so that a person would no longer experience oppressive boredom . . . well, I agree, we're talking "the best thing since sliced bread." If that's not the case, then wearing a helmet in a sport where you're suppose to use your head makes the law similar to forcing baseball players to wrap their bats in bubble wrap.

Which brings us to baseball. There are those rare occasions when children are truly tragically hurt playing sports. And during those times, many elected officials feel an understandable pull to do something to rectify a situation that is beyond their control.

After a baseball line drive hit a Chicago-area high-school student in the face, there was a concentrated effort in the district to ban aluminum bats at baseball games on all district-owned fields.

Is an aluminum bat a weapon? Sure, if someone smashed you over the head with one. In reality, aluminum bats have been used at the collegiate and high-school level for more than twenty years with few serious injuries. More than four million of these supposed weapons are produced in the United States each year. If anything is dangerous it's the hardball. And if we want to protect children from baseball, we're going to have to mandate soft-pitch ball games.

★ ★ ★

In March 2006, during the Missouri Valley Conference championship, a Southern Illinois University cheerleader took a fall from a fifteen-foot human pyramid. Since then, the national cheerleading safety group restricted high-flying stunts. "Basically, we have been practicing this whole semester for nothing. One incident has caused us to have to rework everything," explained Heather Cunningham, Baylor's cheerleading captain, as her squad prepared for a Big 12 Conference tournament. "We are going back to middle school stuff."

They may be surprised at what goes on in some of the middle schools in Texas. In the epicenter of high-school football, legislation filed by Representative Al Edwards would, if it could, put an end to "sexually suggestive" performances at athletic events and other extracurricular competitions. In other words: cheerleading.

"It's just too sexually oriented, you know, the way they're shaking their behinds and going on, breaking it down," explained Edwards, a twenty-six-year veteran of the Texas House. "And then we say to them, 'don't get involved in sex unless it's marriage or love, it's dangerous out there' and yet the teachers and directors are helping them go through those kinds of gyrations."

SPEAKING OF GYRATIONS

Seems as if "breaking it down" is something the Virginia State House wasn't crazy about, either. In 2005, a bipartisan group of legislators came together to outlaw the trend of wearing trousers so low that underwear hangs over the top. Delegates said the habit was "coarsening" society. Youngsters in Virginia showing too much of their boxer shorts or G-strings could be fined $50 a pop.

After hearing complaints from some folks at his local barbershop, Virginia legislator Algie Howell introduced a bill that would criminalize the trend of teenagers wearing their pants low on their hips. He isn't even the first. A similar bill was introduced in Louisiana last year. Howell has also sponsored bills putting restrictions on tricked-out automobiles and overly noisy stereo systems.

"It's not an attack on baggy pants," he argued. "To vote for this bill would be a vote for character, to uplift your community and to do something good not only for the state of Virginia." Baggy pants may be safe but independence certainly isn't. Puritanical laws should be dictated by parents, not some stodgy middle-aged politician in the legislature. The penalty for ludicrous high-school fashion statements will arrive in due time.

If you don't believe me, check out your very own yearbook.

Teenagers cheerlead. They wear clothes parents might not find reasonable. They wear clothes that will make them cringe in twenty years. They flirt. Nowadays they do it online. At Pope John XXIII Regional High School in New Jersey, the Reverend Kieran McHugh unloaded a surprise on nine hundred students at a school assembly one morning in 2006. Effective immediately, McHugh informed the students, they would have to dismantle their personal Web pages on community sites such as MySpace.com and Friendster or face suspension.

McHugh, of course, can dictate policy at a private school in almost any manner he sees fit. Protecting students from online sexual predators that prowl cyberspace in search of personal information and pictures of children is a noble goal, but monitoring student activities outside of school is impractical and perhaps unconstitutional.

The popularity of these online communities is staggering. According to the Nielsen NetRatings, the top-ten social network sites like MySpace grew 47 percent over a year from a unique audience of 46.8 million in April 2005 to 68.8 million in April 2006, which means that these sites reach somewhere around 45 percent of active Web users, which is a tough number to wrangle.

MySpace sat at the top of the heap. The community site drew more than 38 million unique visitors during that time and saw a yearly growth rate of 367 percent. In July of 2006, MySpace.com ranked as the number-one U.S. Web site, displacing Yahoo and Google for the first time. "Social networking is not a fad that will disappear," Jon Gibs, senior media director of Nielsen NetRatings, explained. "If anything, it will become more ingrained in mainstream sites."

With tens of millions of young people come some miscreants and criminals. In June of 2006, a fourteen-year-old girl claimed she was sexually assaulted by another user of MySpace.com and sued the social networking site for $30 million. The girl said a nineteen-year-old man who had lied in his profile about being a senior on a football team had gained her trust—and her phone number. The suit alleges that MySpace has "absolutely no meaningful protections or security measures to protect underage users."

"[MySpace] has got to take this seriously," offered attorney Carl Barry. MySpace, apparently, did take these sorts of events seriously, hiring as its first chief security officer Hemanshu Nigam, who had specialized in finding child predators as a U.S. prosecutor.

This effort wasn't enough for some in Washington, D.C. Representative Michael Fitzpatrick of Pennsylvania believed controlling tens of millions of eager teens could be accomplished through legislation. His bill, the Deleting Online Predators Act of 2006, would require "recipients of universal service support for schools and libraries to protect minors from commercial social networking sites and chat rooms."

Using awfully wide-ranging language, the bill would have included virtually thousands of sites that bring users together in communities or forums. Not only is it unfeasible to regulate the

Internet in this fashion but it has the potential to be counterproductive, driving students underground and to anonymous sites where they would be under the radar of parents and teachers, building MySpace pages that can't be traced or meeting in communities that can't be monitored.

And, as with a large amount of nannyist legislation, Fitzpatrick's bill overstates the so-called emergency. Remember, NetRatings claims that approximately 31 percent of MySpace users are under the age of eighteen, leaving us with more than thirty-five million teen users on MySpace. With a handful of incidents, staying at home and posting on MySpace doesn't seem to be any more dangerous than hanging out at the local mall or in back of the local convenience store.

ANOTHER ZERO-TOLERANCE POLICY

Keeping kids safe from one another, now that's a challenging responsibility. In 2006, a Massachusetts elementary-school girl named Savannah claimed her friend Sophie hugged her on the playground. Savannah hugged Sophie back. The hugs resulted in Savannah having to write a letter of apology—complete with teacher corrections—that read in part, "I touch Sophie because she touch me and I didn't like it because she was hugging me. I didn't like when she hugged me."

The parents in this situation were understandably irate. "I can understand if boys are playing rough or kids are pulling each other around—that's one thing. But when kids are being affectionate, I mean hugging, hey, they shouldn't be disciplined over it and they shouldn't be lying in letters making the kid say the opposite that they don't like to hug," said Savannah's father.

First graders who repeatedly touch classmates in inappropriate ways should be disciplined—by teachers and parents. Certainly it's not appropriate for a child to paw at another kid incessantly. But to hand over the monitoring and punishment of this kind of activity to the federal government can lead to all kinds of ugly places.

A similar overreaction surrounding any public display of affection came down at Sky View Middle School in Bend, Oregon, when fourteen-year-old Cazz Altomare decided to hug her boyfriend in the hallway. "Really, all we're trying to do is create an environment that's focused on learning, and learning proper manners is part of that," said Dave Haack, the principal of another Bend middle school. "This is not us being the romance police."

How about a six- or seven-year-old? Can they comprehend the meaning of romance? In 1996, there were a number of incidents that uncovered the nonsense of treating children with the same strict nannyism we levy on adults. In New York, a second grader was suspended for kissing a girl and ripping a button off her skirt—an idea the boy got from his favorite book, *Corduroy*. District parents were perplexed. That same year, a media firestorm broke out surrounding the plight of a six-year-old North Carolina boy named Jonathan Prevette. The tyke received a one-day suspension and was excluded from an ice-cream party and other activities after kissing a young classmate on the cheek.

The Department of Education was forced to clarify their guidelines for the school. "The factors in the guidance confirm that a kiss on the cheek by a 1st grader does not constitute sexual harassment," the department helpfully explained, exonerating little Jonathan. In order to give rise to a complaint, the new guidelines explained, "sexual harassment must be sufficiently severe, persistent or pervasive that it adversely affects a student's education or creates a hostile or abusive educational environment. For a one-time incident to rise to the level of harassment, it must be severe."

In 2005, a first grader was suspended for three days for sexual harassment after he put two fingers inside a classmate's waistband. Christopher Murray, a civil rights attorney who has handled school discipline cases, explains the major problem with this brand of zero-tolerance policy: "The connotation is you're getting some kind of sexual gratification, or wanting sexual gratification, or are putting pressure on for some kind of sexual gratification, when a six-year-old doesn't have that capacity."

As Nan Stein, a senior research scientist at the Center for Research on Women at Wellesley College explained, these sorts of troubling cases aren't "sexual harassment" as first graders simply can't mentally digest the concept.

And don't think this strain of over-the-top policy only targets boys. When a ten-year-old girl at an elementary school in Thornton, Colorado, "repeatedly" asked a certain boy on the playground if he liked her, the boy complained to a teacher (boy, is this kid gonna change his tune in a couple of years). Naturally, school administrators, citing the district's "zero-tolerance sexual harassment policy" suspended the irritating young girl.

Only after the parents rose up in anger did school officials admit that they had "probably" overreacted. Then again, officials claimed "it's all in how you look at it."

Yes. And anyone with a modicum of common sense looks at it as nannyism.

* * *

Political speech, unlike first-grade sex crimes, is all about perspective. Fortunately, here in the United States we have always worked out our problems through invective on talk shows and expressed our displeasure through bumper stickers. Rarely do we use bullets to solve political battles. So while partisan politics can deteriorate into hostile name-calling on occasion, children do not need to be hermetically sealed from the slightest unpleasant political commentary.

Take for example, the reaction of administrators in a Prosser, Washington, high school when a fifteen-year-old boy turned in a few puerile political sketches in art class. The boy was interrogated by the Secret Service after his hypersensitive teacher reported the sketches featuring President Bush dressed as the devil, firing off rockets.

The caption on one sketch read, "End the War—on Errorism." There were more sketches, including one of the Bill of Rights and the Constitution in flames. The police claimed that the boy's sketches were seen as "a threat against the president of the United States" and they notified the Secret Service because "that's their bailiwick."

In February 2003, school officials at a Dearborn, Michigan, high school ordered a sixteen-year-old student to either take off the shirt which featured the face of President Bush and the words "International Terrorist" or face suspension. The student, Bretton Barber, said the shirt expressed his objections to the war in Iraq and went home. And everyone knows what a crushing blow missing school must have been for a sixteen-year-old.

The American Civil Liberties Union (ACLU) filed a suit on his behalf and won—because, hey, that's their bailiwick.

Wasn't the First Amendment crystal clear on this point? Or did I miss the part that says freedom of speech will not be abridged unless you're a knucklehead?

There's no ideological discrimination when it comes to suppression of adolescent political speech—though there seems to be bias in the cases the ACLU deems important to take on. In Illinois, high-school student James Lord (it's almost creepy how appropriate his name is) was suspended for one month after he closed his daily news broadcast on the school's closed circuit television with "Have a safe and happy holiday, and God bless."

Similarly, the Clark County School District defended school officials' decision to cut short a high-school valedictorian's commencement speech, saying the speech would have amounted to school-sponsored proselytizing. Officials and a lawyer with the ACLU claimed that administrators followed federal law when they cut the microphone on valedictorian Brittany McComb when she began mentioning—gasp—God.

"There should be no controversy here," the ACLU's Allen Lichtenstein claimed. "It's important for people to understand that a student was given a school-sponsored forum by a school and therefore, in essence, it was a school-sponsored speech."

It seems that McComb exhibited a far better understanding of the parameters of free speech. "I went through four years of school at Foothill and they taught me logic and they taught me freedom of speech," McComb told the *Las Vegas Review-Journal.* "God's the biggest part of my life. Just like other valedictorians thank their parents, I wanted to thank my lord and savior."

In Virginia, a high-school student was barred from wearing a shirt with a pro-life message because it violates the school's policy against "profane or obscene" language. The shirt opined that "Abortion is Homicide. You will not silence my message. You will not mock my God. You will stop killing my generation. Rock for Life."

Provocative maybe, but certainly not obscene.

When Tyler Harper wore an anti-gay T-shirt to his San Diego school, in response to a pro-gay-rights rally hosted by the Gay-Straight Alliance, he ran into some more trouble. The front of the T-shirt read "Be Ashamed, Our School Embraced What God Has Condemned," and on the back, it said "Homosexuality Is Shameful." When the school forced Harper to take off the T-shirt, he took legal action, claiming this violated his First Amendment rights.

The Ninth Circuit Court—which has a long history of overturned decisions, leading some to wonder if they have an altered or incomplete version of the Constitution—claimed that Harper's type of speech, which aimed "derogatory and injurious remarks" at students' minority status, such as "race, religion, and sexual orientation," is not protected by the First Amendment. The idea that we can cherry-pick comfortable speech and deny freedom of expression for what some may consider ugly flies in the face of everything the Founding Fathers intended and contributes mightily to the growing nanny state.

HEAVY HANDS

Not long ago, two professors at Boston University noticed a disturbing trend regarding free speech in schools. "The events at Columbine gave high school administrators all the reasons—legitimate or illegitimate—they needed to trounce the First Amendment rights of public school students in the name of preventing violence."

Though belligerent speech rarely manifests into authentic violence, there is always the reasonable fear that it might. In this country's most infamous act of school violence, two teenage gunmen murdered twelve students and a teacher before killing themselves at Columbine High School outside of Denver in 1999. A few years later, at Red Lake High School on a Native American reservation in Minnesota, an unbalanced teenage shooter murdered two school officials and six students. Thus, school officials have a duty to ensure safe learning environments. Could stricter school rules on speech have prevented such tragedies?

When a ten-year-old North Carolina boy is suspended from

school for reportedly using his thumb and forefinger as an imaginary gun and aiming it at the ceiling, are we preventing another Columbine? Jonathan Motes had violated the school's zero-tolerance weapons policy. "I finished my work. I was bored. I was playing around and saying 'bam' in my hand. I did this twice," the fifth grader said.

Is violence prevented when an honor-roll student in a Kansas high school is suspended for writing a poem entitled "Who Killed My Dog"? School officials determined the poem to be a threat to other students (did they resemble dogs?) and suspended the student.

Have we nipped tragedy in the bud when a third grader in an Alabama elementary school is suspended for bringing a G.I. Joe toy handgun to school? "It's about an inch long," the boy's grandmother explained. "[The school] had to tape it to a piece of paper to keep from losing it." According to a notice sent from the school to Austin Crittenden's family, he was suspended for "Possession of a weapon Firearm replica."

What have school officials really accomplished when four kindergarten boys in New Jersey were suspended for three days for playing "cops and robbers"? While the school district claims to have no official written policy mandating "zero tolerance" of violent behavior or "threats," the actions by the school officials are consistent with those of many other school districts who have adopted such blanket policies. In the same state, a student was suspended from school for a day and ordered to undergo a psychological evaluation after mentioning to a classmate his intent to "shoot" a fellow classmate with a wad of paper.

Notwithstanding the fact that the "weapon" considered suspect consisted of a wadded-up piece of moistened paper and a rubber band with which to launch it, district officials notified local police, suspended the student under the school's zero tolerance policy, and required him to undergo a psychological evaluation before returning to class.

Don't "shoot" paper and don't try to "shoot" baskets and never ever "shoot" the breeze, either. Unless, of course, you're prepared to pay the price.

★ CHAPTER FIVE ★

YAHWEH (OR THE HIGHWAY)

I'm completely in favor of the separation of Church and State. My idea is that these two institutions screw us up enough on their own, so both of them together is certain death.

—George Carlin

★

HOLIER THAN THOU

"It is a ridiculous notion to say you can't legislate morality," Texas Governor Rick Perry once said during a discussion on a gay-marriage ban passing. "I say you can't *not* legislate morality." Former senator and future attorney general John Ashcroft would certainly agree. He once explained to the Christian-centric magazine *Charisma* in 1999 that "I think *all* we should legislate is morality."

One can just about feel the blood pressure rise in blue states. The notion that government should *ever* legislate morality—much less *only* legislate morality—flies in the face of the liberals' ingrained notions about the purpose of government. But as it turns out, Perry is right. Sort of.

In spite of sanctimonious grousing about the horrors of "legislating morality," all political stripes engage in the practice. When government taxes prosperous citizens at a higher rate than less prosperous ones in an effort to more fairly disperse wealth among citizens, morality is being legislated. Zoning regulations that determine which types of business are suited for certain neighborhoods is another way to legislate communal morality. Equal hiring opportunities, minimum wages, statutory rape laws are all shared understanding of morality.

Why then do conservatives deserve special scorn? Unlike their contemporaries on the left, modern conservatism regards itself—and still sells itself—as the ideology of less intrusive government. The first question a conservative might have asked years ago is *should* government get involved, not *can* government get involved. Personal responsibility was a pillar of the right-wing rhetoric and though there has been plenty of ideological infighting among right-wingers over the years (freedom versus virtue, isolationists versus free traders), the idea that government should get off the backs of Americans was a principle everyone could share.

Times have changed. Former Republican icon Ronald Reagan—the measuring stick for all that is modern conservatism—once said that "government exists to protect us from each other. Where government has gone beyond its limits is in deciding to protect us from ourselves." Today many on the right embrace nannyism as a tool for social good.

Indeed, from his first day in office, President George W. Bush not only would continue to bankroll many of the nanny health and safety initiatives of the 1990s, often building the size and scope of programs, but would oversee the largest increases in federal spending since Lyndon Johnson. And as government grows so does nannyism. Bush has federalized education with the No Child Left Behind Act, doubled money for abstinence training programs, and enacted faith-based initiatives as expansions of government.

Bush was driven by values. In his 2001 State of the Union address, he stated that "values are important, so we have tripled funding for character education to teach our children not only reading and writing, but right from wrong." It's safe to say that Reagan, whatever his feelings may have been on good and evil, would never have put government-run schools in the position of indoctrinating children on the topic. Reagan, in 1980, ran in opposition to the idea of a federal Department of Education.

It would be hard to imagine even the conservative's über-villain Bill Clinton making such a bald-faced nannyistic claim without howls of condemnation coming from the right. Yet nearly all Republicans remained silent. Social conservatives, as a matter of fact, applauded. Here's how Pennsylvania's Republican senator Rick Santorum, a devout Catholic and one of the leaders of the religious conservative right, dismissed limited government and personal autonomy:

> This whole idea of personal autonomy, well I don't think most conservatives hold that point of view. Some do. They have this idea that people should be left alone, be able to do whatever they want to do, government should keep our taxes down and keep our regulations low, that we shouldn't get involved in the bedroom, we shouldn't get involved in cultural issues. You know, people should do whatever they want. Well, that is not how traditional conservatives view the world and I think most conservatives understand that individuals can't go it alone.

Santorum is correct. Government should not be left out of the equation entirely. Government should help those in need. But to so cavalierly dismiss individual independence is something else altogether. Because guess what? We *can* go it alone.

Still, the U.S. attorney general's office guaranteed that the individual didn't go it alone as it pressed for a multitude of legal and law-enforcement assaults on individualism and states' rights. The attacks of September 11, 2001, changed the way law enforcement did business, and the pros and cons of curbing personal freedoms is still hotly debated. But Ashcroft's office also began a less-discussed assault on federalism that had absolutely nothing to do with global terror—the most obvious being the cases of medical marijuana in California and assisted suicide in Oregon, both passing through the local electorate, and both shut down by federal intervention.

Social conservatives may see short-term gains in this form of power grab, but intrusive government may come back to haunt them. In their sprawling study of modern conservatism, *The Right*

Nation, authors John Micklethwait and Adrian Wooldridge detail how big-government Republicanism morphed into big-government conservatism and how Ashcroft may one day see the flip side of his intrusions into personal responsibility.

> . . . as an Evangelical who refrains from smoking, drinking, dancing and looking at nude statues, Ashcroft represents a minority in his own party, let alone the country at large. The best he can hope for is a live-and-let-live attitude that gives minorities like his room to flourish. Ashcroft may well come to rue this Faustian bargain with big brother government next time a Democrat sits in his office.

And the authors go on to point out that Ashcroft engaged in all kinds of "meddling that had nothing to do with fighting terrorism." Many social conservatives didn't display any fear of the future repercussions of big government. They employed the nanny state in their own creative ways. When in 2005, Governor Perry needed to make up revenue loss in Texas, he didn't dare raise income taxes—which would have amounted to political suicide in a predominantly conservative state—instead, he got the job done by nibbling on the margins of the nanny state. He increased cigarette taxes by $1 a pack, raised taxes on alcoholic drinks, *and* collected a tax of at least $5 each time a patron entered a topless bar.

A nanny-state hat trick: health, temperance, and morality.

ATTACK OF THE KILLER NIPPLE

One of the more brazen expansions of paternalistic conservatism was taken by the Federal Communications Commission (FCC). After rejecting more than 80 percent of indecency complaints thrown their way in 2002, one incident became the impetus for an extraordinary crackdown on speech. In February 2004, during the Super Bowl halftime show sponsored by MTV, singer Janet Jackson experienced what she generously referred to as a "wardrobe malfunction" when duet partner Justin Timberlake ripped off a patch covering her right breast. Millions of Americans were exposed to a bewildering sight for a milli-instant.

The CBS network—once considered the most family-friendly of the majors—was hit with a $550,000 fine by the FCC (a pair of nipples, I imagine, would have cost a million). And soon enough, self-proclaimed guardians of American decency began their handwringing and we heard the five most frightening words in the English language: "Something needs to be done." Many viewers, it seems, had difficulty unraveling the mysteries of the remote control.

Between 2002 and 2005 the agency received 300,000 official complaints about television shows alone. To this FCC commissioner Michael Copps offered up some self-flagellating comments, explaining that "nothing this Commission has done so far has accomplished anything to slow down Big Media's race to the bottom."

If the FCC was not prepared to do the right thing, Congress would have to step in. James Sensenbrenner, a Republican from Wisconsin, took the lead by letting industry executives attending the National Cable & Telecommunications Association conference know that if fines were no longer enough of a deterrent, he wanted criminal prosecution for unruly behavior on the air. This tact, he claimed, would induce networks to fall in line when it came to programming. "I'd prefer using the criminal process rather than the regulatory process," Sensenbrenner said.

Sensenbrenner may be right. When government threatens corporations with criminal prosecution, the tendency is for them to tread cautiously. And the more serious—and in this case unwarranted—the charges, the more careful they would be. But if Congress threatened television producers with criminal charges, the ensuing outbreak of "cover your own ass" would mean a perpetual loop of *Mr. Rogers' Neighborhood* reruns.

Implementation of such laws would also hold some potential difficulties. Who would be charged? The network? The producer of the program? The director? The nipple-baring pop star? And then we are faced with the age-old dilemma of defining indecency. To many folks the thought of Janet Jackson performing at the Super Bowl is indecent enough, and to others that nipple was the highlight of the game. Who gets to choose what is offensive?

Practicality wasn't important. Politics were. And Sensenbrenner wasn't alone in overreacting. Smelling the political upside of such a campaign, morally hawkish politicians lined up to make some nanny-state hay. There was only one mystery remaining: Which legislator could feign higher levels of indignation and reach optimum political output? During the hearings for the Broadcast Decency Enforcement Act, the bill that would purportedly fix the problem, Congresswoman Heather Wilson from New Mexico looked to be leader of the pack.

Wilson was so incensed, according to *The Hill* (a newspaper covering Congress), that "her voice cracked and her eyes filled with tears." She sat there listening courteously to prepared speeches by various industry types until it was her time to shine. Discarding her prepared statement, she dressed down Viacom president Mel Karmazin. "You knew what you were doing!" Wilson accused him. "You knew that shock and indecency creates a buzz that moves market share and lines your pockets."

It's not often you see a so-called conservative attacking the profit motive.

Texas Republican congressman Ron Paul—admittedly more a paleo-libertarian than a Republican—was the only member of his party to vote against the Broadcast Decency Enforcement Act. "My boss would say [Wilson's speech] was somewhat Orwellian," explained Paul's spokesman. "The notion that government can make us more of a decent society is largely false. Government makes us less decent, not more." Just watching the nannies at work makes me think that Paul is right.

Paul was in the definite minority. Increasingly, conservative legislators believed government could inject much-needed purity into our souls through regulation. The FCC's fines for indecency have grown exponentially. From a meager $4,000 in total fines in 1995 the number went to $7.9 million by 2004. In 2005, Bush signed the Broadcast Decency Enforcement Act into law, which allowed fines to be raised tenfold for radio and television broadcasters who aired indecent programs, from $32,000 per violation to $325,000 a pop.

★ ★ ★

There are instances, like Jackson's Super Bowl performance, in which parents are hit with the unanticipated adult moment. But those are few and far between.

The Jackson nipple controversy and the subsequent pundit-induced hysteria elicited far less anger than the public may have realized. A *Time* magazine poll found that 66 percent of Americans thought the FCC had overreacted to the Jackson incident. In a 2006 Pew Research Center poll Americans stated that they held themselves to blame when children were exposed to explicit sex or graphic violence. And by more than a ten-to-one margin the public believed that parents, rather than the entertainment industry, bears the most responsibility for keeping children from seeing sex and violence on television. That was a good sign.

While there is a considerable slice of the nation's viewership that is fed up with sexually provocative television, evidence suggests many of them were more upset by the mere thought, not the existence, of offensive programs. For example, when the FCC forced Fox Network to fork over $1.2 million for its "sexually suggestive" program *Married by America,* the penalty was prompted by only *three* complaints from the public.

One of the largest fines imposed by the FCC was a $3.6 million slap—again paid by CBS—for an episode of *Without a Trace,* a show about a special unit of the FBI that featured a "teen orgy" party scene. When CBS filed a Freedom of Information Act request to review the complaints that spurred the exorbitant fine, it discovered that every single one of the 4,211 e-mails provided by the FCC had originated from the Web sites of either the Parents Television Council or the American Family Association. Both are nosy socially conservative organizations that keep an eye on explicit television so your children don't have to. Even more surprising was that only two of the more than four thousand letter writers had taken the time to watch the program. And in both those cases the complainer only viewed a "brief, out-of-context segment" posted on the Parents Television Council's Web site.

The FCC has also taken their witch hunt further and gone after broadcasters. In 2006, the FCC requested a whole host of tapes from major broadcasters of live football games and NASCAR races to see if coaches, athletes, or spectators might have used expletives on television. (Any avid sports fan could tell you without seeing the tapes, the majority certainly did.) The FCC jumped into this important investigation without a single complaint from the public.

Here we enter a murky area. When it comes to naughty language, it isn't only that the FCC employs strict guidelines on speech, it's that the FCC often makes arbitrary and inconsistent decisions about the words the public is capable of handling.

Legendary director Martin Scorsese produced a documentary

miniseries about the history of American blues music called *The Blues*. When one of the episodes, *Godfathers and Sons*, was aired by a community college public television station in California, it was also singled out by the FCC for a $15,000 fine because of some blue language used by the featured musicians. "The language of the film was an essential element of the story," explained an agitated Scorsese. "The language of blues musicians often was filled with expletives that shocked and challenged America's white-dominated society of the 1940s, 1950s and 1960s."

Around the same time, Steven Spielberg's World War II epic *Saving Private Ryan* was found not to be subject to indecency fines despite being littered with the f-word, the s-word, and explicit violence. Here, the FCC noted that "in rare contexts, language that is presumptively profane" will still be allowed "where it is demonstrably essential to the nature of an artistic or educational work or essential to informing viewers on a matter of public importance." Why do they get to decide which context is appropriate?

The FCC, in what amounts to nothing more than censorship, takes on the task of deciding what is essential, artistic, educational, smart, or even profane. In reality, it is impossible for the FCC to gauge how a particular viewer in a particular community will perceive or react to a subject matter. What we end up with is an overreaching and confusing policy.

Consider Princeton University philosophy professor Harry G. Frankfurt's book *On Bullshit*. An insightful study of "purposeful obfuscation and pretentious duplicity," his slim tome became a surprising bestseller in 2005. Its contents were discussed in detail on popular television shows like *Today* and *60 Minutes*—well, discussed in detail without ever mentioning the title of the book. The word "bullshit" is banned by the FCC—even if used in an intellectual or non-offensive context.

As Jeff Jarvis, a columnist and media critic, once commented, no word really conveys the gist of "bullshit" as well as "bullshit" does. Moreover, he believes that the FCC has outlawed the "single most essential word in political discourse and protest." Jarvis points out that offensive racial and religious smears like "nigger" and "kike" are constitutionally protected as political speech, while "fuck" and "shit" are not. "I believe that the FCC has now violated my civil right to speak truth to power any time I am on TV or radio. They went too far when they banned not just 'shit' but 'bullshit' and banned it presumptively."

The incongruity of the FCC's policy is even more evident in the fact that the word "fucking"—the adjective, not the verb, that is—is technically permissible on broadcast television. Yet how many times have you heard it used? This tells us that network executives realize the consequences of allowing offensive words on their television programs: low ratings. That's exactly how it's supposed to work in a free nation. At least, in a nation where leaders trust that citizens will have the common sense to vote with their feet and wallets.

But the minute someone falls off the wagon legislators jump to action. When the rock group U2's lead singer, Bono, did let the f-word fly at the 2003 Golden Globe Awards (as in "This is really, really, fucking brilliant"), he upset a lot of people but no one more than California congressman Doug Ose. The legislator decided he'd repair the glitch. "I don't want to be sitting there when a guy blurts something out over the TV and have my daughters ask me what those words meant," he explained.

Ose has a point. If my two young children heard a nasty word like "fucking" (not counting the one that slips out of my mouth from time to time), I would be forced to boycott the guilty station until I was sure it would not happen again. The market would not allow a station to get away with it. You can be assured a boycott by thousands of concerned parents would soon have a direct impact on ratings—and there is no better way to get a network executive's attention.

Instead of appreciating that independence, Ose decided to draft legislation that closed every imaginable loophole on cursing, "leaving our children free from exposure to offensive and crude speech broadcast over America's airwaves." And like an out-of-control English professor, his bill leaves no rock unturned:

> As used in this section, the term 'profane', used with respect to language, includes the words 'shit', 'piss', 'fuck', 'cunt', 'asshole', and the phrases 'cock sucker', 'mother fucker', and 'ass hole', compound use (including hyphenated compounds) of such words and phrases with each other or with other words or phrases, and other grammatical forms of such words and phrases (including verb, adjective, gerund, participle, and infinitive forms).

I apologize for reprinting the congressman's offensive language, but every so often adults find it necessary to use profanity. For example, if an adult acquaintance asked you to explain Ose's bill, the phrase "absolute bullshit" would be perfectly acceptable. Because allowing an uptight congressman to micromanage speech should be more offensive to Americans than the occasional profanity that slips out of a celebrity's mouth.

KILLJOYS ON THE LOOSE

The overreactions and overreaching of the FCC and legislators may lead to their irrelevance. In 2004, radio jock Howard Stern, the wildly successful and provocative radio personality, emancipated himself from the regulatory reach of the FCC by signing a massive contract with the burgeoning SIRIUS Satellite Radio. Listeners would now have to fork over a couple of bucks a month, but they would do so with the knowledge that government strictures would no longer govern the Wheel of Sex or the Homeless Game.

New technology is making it possible for entertainers to circumvent the FCC on a multitude of fronts. When the WB network first aired a show with some sexually sensitive material called *The Bedford Diaries,* the FCC, it seems, was the only one watching. The network ran an edited version on television and posted the uncut version on its Web site. Other shows of a similar nature soon followed suit.

These instances portend a mass migration of adult-themed—not necessarily "pornographic"—shows to alternative mediums. Cable television, satellite radio, streaming video, and podcasts are the nanny's worst nightmare as they're not within the regulatory reach of the FCC. There is obviously only one answer: expand the FCC's scope to cover all mediums. "We believe Congress should authorize the FCC to have authority over cable broadcasts," said Randy Sharp, the director of special projects for the American Family Association (AFA), a conservative organization with two million members. "We want to see TV cleaned up for our children."

At first glance a request to make television safer for children may seem laudable, but once you deconstruct what it means to have the FCC govern private cable companies, you realize the absolute chutzpah of it all. There are hundreds of thousands of adults who don't have children or who simply believe that television doesn't feature *enough* adult-oriented television. If local cable outlets and satellite operators will now be under similar restraints, where will adults go for their television?

Granted, it is the AFA's prerogative to pressure advertisers and initiate economic boycotts to *convince* cable networks to provide wholesome programming. It's the American way. But when the

AFA and countless other social conservative groups decide to pressure the Bush administration and the FCC to intrude into consumers' viewing habits, they cross the line from regulation to nannyism.

With the way things have shaped up over the past half decade, it's hard to believe that when the Republicans took over Congress back in 1994, there were serious discussions about cutting back the authority of FCC and perhaps eliminating the agency altogether. The fear at the time was that the FCC was quashing political speech. At the time the Republican-led House Committee on Energy and Commerce went as far as holding a series of closed-door meetings with industry executives to explore ideas intended to curb the agency's powers.

Attitudes have changed within the GOP. Today many Republicans with an unhealthy reverence for political power see the FCC as a force of good that wields too little sway. One such legislator was Joe Barton, a Republican congressman and head of the House Committee on Energy and Commerce, which oversees the FCC. Barton told the National Association of Broadcasters that he saw virtually no difference between public airwaves and private broadcasts. "If I can see it on my TV and my grandson can click and watch a channel, whether it's satellite, over-the-air or cable, the same rules in terms of decency should apply."

Barton's grandson wouldn't be subjected to any cable programming whatsoever if his parents hadn't subscribed to the service. Nor would his grandson be exposed to tawdry programming had his parents learned to child-lock stations. It's not too much to ask the individual to make these choices for themselves and their families. And it's certainly not too much to expect Barton, a conservative, to understand that the idea of personal responsibility should extend to all aspects of life not only the ones he finds important.

Barton had plenty of allies. The bipartisan Indecent and Gratuitous and Excessive Violence Broadcasting Control Act of 2005 was co-sponsored by Republican senator Kay Bailey Hutchison of Texas and her colleague West Virginia Democrat Jay Rockefeller. And the bill lived up to its Orwellian title. "The overwhelming majority of Americans get their broadcast channels and others through cable and satellite," a spokesman for Hutchison said. "If you are going to do something to protect children, you also have to do it on cable and satellite or you will only hit about 5 to 10 percent of the country."

Au contraire, senators. You don't *have* to do anything. Even Michael Powell, the former conservative commissioner at the FCC, said that it was a potentially "dangerous thing" to extend government oversight to other media just to level the playing field. Dangerous, because protecting children—as we've seen—is a regulatory addiction with no end. Adam Thierer, senior fellow at the Progress & Freedom Foundation, a market-based think tank in Washington, D.C., best summed it up when he told *The Boston Globe* in 2006, "They're [the FCC] just continuing to try to exert whatever authority they have, and all they really have is authority over broadcast television and radio. This policy is now highly illogical, increasingly unworkable, and blatantly unfair."

Unworkable and unfair are concepts that have never stopped nannies before.

THE PERFECT ADDICTIVE SUBSTANCE

Looking out for the welfare of children is almost always a self-satisfying (and often self-righteous) enterprise. Defending pornography, not so much. Yet the war on porn is an important illustration of how a small but powerful and tenacious group of busybodies will attempt to decide what adults are equipped to see and hear.

These meddlers are right about one thing: porn is indecent. At least, if it's done right. Though a significant number of Americans enjoy watching the stuff, there hasn't been a popular push for prime-time airings of *Three Men and a Barbie.* A good number of adults have come to the conclusion that porn has its place in society—and that place is out of the reach of children. Moral nannies have proven that they don't believe adults should have access to this variety of titillating entertainment in any form, at any time, anywhere.

Just listen to the redoubtable moralist John Ashcroft, who once asserted that porn "invades our homes persistently through the mail, phone, VCR, cable TV and the Internet." What utter garbage. While there is a case to be made that porn invades our e-mail through spam—technology to combat that particular invasion is improving—it has never overrun a VCR or television. Ever. It's only been invited.

And it's invited quite often. No one can deny that the United States supports massive porn commerce. According to *Adult Video News*—a porn industry trade magazine—business revenue for sex movies hovers around a jaw-dropping $13 billion a year. So let's face it, porn is easy to get hold of. Asserting, as many puritanical politicians have, that pornography has become "more accessible" is not only true, it is a colossal understatement.

These days a consumer of adult movies needn't trek downtown to a seedy bookstore wearing a hooded sweatshirt and sunglasses. Porn can be watched through pay-per-view services at the Sheraton, Hilton, Marriott, and Hyatt chains, among others, and almost every cable and satellite television service brings diluted raunchy movies right into your home if you desire. If that's not enough, a porn consumer can use technology in a host of other ways to satisfy his or her cravings: a Netflix-like pornography service called WantedList, downloadable movies through your computer, and podcasts—all without leaving the comfort of their home.

A tracking firm, comScore Media Metrix, estimates that around 40 percent of online users visit adult sites at least once a month. "The simple fact is porn is an early adopter of new media," said Paul Saffo, director of the Institute for the Future in Palo Alto. "If you're trying to get something established . . . you're going to privately and secretly hope and pray that the porn industry likes your medium."

Pornographers remain on the vanguard of media technology for many reasons. One is that nannyistic constraints make it a necessity for them to stay ahead of regulators and technological trends. Conversely, on the production side, porn is remarkably lo-fi. It has always been the ultimate do-it-yourself medium. No special training is required to star in, direct, or write a porn flick. (That's not to say a person can't excel at this endeavor; like anything else in life, you may have a gift.) Big budgets, clever scripts, high-tech equipment, or intricate props—unless silicon enhancement is considered a prop—are essentially worthless.

Low-cost production, hi-fi distribution adds up to one indisputable fact: porn can't be controlled. Yet it seems that as much as citizens take pleasure in watching pornography, government types are fond of studying it and creating a false sense of fear regarding its effects.

In 1969, a Supreme Court decision established that Americans were free to view porn in the privacy of their own homes *(Stanley v. Georgia)*. Soon after, Congress, unhappy with this verdict, proceeded to fund a commission that would study the true effects of pornography. "The Report of the Commission on Obscenity and Pornography," released in 1970, recommended more sex education, more restriction of children's access to pornography, and absolutely no restrictions for adults.

With the Child Protection Act of 1984, President Reagan announced he would commission a group to "study pornography" again. For this task, he appointed Attorney General Edwin Meese in the spring of 1985, who assembled a panel of eleven members, the majority recognized as antipornography crusaders.

The commission's 1987 report is fairly broad X-rated reading. I wouldn't be shocked if thousands of teenage boys had it tucked under their mattresses. After issuing a 700-page hardcover version of the report, with an introduction by Clive Barnes of *The New York Times,* the only tidbit worth noting was that two-thirds of the commission claimed that there was no need to label these products as obscene. They advised that federal, state, and local legislation *should not seek to interfere* with the rights of adults who wish to read, obtain, or view sexually explicit material.

These days, Kansas senator Sam Brownback has taken the lead in scaremongering Americans about porn. Brownback, before the Democratic takeover of 2006, was chair of the Senate Subcommittee on the Constitution, Civil Rights and Property Rights. But recently he has put together a couple of investigations into, you guessed it, uncovering the deleterious effects of porn, a "morally repugnant and offensive" form of entertainment.

What differentiates this porn crusade from the ones before it is a refinement in message, a tactic used on many nanny-state fronts. According to experts assembled by Brownback, porn is the smack of the cyberage, the "most perfect addictive substance." They even suggest it is a gateway drug, a compulsion that leads viewers to dabble in sadomasochism, pedophilia, bestiality, and misogyny. Yet one of the most dangerous aspects of pornography seems to be that it induces adults to masturbate. And when government officials begin discussing the intimate aspects of our lives, we should be incensed.

"Hey, don't knock masturbation," Woody Allen once quipped in the '70s. "It's sex with someone I love." Self-love shouldn't be knocked for a multitude of reasons. Masturbation, many health professionals claim, is extraordinarily common behavior. In one national study, 95 percent of males and 89 percent of females reported that they masturbate on occasion. So it's perfectly normal. As it states right there on one of America's leading health sites, WebMD's Your Guide to Masturbation, "In general, the medical community considers masturbation to be a natural and harmless expression of sexuality for both men and women."

You would never know how innocuous this widespread activity was if you listened to Jeffrey Satinover, a psychiatrist and adviser to the National Association for Research and Therapy of Homosexuality, who argued during Brownback's investigation that "Pornography really does, unlike other addictions, biologically cause direct release of the most perfect addictive substance. That is, it causes masturbation, which causes release of the naturally occurring opioids. It does what heroin can't do, in effect."

Jill Manning, a sociologist from Brigham Young University, told the Senate Subcommittee on Science, Technology, and Space, which Brownback chaired, that we're dealing with a "potentially addictive substance. People watch a movie, read a book, listen to music, but they masturbate to pornography. In that difference, you have a different stimulation to the brain."

Even with plenty of evidence to the contrary, the linking of sexually explicit entertainment to all of society's ills continues. In another, earlier porn investigation before the same subcommittee, Brownback queried panelists for suggestions on how to stem the growth of pornography. Judith Reisman, of the California Protective Parents Association and one of the leading lights in the sex-is-evil-in-any-form junta, explained that the "study of 'erototoxins' could show how pornography is not speech-protected under the First Amendment."

For those who may not be familiar with erototoxin, it is an addictive psychoactive neurochemical that is formed in the brain when watching porn. It has been tied to murder, rape, child molestation, and erectile dysfunction.

Erototoxins are also unique in that they seem to exist exclusively in the imagination of Reisman. Now, we understand the nanny is prone to utilize junk science as a springboard to meddling public policy—implausible studies from the Centers for Disease Control on obesity or from Joe Califano on alcohol come to mind—but using a neurochemical no one's ever heard of as the impetus to circumvent the First Amendment, well, that's just something special.

As it turns out, erototoxins were perhaps one of the more reasonable topics discussed at the porn confab led by Brownback. All the panelists were in agreement that government was obliged to get involved. They decided that government should fund health campaigns to educate the public about the dangers of pornography. The question was: How? "The campaign should combat the messages of pornography by putting signs on buses saying sex with children is not OK," chimed in Mary Anne Layden, co-director of a sexual trauma program at the University of Pennsylvania.

Imagine, if you can, a yellow school bus pulling up in front of your house. When you open the door to see the little ones off to school, you notice a public service announcement plastered on the side of the bus: "Sex with children is NOT OK!"

Would you feel safer for your children? Certainly child molesters will not abandon pedophilia. No, a campaign combating the "message of pornography"—namely that sex with children is OK—intentionally perpetuates the myth that all pornography spreads such a sinister message in the first place.

There is a market for child porn, which is illegal, despicable, and broadly condemned by society. But linking porn to children and comparing it to heroin or crack cocaine addictions is rhetoric that deliberately overstates the crisis—and from all indications the problem is small. For instance, sex crimes, which some link to pornography, have plummeted. Rapes per capita, according to the

Justice Department, have decreased by more than 85 percent since the 1970s—which coincides directly with the explosion of the porn industry.

SMIRKS ALL AROUND

When FBI supervisors met with new interim U.S. attorney Alex Acosta in July of 2005, they were pretty sure they had a handle on what the top enforcement priority of Attorney General Alberto Gonzales was: terrorism. Many agents were somewhat perplexed when they were told that pornography was perched high on the list. "Compared to terrorism, public corruption and narcotics, [pornography] is no worse than dropping gum on the sidewalk," said Stephen Bronis, chair of the white-collar crime division of the American Bar Association. "With so many other problems in this area, this is absolutely ridiculous."

That same month, the FBI posted a help wanted ad through the electronic communication bulletin at FBI headquarters to all of its field offices. The attorney general was looking for agents to fill an antiobscenity squad—eight agents all told—that would gather evidence against "manufacturers and purveyors" of pornography.

To be perfectly clear, Gonzales was not assembling a porn squad for the purpose of flushing out manufacturers and purveyors of child porn or sexually exploited children. The squad was targeting adult porn, produced by adults and purchased by consenting adults. Soon enough, mischievous messages began circulating around the FBI's second-largest field office. "I guess this means we've won the war on terror," said one exasperated FBI agent. "We must not need any more resources for espionage." *The Washington Post* relayed some of the other comments: "Things I Don't Want On My Résumé, Volume Four." "Honestly, most of the guys would have to recuse themselves."

Curious about the evangelical attitudes toward government's

role in abetting this sort of behavior, I spoke with Carrie Gordon Earll, an expert from Focus on the Family, the social conservative superpower bunkered in Colorado Springs. "We concur with the message being conveyed by those other groups, yes. *This is exactly what federal government does.* They have a responsibility to prosecute and it's positive: it shows the Justice Department is going to actively and aggressively prosecute obscenity." (Emphasis mine.)

This may be exactly what federal government does, but it's exactly what federal government should be avoiding. Focus on the Family and similar groups have a hard time differentiating between preaching the message that pornography is harmful to society, and urging the federal government to impose its will on law-abiding citizens and limiting their personal freedoms. The freedom to sully the holy union, for instance. The freedom to be a shut-in or a pervert or even an Internet porn addict.

"If anything, the danger is that this type of material is marketed to everyone," says Earll. "The pendulum right now is so far toward the personal-freedom side that laws are not being prosecuted."

It's important to understand that many (not all) social conservatives believe that the pendulum has swung dangerously toward the side of personal freedom—as if that's possible. But it is telling to understand that they view the moral decline as more important than personal freedom. This is the same brand of hubris all nannies show toward liberty.

A SERIES OF TUBES

The proliferation of porn in video, DVD, or magazine form is problematic, so we can only imagine that cyberspace will be utterly uncontrollable. And the thought of an unregulated flow of information streaming freely into your home is a frightening thought for any nanny.

As far back as 1995, when Nebraska senator James Exon became the first government official to attempt to regulate free speech online, there have been efforts to corral this infinite flow of information. Exon's bill, which aimed to stop the Internet from becoming a "red-light-district," was the genesis for the 1996 Communications Decency Act. It was approved overwhelmingly by a Congress that had little understanding of the dynamic technology and cultural phenomena unfolding. Fortunately, it was struck down by a court soon after. The good-intentioned follow-up, the Children's Online Protection Act (COPA) of 1998, was more practical than its predecessor in trying to stop pornography from filtering down to children, but it mattered none. COPA was found to be unconstitutional on free-speech grounds.

In spite of the ruling, political demands—namely from evangelical groups that helped the Bush administration win the White House twice—required that the administration concoct ways to circumvent the ruling. The Justice Department then approached leading Internet providers and search engines about handing over their URL records of ordinary users. Ostensibly, the administration notified companies that it would require the data to determine how often pornography shows up in online searches. Prosecutors requested a "random sampling" of URLs that were requested through Google's search engine.

Google initially refused to comply with the request. That was until the Justice Department delivered a subpoena for the information. In the end, Google was forced to turn over a sample of 50,000 Web site addresses and 5,000 search queries—though according to Nicole Wong, Google's associate general counsel, in a March 2006 post on the company's blog, the original request was "billions of URLs and two months' worth of users' search queries."

Such nannyistic incursions into our privacy might at least have piqued the curiosity of the average citizen. Not so the folks in the moral nanny movement. Jack Samad, senior vice president for the National Coalition for the Protection of Children & Families, echoed the sentiments of similar groups, by urging search engines to hand over private information to the Bush administration. "Young people are experiencing broken lives after being exposed to adult images and behaviors on the Internet," Samad said. "I'm disappointed Google did not want to exercise its good corporate branding to secure the protection of youth. I think [complying with the subpoena] would substantiate the basis of COPA if they get a free exchange of information on youthful use of the Internet."

Samad only has it half right. It's good corporate branding if it is legitimately attained through consumer pressure—not government intimidation. If the genuine goal of moral crusaders was to fight porn because of child access, they would be more amenable to good ideas that protected children and the rights of adults.

★ ★ ★

When the idea of creating a real red-light district online was close to being a reality—by using the legitimate option of replacing the prefix ".com" with ".xxx" for sites that deserved such a designation—social conservatives wanted nothing to do with it. When President Bush would not support the idea, the Family Research Council went out of its way to thank W. for "calling a halt to the '.XXX' domain idea." The Bush administration should not, they said, be seen "facilitating" the porn industry, which "has been a plague on our society since the establishment of the internet." They viewed the .xxx domain as a proposal that pandered to the porn industry and "offers nothing but false hope to an American public which wants illegal pornographers prosecuted, not rewarded."

Simply acknowledging that porn sites exist or have a legal place in society is intolerable to the didactic nanny. Clearly differentiating pornographic sites from all others seems like a sensible idea—though practicality issues would certainly arise in defining them. It seems to be an idea that would make it easier to protect children from online porn if that was really the target of these crusades.

PUTTING THE SIN IN SIN TAX

As we've seen on other fronts of the nanny state, a sin tax is normally used as a tool for mass behavior modification. The expectation is that a punitive levy will discourage an unsavory behavior or, at the very least, assist in funding programs that dissuade those who can't say no to a cookie, a glass of wine, or a trip to the Bada Bing.

Ironically enough, while using a sin tax to modify your two-pack-a-day Camel Lights habit is fine, taxing authentic sin may be unconstitutional.

When congressional Democrats first broached the idea of tagging Internet porn with a 25 percent tax a couple of years ago, there was instantaneous criticism from First Amendment experts, who maintained that while sin taxes on drinking, gambling, and smoking were legally acceptable, skin taxes were not. Sexual entertainment is a form of free speech. "You cannot have that [porn] tax anymore than you can have a special tax, on, for example, Methodists," Marilyn Ireland, professor of law at California Western School of Law told *Wired News*.

Methodists everywhere breathed a collective sigh of relief.

Incredibly enough, some in the sin business are practically begging to be taxed so they can join the reputable world. Which gives us a good idea just how normalized the idea of taxing behavior has become.

"We'd not necessarily be pleased if the U.S. gets into what some people would call a 'sin tax.' There would be the concern that the government would change its focus to tax pornographic materials rather than control production and distribution." That is the primary concern of Rick Schatz, president of the National Coalition for the Protection of Children & Families, a religious group that believes a sin tax puts pornography on the road to respectability.

Now listen to what Bill Margold, a former porn star and now an advocate for adult performers, had to say to *Wired News:* "As soon as we get a universal or national porn tax, we get what we've always wanted—that comfort zone of respectability that cigarettes, alcohol and gambling have." Margold goes on to accuse "greedy" adult-industry types of opposing any kind of tax—which doesn't make them greedy, just smart.

If what Margold says is true, we may soon have to identify strip clubs as "gentleman's" clubs without the sarcastic smile. And those who enjoy strip clubs might find themselves handing over a few extra bucks per lap dance. Sin City is one of the least likely places you would expect such a travesty, but yet when the Nevada State Senate minority leader, Democrat Dina Titus, put forward a plan to impose a 10 percent sin tax on strip clubs, the American Civil Liberties Union (ACLU) came out and challenged the constitutionality of the proposal.

"This bill is way off base from a constitutional standpoint," ACLU of Nevada general counsel Allen Lichtenstein told the Nevada Senate Taxation Committee. It turns out that stripping is a constitutionally protected right of free expression—like the DVD of *Swedish Erotica #55* but not like a pack of Marlboros. While strip clubs can be required to pay a general tax, like any other businesses in the state, they can't be picked on with a special tax just because people don't like what they're up to in various "gentleman's clubs" in Sin City.

A perplexed Titus—who later ran for governor of Nevada—somewhat innocently stated: "I don't know why the Constitution should be a problem."

The Constitution never seems to be a problem.

The Lone Star State mulled over the intricacies of instituting a sin tax on exotic dancing. Texas ultimately decided that Governor Perry's so-called "tassel tax" could raise $25 million a year by setting up a toll for topless dancers. Then in 2005, the progressive Seattle City Council passed a new ordinance for strip clubs replacing the seventeen-year-old moratorium on new strip clubs. At the time Seattle featured only four strip clubs and has long prevented new ones from opening through nannyistic legal maneuvering.

But there was little to celebrate for those interested in taking it off for a living. In the strip clubs that remain, a local ordinance prohibited strippers from touching patrons. And as any stripper knows, the big bucks are found in lap dancing. States like Kentucky, Maryland, Tennessee, Utah, and West Virginia had similar restrictions, but as an added bonus were shifting part of the cost of public education from income, sales, and property taxes to levies on topless dancing.

What made this piece of nannyism special is that it would also stop strippers from collecting tips while working and would cordon off dancers behind a rail at least ten feet away from their patrons. The legislation also would impose a $5 per customer charge for sexually oriented businesses, from strip clubs to adult bookstores, and a 20 percent tax on revenues. What precisely is unacceptable? A Victoria's Secret catalog? Or worse, something from Frederick's of Hollywood? What about a Dr. Ruth radio call-in show on oral sex? Where does it end?

★ ★ ★

Maybe with prostitution. Could a sin tax legitimize the world's oldest profession? Nevada is a peculiar and surreal place for many reasons—none more than that prostitution is legal. There are in the neighborhood of thirty brothels operating in ten of Nevada's sixteen counties and it's estimated that they generate tens of millions in profits. The state Health Division estimates—can you believe someone is keeping count of this?—365,000 sex acts are "performed" in Nevada's brothels yearly. Business is brisk.

This was a bit much for some legislators to take. Because, well, that's a lot of dough. In 2005, a number of Nevada lawmakers, looking for avenues to deal with a $700 million deficit, wanted to tax the fees of prostitutes. "Everybody should pay," said Assemblywoman Sheila Leslie, a Reno Democrat. "It should be taxed just like any other entertainment."

Prostitutes in Nevada are already subject to federal income tax on their earnings, and have to pay various county taxes and fees like the rest of us grunts. And as they did with porn, some Republicans opposed the state tax because directly attaching a duty to sex acts would only further legitimize an immoral industry. "When you talk about paying taxes on a state level, this would be more official recognition as a legitimate business," Nevada historian Guy Rocha said.

And like any other legitimate business, these poor souls would have to figure out the practical implementations of sin taxes. "What are the girls going to do?" asked the president of the Nevada Brothel Association (proving once again that *every* trade group in the nation has an association). "Have a calculator in the room? The girls aren't the best at math."

For now, Nevada prostitutes are safe from the nanny state.

DILDO A NO-NO

Swinging to the other extreme, we head to Alabama. Though the state's motto is "We Dare Defend Our Rights," in Mobile it is illegal for women to don a "lewd dress," pay a person of the opposite sex for a massage, or sunbathe nude. But if you think these are lingering intrusions of a bygone day, you should know that the latter two were passed in 1991. And a couple of years later, lawmakers decided that the threat of dildos was within their purview as well.

The sale of sex toys is a misdemeanor punishable by a fine of up to $10,000 and one year in jail. This invasive law was part of an obscenity provision that made it illegal to sell or produce "any device designed or marketed as useful primarily for the stimulation of human genital organs."

Quite appropriately, someone took legal action: Sherri Williams, the chief plaintiff and owner of two stores called Pleasures. Other plaintiffs included dildo vendors and even users of sex toys. The challenge of this retrograde law was based on the argument that sex toys "have many recognized beneficial uses and are used by consenting adults in deeply private acts that are beyond the reach of governmental regulation." Indeed, if the "stimulation of human genital organs" is within the scope of government regulation, really now, what on God's Earth isn't? Imagine if every business had to demonstrate that the products they stocked had a "recognized beneficial use." Half the mall would be out of business within days. And one could certainly argue that stimulating genital organs was just as beneficial as stimulating muscles, your brain, or any other part of the self.

And Alabama was not alone. In Texas, there are comparable regulations inhibiting an adult from exercising their God-given right to purchase a sex toy. Yet in certain places those who possess "with intent to wholesale promote any obscene material or obscene device" would engage in committing a criminal offense.

One of the rowdy perps rounded up by Texas authorities was Joanne Webb, a forty-three-year-old former schoolteacher from Burleson, a small town of about 27,000 people, a few minutes south of Ft. Worth. Burleson's motto, by the way, is "A City of Character." Webb soon found out how much character we're talking about.

A self-proclaimed practicing Christian, registered Republican, and mother of three, Webb was hauled off to jail after being accused of selling a vibrator to two undercover cops posing as a disgruntled, sexually repressed couple.

Webb, after explaining how to use the dildo to the officers, was facing a year in jail. This dildo-peddling mom was making some extra money working as a saleswoman for a company called Passion Parties, a nationwide sex-toy company that sells "marital aids." The dildo Tupperware-style get-togethers were held at private homes with only adults present. "What we do is not obscene," explained Pat Davis, president of Passion Parties. "We're all about education and freedom. The law in Texas should not exist."

Lisa Lawless, the president and founder of the National Association for Sexual Awareness & Empowerment, said, "One of the things that was so outraging to me was to watch women like Joanne Webb . . . go through these witch hunts concerning the sale of sex toys, which in themselves are not only beneficial to health and sexuality, but also a constitutional right of adults in this country. These backward laws blatantly violate our constitutional rights and are absolutely ludicrous."

The county finally dropped the criminal charges against Webb. They would never comment publicly on why the charges were dropped, but according to sources town leaders had grown tired of the so-called dildo spotlight.

EL DIABLO

Though the use of sex toys could still land you in the Big House in a couple of states, attitudes about sex make it unlikely such intrusions will continue on a large scale. The thought of intruding in the bedroom is not an idea that is gaining any traction. In June of 2003, the Supreme Court finally struck down the Texas ban on consensual sex between adults of the same sex. It was a milestone that brought constitutional protection to sexual privacy. A majority of justices ruled that Texas had violated the rights of two Houston men arrested for engaging in sodomy in the privacy of their home.

That doesn't mean there won't be the occasional second-rate Cotton Mather nibbling away at our rights. Recently, an Alabama legislator—the state has quite a track record—demanded that libraries engage in crass censorship against gay or even vaguely gay-themed books. Representative Gerald Allen called for the removal of all history books, biographies, literature, and plays that discussed or "promoted" or were authored by homosexuals.

Keeping tabs on such things is preposterous: at one time or another there have been rumors floating around that Socrates, Aristotle, Proust, Michelangelo, da Vinci, Noel Coward, and Walt Whitman might be gay. A book like Truman Capote's *In Cold Blood* would be pulled from the shelf and buried, not because it is a story of a brutal mass murderer but because the author happened to be homosexual.

Such a bill, which failed in the Alabama legislature, is extreme even in the nanny state. Not only was the bill unquestionably idiotic, denounced by all reasonable pundits on the left and right, but it failed to grasp the nuances and incremental game plan necessary when aspiring to be a middling Fascist.

Allen is an aberration, but social conservative engineering through the FCC, religious right groups, legislators, and the Bush administration are not. And their efforts are no better than the garden-variety nannyism that conservatives have traditionally railed against. Critics of the nanny state need not shy away from condemnation and finger-pointing—say, the delirious effects of the dildo—only legislative overreach.

There is nothing insulting or injurious about preaching "values." Sometimes social conservatives confuse limited government with moral absenteeism. They are missing the point. True believers are free to knock on our doors and convince us that God is King and *Desperate Housewives* is wickedness incarnate.

They can attempt to convince me that watching raunchy reality television or gay-themed sitcoms is the highway to Hell. They'd be wasting their time, in my case. But I have plenty of neighbors. Who knows? They may convert a few.

⋆ CHAPTER SIX ⋆

MISSION CREEP

One of the annoying things about believing in free will and individual responsibility is the difficulty of finding somebody to blame your problems on. And when you do find somebody, it's remarkable how often his picture turns up on your driver's license.

—P. J. O'Rourke

★

THE BUSINESS OF YOUR LIFE

Nannyistic barriers that constrict spontaneity and ingenuity—both critical ingredients for a successful small business—are being erected nationwide. Often there is little or no justification for their existence—putting aside, of course, the necessity some bureaucrats have to control every aspect of our lives.

In 2003, the Institute for Justice, a civil liberties law firm based in Washington, D.C., filed a civil rights lawsuit against the Louisiana Horticulture Commission on behalf of plaintiffs who had repeatedly failed the licensing exam. The institute asked the court to declare Louisiana's licensing law unconstitutional. It claimed that the plaintiffs' "right to economic liberty—the right to earn an honest living free from excessive government regulation" had been violated.

The state had insisted that would-be florists secure government-imposed licenses before practicing their craft. Not exactly a precarious vocation crying out for government oversight. And yet this is no perfunctory drive down to the government office to obtain a license. The test, some florists claim, is so complicated that nearly two-thirds of those who take the exam fail. Many experienced florists were forced to find lawyers just to stay in business after the test became mandatory.

In August of 2006, the Fifth U.S. Circuit Court of Appeals dismissed the institute's lawsuit as "moot"—no longer viable to be pursued. In this case, none of the women who filed suit can still pursue flower arranging in Louisiana.

The Institute for Justice takes on many similar cases of intrusive government. One of their clients is Margurite Sylva, a native of Senegal, and her partner, Ali Rasheed. Like any entrepreneur worth their salt, Sylva glimpsed an economic opportunity in her neighborhood: she could make a living putting her braiding skills to use. Soon enough, her African hairstyles became so sought after that Sylva's 400-plus customers had a three-month wait for her services.

The difficulty was that after attempting to earn the proper licensing to braid hair by attending state-mandated cosmetology school in California, Sylva realized that there were no lessons in braiding, or cornrowing, or other hairdressing techniques that are popular in the black community. It was a waste of her time. Instead of celebrating this story of American ingenuity and business prowess, the state soon caught up to Sylva and charged her with "aiding and abetting" unlicensed braiding activity. "You go from a few thousand dollars to a business that is supporting seven or eight people, plus people in a foreign country who can't make a living. We think that's the American dream," explained Rasheed. "And to be penalized for doing this by somebody who has no idea what you do, somebody who is really trying to protect their industry, we think is un-American."

If a recent immigrant to this nation understands that such silly laws are un-American, why can't legislators?

Often the enforcement of these piddling regulations is as arbitrary as it is ludicrous. Take the case of Mike Fisher. The resident of New Hampshire decided to challenge a law that bars manicuring without a license. Fisher accepted $1 from another agitator and began buffing nails—without a license—right outside the office of the Board of Barbering, Cosmetology and Esthetics. The Concord, New Hampshire, police claimed Fisher was "actively engaged" in giving a manicure and arrested him. The crime is a misdemeanor and carries a fine of up to $1,000.

★ ★ ★

The nanny state also seems remarkably interested in how culinary establishments—above and beyond using those insidious fatty foods—do business.

The first time I'd ever run across the term *sous vide* (pronounced *sue veed)*, for example, was after reading a story about a newly instituted New York City ban. The French culinary technique entails placing meat in a vacuum-sealed plastic bag then cooking it gradually in lukewarm water. To put this trend into more glowing terms, as Gabrielle Hamilton of Manhattan's Prune restaurant wrote in *The New York Times* in April 2006, cooking *sous vide* "makes food taste more intensely of what it should taste like, preserves its nutritional value, and often creates a texture of unspeakable silkiness that everyone ought to experience."

With such a ringing endorsement, New York City's culinary establishment was collectively bewildered when the Department of Health and Mental Hygiene (DHMH) banned the procedure. The DHMH maintained that this method could lead to food poisoning—regardless of the fact that not a single complaint had been filed. *Sous vide* became perhaps the first culinary technique on record prohibited by law. A growing niche market was quashed before it had a chance to take off.

Public safety has become a catchall that allows pencil-pushing civil servants to proactively shut down businesses and sideline lifestyle choices—as well as satisfy a perpetual need to justify their existence. But even in areas of public life where government is typically needed to act in defense of the consumer, well-meaning intrusions can sometimes bring about unintentional consequences.

As a society, there ought to be an acknowledgment that the world is far from a perfect place. There will always be botched braiding and shoddy manicures, I can assure you. At the very least, advocating for consumer interests offers a quasi-legitimate justification for nanny intrusions. But laws steeped in politically correct sensitivities are much more difficult to rationalize. Typically, it's not required.

In 2006, members of the Chicago City Council voted forty-eight to one to outlaw the sale of foie gras (pronounced *fwah grah)* in all "food dispensing establishments" in the city or face fines of $500. Foie gras translated from the French means "fatty liver." It's been a delicacy since the days of the ancient Egyptians. Goose-liver foie gras is most commonly found in the States as an appetizer in high-end restaurants specializing in French cuisine. Few people enjoy this expensive treat, making it an easy target.

Not everyone in Chicago has lost their mind, however. When Doug Sohn, owner of the North Side restaurant Hot Doug's, received a letter from city hall threatening him for serving foie gras, not only did he ignore it but he framed it. "We displayed it proudly," said Sohn. Letters are just the first step. Visits from the city that turn up goose liver will result in fines. Another owner who was also ignoring the city said, "We look at it as a choice. We live in a free-market society and if people are truly offended they won't buy it. If they don't buy it, I won't buy it."

The movement to expunge foie gras from American restaurants is growing. In 2006, New Jersey assemblyman Michael Panter introduced legislation that would prohibit the sale and distribution of this refined treat in his home state. The age-old force-feeding of birds, he observed, is a "barbaric practice that has no place in any civilized society." So important was this issue that Panter's proposal was the *second* bill concerning foie gras introduced in the Garden State in the year 2006. California has already passed legislation that will end the practice by 2012 and other states are looking into their own bans.

As barbaric as force-feeding a goose might appear to some (no less barbaric than, say, leading cattle to the slaughterhouse), even Chicago mayor Richard Daley, one of the leading nannies in the nation, was quoted as saying, "We have children getting killed by gang leaders and dope dealers. We have real issues here in the city. And we're dealing with foie gras? Let's get some priorities."

But for groups like People for the Ethical Treatment of Animals (PETA) enacting such bans *is* the priority. In reality, PETA would bring forth a plethora of prohibitions that I'm certain most rational Americans would find unreasonable and gratuitous. Ingrid Newkirk, the president of the group, once called for "total animal liberation." Let your imagination chew on that for a while. And though most of PETA's over-the-top lobbying is beyond the scope of this book, and beyond the scope of common sense, many of their legislative goals are the seedlings of future nannyism.

Besides advocating for pulling first-rate products from the marketplace, there are numerous other potential costs to politically correct bans. One of PETA's pet peeves, for example, is the practice of buying fresh lobsters—"fresh" as in still alive and kicking—from tanks at markets. "The ways that lobsters are treated would warrant felony cruelty to animals charges if they were dogs or cats," said Bruce Friedrich, a spokesman for PETA.

It is worth exploring the consequences of this legislation should it find its way to a signature. Whole Foods Markets, one of the largest natural-foods grocery chains in the nation, provides a great case study since its executives have decided to surrender to PETA's demands and have halted the practice of selling fresh lobsters in its stores. "We place as great an emphasis on the importance of humane treatment and quality of life for all animals as we do on the expectations for quality and flavor," John Mackey, Whole Foods' co-founder and chief executive, said in a statement. As a corporation, Whole Foods has every right to conduct business as it sees fit within the law. Besides, this is how the free market works. The question is: What would happen if such policy were codified into laws?

According to the Lobster Institute at the University of Maine (I kid you not, there is a Lobster Institute), approximately 183 million pounds of lobsters are caught each year in North America, and about 25 percent of that is sold live. Jasper White, proprietor of the Summer Shack restaurant chain in New England, told *The Boston Globe* that he sells $4 million to $5 million worth of fresh lobsters each year. The article went on to claim that 10,000 families in New England and Canada depend on lobstering for income, and Whole Foods should be more concerned about them than about an animal that he called "basically an insect."

CROP SHOCK

In Florida, selling live lobsters is still legal, but exporting ugly tomatoes is not. Why would anyone want to purchase unsightly tomatoes? Evidently there is a high demand for vine-ripened brand names like UglyRipes because they are not picked too early, ensuring heightened freshness and a naturally sweet taste that conventional brands lack. The problem for those interested in purchasing uglies is that the Florida Tomato Committee, a trade group that controls sales and shipments of round tomatoes—via government mandate—has determined that these tomatoes do not meet standards for the association's "lack of blemishes" clause.

"They are prohibiting trade," accuses Joe Procacci, co-owner of the Procacci Brothers Sales Corporation, the villains behind the UglyRipes. The owner told an investigating twelve-member board of tomato growers that "Last year, we had to dump $3 million worth of tomatoes, and we had customers . . . who were begging for them."

The Florida committee is one of numerous state-sponsored

trade groups across the nation that have jurisdiction over quality standards. Though you could wonder if an aesthetic value judgment (typically a subjective call) should be akin to a "quality" standard. This prohibition was so ludicrous that it generated an outcry from editorial boards across the country, including habitual nanny-state boosters like *The New York Times*. *The Christian Science Monitor* ran a house editorial titled "Let Them Eat (Ugly) Tomatoes," summing up the absurdity of banning tomatoes:

> The committee appears to be technically within its rights. It's backed by a 1937 federal provision that allows farmers to join together and set marketing and quality standards for their produce.
>
> But to Americans who might want a tastier tomato in the middle of winter it just looks like the committee is getting in the way of free trade.
>
> There's a new tomato on the block. Let the people decide if it's any good.

"Let the people decide" was once an American credo. It's also sporadically referred to as free market or free choice. But consumers are often at the mercy of the whims and apprehensions of a handful of people. And with each intrusion their reach grows.

LOVE ON THE ROCKS

Imagine you've planned a romantic New York City evening with your spouse. A couple of years ago this may have entailed such delicacies as foie gras, or *sous vide* beef, maybe an ugly tomato—and, God forbid, a post-meal smoke. And you, taken by the moment, grab your fetching mate's hand and began an impromptu dance to woo her.

Sit down, dummy.

Like smoking and slow-cooked meat, dancing can be illegal in New York City, where an ordinance makes a cabaret license mandatory for any establishment where there would be dancing. "This is like *Footloose* coming to New York," said Norman Siegel, a civil rights lawyer who fought an ordinance banning "social dancing." The law, Siegel, said "runs contra to the image internationally that New York City has as a place of nightlife. People don't believe it. It's not real to people that we have this kind of system."

Whether it seems real or not, the ban on dancing is now ingrained into law and precedent. Superior court judge Michael D. Stallman ruled in 2005 that "social participatory dancing" was not a protected form of free expression under the New York State constitution.

New York takes this variety of reckless lawlessness seriously. According to a 2002 story in *The Village Voice*, in the winter of 1999 a "small army" of police, firefighters, and inspectors raided a now-defunct meatpacking-district club called the Cooler. They weren't looking for drug dealers or prostitutes. They were on the lookout for ordinary folks dancing. (That's something you don't see on *Law & Order*.) And New Yorkers, as they often do, simply adapted. When the police burst in, a sentinel flipped a switch alerting the sound tech via a flashing light. Instantaneously, the Cooler transformed from an orgy of salaciously illicit dancing to a collection of people standing motionless.

No one was busted for dancing that time.

* * *

From the dance floor to the Internet, courtship is on the agenda. For many singles, online dating is a blessing. The process allows you to control from the comfort of home the exact physical proportions, likes and dislikes, and personality traits of those you plan on dating. True, this process often lacks the spontaneity and romanticism of traditional dating, but the tens of millions of people who use dating sites like Match.com and PerfectMatch.com each year can't all be wrong.

Legislators, always more dogmatic than romantic, quickly inserted themselves into this harmless situation. "There are inherent dangers in the whole area of the Internet. Something needs to be done," claimed Michigan Republican senator Alan Cropsey. Consequently, Cropsey introduced legislation requiring all Internet dating companies to disclose on their Web sites whether they had conducted exhaustive criminal background checks on users. California, Ohio, Virginia, Florida, and Texas have had similar legislation on the agenda.

That "something needs to be done" about the "whole area of the Internet" is the sort of sweeping generalization that exposes not only the blundering ignorance of legislators but also the tragedy of a public that allows numskulls to craft serious legislation. Certainly, dating has never been easy. Even in the real world adults must remember to protect themselves. And really, there is no greater danger in meeting someone online than there is meeting a stranger in a bar or at a party. Yet we would roll our eyes at the idea that we need to start checking the background of every patron or partygoer.

Then again, who knows? That might be next on the agenda.

In New York, concerns about online dating were codified into legislative protections called the Dating Service Consumer Bill of Rights, passed in 1996, which among other things imposes price controls and background checks on users: "If your social referral service contract costs more than twenty-five dollars," for instance, "the seller must furnish a minimum number of referrals per month to you." That's right, no matter how brainless, or how unattractive, or how disheveled you happen to be, New York says online dating sites *must* forward a certain number of referrals for your perusal.

And this law is not just for show. In 2006, Great Expectations, an Internet dating service, found itself in a legal mess when two disgruntled Manhattan women sued the company for failing to provide them with enough dates. A Manhattan judge agreed to have their membership fees refunded. Another fifty-five-year-old divorcée from Brooklyn, named, appropriately enough, Sara Valentine, also sued the company that year. After voluntarily signing a contract in 2005, requiring her to pay a $3,000 fee, not a single bachelor contacted her. "Maybe there are people who have met the man or woman of their dreams, and they didn't care what they paid," said Valentine's lawyer, Richard Altman. "Well, she was dissatisfied with what she got."

Imagine if we proposed new legislation and were able to sue every time we were dissatisfied with a service. The end of Western civilization—or at the very least chain restaurants and video stores plagued by the scourge of apathetic employees—would be in the offing.

It is fathomable that the majority of Internet daters would find comfort in the idea of background checks. Certainly it would be nice to have a guaranteed number of referrals for potential dates. If this is so, it would be in the best interest of dating services to offer such extras to entice customers. It may even be in the interest of online dating services to provide background checks as a means of legal protection. But it isn't the sort of pressing issue government is required to fret about. Indeed, it seems downright invasive.

For now, at least, New York dating protections are fairly moderate compared to international online dating regulations. In March

2006, Congress passed the International Marriage Broker Regulation Act, a law which criminalized the act of one person meeting another in foreign countries if they happen to first meet on the Internet.

The law makes it a criminal offense for an American male to send an e-mail or snail mail or to use a phone to connect with a woman in a foreign country unless he's submitted a criminal background check and sex offender check, provided a signed statement listing all prior marriages and any children he may have sired, and listed every state he's ever lived in—translated into the native language of his prospective date.

The law spurs a concern that many transnational relationships involve abuse, but there is no dependable study that proves matchmaking services, like the ones this law targets, contribute to abuse. In fact a 1999 study by the Immigration and Naturalization Service "failed to establish that the international matchmaking industry contributes in any significant way to these problems."

IN THE BATHROOM

Problems. So many of them and so little time to pass laws to correct all of them. Really, if the authorities are within their rights to maintain that corporations must guarantee a specific number of replies to classified ads and prohibit you from dating a foreigner without telling her your life story before you meet, it is surely within its rights to guarantee a precise number of toilets.

In a 1990 *National Law Journal* article, nanny-state provocateur John Banzhaf cooked up yet another recipe to sue his personal belief system into law: toilet exposure. He wrote, "For more than 20 years we have recognized that, with respect to race, it is unconstitutional to have restrooms that are separate but equal. On the other hand, with regard to the two sexes, the universal norm is restrooms that are separate and equal. But, in this context, what does 'equal' mean?"

Equal can mean a million things in a million circumstances. But certainly equal doesn't mean dictating what ratio of toilets independent businesses should install. In our own self-interest, we make sense of toilet issues amongst ourselves. Or, at least, we used to.

In 2006, New York mayor Mike Bloomberg, who's made it his legacy to micromanage everyone's life, made it an imperative to sign a so-called "potty parity" bill, impelling NYC establishments to feature more women's toilets in newly built arenas, bars, convention halls, and movie theaters. For every toilet in the men's room there would now have to be two in a women's room.

"We're talking about the quality of life for women. It's as simple as that," said Democratic council member Yvette Clarke at the bill-signing ceremony. Women, claimed Clarke, "have had to really endure sometimes degrading situations just trying to take care of their personal business. A number of times I've been in a restaurant waiting for a small men's room to open up and a woman comes out." And Paulette Geanacopoulos, executive director of the Women's City Club of New York, called it "a major health bill."

It's exceedingly improbable that there is a patriarchal toilet conspiracy afoot in America. Why would business owners want to humiliate customers? This crack at social engineering feeds off populist notions of equality that are based in pure fantasy. Sure, waiting for a bathroom can be annoying and even a little embarrassing. But since when do we need government protection from debasing situations? Alas, I'm sure we could all concoct rather long lists of humiliating situations that necessitate mending.

I would also bring to your attention the experience many men go through when they attend professional sporting events. We wait on an endless line while a perfectly free (and typically cleaner) toilet is waiting for us in the women's room. Each situation is different. Each place is different. And the state of affairs as concerning the ratio of men to women is always in flux.

Incredibly, Banzhaf has successfully brought parity lawsuits against dry cleaners and hair salons in Washington, D.C. And he also threatened city council members who were in the midst of planning on building a stadium for the Washington Nationals baseball team. Bathroom-equality bills have already passed in Virginia (where a number of Founding Fathers gave us an extra roll in their graves), Texas, Pennsylvania, and California.

PET LOGIC

Designing gender-specific regulations for toilets is one silly thing, but in legislating the life of pets, well, we're taking yet another important step toward total absurdity. It's completely reasonable to love your pets. You're searching for rewarding and honest companionship. Pets are loyal. Easy to please. Fun. You should be warned, though, if you live in Boulder, West Hollywood, or San Francisco—or other such cuddly enclaves—you're no longer a "pet owner," you're officially a "pet guardian." A title mandated by government.

Euphemisms notwithstanding, the two square miles of West Hollywood is a sanctuary for our less-evolved companions. In 2003, it became the first U.S. city to ban cat declawing, a procedure that strips felines of equipment necessary to destroy your couch and wreak havoc on other household items. The ban was the brainchild of city councilman John Duran, who claimed, "We don't consider cats and dogs to be just property. To the extent that we can protect them from harm here in West Hollywood, we do."

Later, when Duran became mayor of West Hollywood, he came loaded for bear (if you'll excuse the saying), swiftly launching a motion that would prohibit nearly all pet plastic surgery, including procedures like ear-cropping, tail-docking, debarking, and defanging. Considering that similar plastic surgery is safe and legal—sometimes, it seems, mandatory—for humans in West Hollywood, the law smacks of prejudice against our pets. Not to mention, the ease with which someone could drive outside the city limits to have their Doberman's ears cropped—not exactly a quest-length journey. And vets in these neighborhoods will certainly feel the economic pinch.

Up the coast, in forward-looking San Francisco, pet guardians are mandated to provide tip-proof water bowls that are changed once daily, "healthy" pet food (palatable and nutritious), and expansive doghouses that have at least three walls, a floor, and a roof. San Francisco city supervisor Bevan Dufty, the sponsor of the legislation, explained: "What it really does is tell these owners what the minimum requirements are if they're going to keep their dog outside."

Are pet owners—or rather, pet guardians—really so negligent that such specialized decrees are necessary? According to the *San Francisco Chronicle,* of an estimated 100,000 dogs in the city, only roughly 100 animals are holed up at Animal Care and Control at any given time. That doesn't seem like rampant abuse to me. As for those miscreants who are negligent in providing Fido the proper care, an added misdemeanor is unlikely to curb their bad behavior, especially since there are a multitude of animal cruelty laws already on the books.

Supervisor Michela Alioto-Pier, one of two to dissent in the vote to mandate heightened level of pet care, says, "I was reading this, and I thought: Now we're treating dogs better than we treat the homeless. It's a classic case of taking an issue we need to deal with and overcompensating. It's one thing to say you have to have clean water for your dog, another to say you have to have it in a container that won't tip, or if it does, then you have to bolt it to the wall. I think it's too Big Brother."

In 2006, (really) Big Brother governor Arnold Schwarzenegger signed into law a regulation that would prohibit dog owners from tethering their pets to stationary objects for more than three hours. "Owning a dog can be a very rewarding experience. As a dog owner, I know firsthand that having a pet requires a lot of responsibility," said Schwarzenegger. "This bill helps protect dogs from cruelty, and enhances public safety by preventing aggressive animal behavior that can result from inhumane tethering."

I can think of worse fates than being tethered to a pole for three hours and fifteen minutes on a beautiful seventy-five-degree San Diego day with a fresh tip-proof bowl of water and nourishing snacks to munch on. But that's just me. Now this act is punishable by a fine not to exceed $1,000 per dog and/or up to six months in a county jail.

This cast of law, dubbed "backyard laws," has yet to make it to the national level, though it's only a matter of time. The closest we come to a federal nanny-state pet project is from New Mexico congresswoman Heather Wilson, who tried to persuade her peers to approve a federal version of her state's Scooby's Law.

Named after an ill-fated golden retriever who perished in Bernalillo, New Mexico, after drinking antifreeze in 2003, the law would mandate that antifreeze manufacturers add a bittering agent into the mix to dissuade animals from partaking of the liquid.

This would cost companies millions of dollars. But interestingly enough the Centers for Disease Control provides a list of dozens of poisons that humans ingest all the time. Why not have legislators pass laws that would force companies to add bittering agents to all of these products? Folic acid? Come to think of it, shouldn't we inject bittering agents into all unhealthy foods or alcohol, as well? We could save millions of lives.

You see how easy it is to be a nanny?

GAMING FUN

From culinary innovation, to pet safety, to the perils of dating, to bathroom equality, to games, nannies are always looking out for us. Sometimes the sheer volume can be a bit overwhelming, even for them. Example: when you mix the ancient pastime of gambling with the sheer unmanageability of the Internet, nannies have quite a bit on their plates.

California businessman Jay Cohen and some of his investor friends hatched a sure-fire moneymaker in the mid-'90s: online gambling. In 1997, the group set up shop, establishing the World Sports Exchange, an Internet-based sports betting casino. The company was based outside of the United States, in Antigua, but the profits, naturally, flowed from the motherland.

Within a year, U.S. officials charged the innovative Cohen with violating the 1961 Wire Act, which prohibits wagers from being taken over telephone lines. Cohen argued that federal laws shouldn't apply to offshore gambling sites and voluntarily returned to the States to contest the charges. Returning turned out to be a big mistake. Cohen lost his case and after losing subsequent appeals, was convicted in 2000, serving a seventeen-month federal sentence.

The authorities have excavated a multitude of archaic laws to curb online gambling: the Travel Act of 1952, which outlaws distribution of proceeds from an unlawful activity across state lines or international borders, or the Illegal Gambling Business Act of 1955, which states that it's a crime if five (not four) people engage in criminal behavior during a thirty-day (not twenty-nine) period and generate more than $2,000 in a single day.

With all this creative nannyism, by 2006 Internet gambling, already nominally illegal, was being used by somewhere between fifteen and twenty million Americans each year. A study by the National Gambling Impact Study Commission claimed Americans were wagering anywhere from $80 billion and $380 billion, far outpacing professional legal bookies in Vegas.

So as a "values" issue, which would hit both personal liberty and business, one of the last acts of the Republican-led Congress in 2006 was to pass the Unlawful Internet Gambling Enforcement Act, making it illegal for financial institutions and credit card companies to process payments to settle Internet gambling bets. President George W. Bush signed the bill, which was snuck into a larger port-security bill.

"It is extraordinary how many American families have been touched by large losses from Internet gambling," said Iowa congressman Jim Leach, the bill's main sponsor in the House. Well, no more than the many families that have been touched by gambling in Las Vegas or Atlantic City, or in the thousands of other casinos that have now popped up across the country. We have yet to quantify how many families waste thousands of dollars on Iowa State lotteries, as well.

But as with all stabs at controlling online gambling, the new Internet ban won't keep bettors from continuing their habit. Rather it will only create black markets and damage American businesses. And not only online gambling businesses. Americans are sure to turn now to overseas payment services and continue their habits. "It has put a terrible scare into people," I. Nelson Rose, a gambling law professor at Whittier Law School, said. "But it won't by any means wipe out Internet gambling." Others warned that Internet gambling would turn unregulated offshore sites into the modern equivalent of speakeasies.

★ ★ ★

Speaking of speakeasies . . . in recent years, Texas Holdem and other poker-related games have enjoyed widespread popularity. ESPN's World Series of Poker and other national tournaments featured on television have fueled a renewed interest in gambling. Participation by thousands each year has helped local bars, steak houses, and legion halls bring in business during typically slow times.

This trend has a created consternation among nannyists. "It's glamorized on TV and in the media in a way that other addictions are not," explains Keith Whyte, executive director of the National Council on Problem Gambling. "There's the impression that through skill you can beat the odds. But randomness is always going to have a bigger factor in determining the outcome than your skill . . . And unfortunately, that's not the message these kids get."

Here we go with the "kids" again. Surely the children must have been on the minds of a Virginia Beach SWAT team when they fatally shot a security guard during a raid to serve a warrant on gambling in 1998. And it was not an isolated incident. Across the nation cops are gearing up to stop gambling. One of the most infamous episodes played out at a Texas Holdem game at the Guadalajara Restaurant in Palmer Lake, a small community south of Denver. A game where "you had to try real hard to lose $30," according to owner Jeff Hulsmann.

Fifty officers in SWAT gear showed up at the restaurant one night, arrested twenty-four players, and confiscated all cards and money. Hulsmann maintains that the game was legal and he has done nothing wrong. He claimed not to receive a cut of the game. Nor did he charge players rent to play there. "I'm a small businessman, and it's going to cost me a lot of money to fight this," he said. "But I'm a stubborn man."

Stubborn is the best kind of American. A volunteer with the parent-teacher organization at his kids' school, Hulsmann also coaches the YMCA girls soccer team and serves on the Tri-Lakes Chamber of Commerce.

"I'm not a punk," he says.

That's where he's wrong. The nanny state doesn't discriminate. In the nanny state, we're all punks.

★ CHAPTER SEVEN ★

HOW WE PAY

Even if there's no such thing as free will, we have to treat each other as if there were free will in order to live together in society. Because otherwise, every time somebody does something terrible, you can't punish him, because he can't help it, because his genes or his environment or god made him do it, and every time somebody does something good, you can't honor him because he was a puppet, too.

—ORSON SCOTT CARD, *XENOCIDE*

★

THINGS CHANGE

It would be a waste of time to calculate the number of new pernicious ideas that are percolating in the minds of nannies. But if recent history is any indication, you'll be hearing about most of them quite soon. The trouble with combating this growing paternalism is pointing out the long-term consequences. So let's end this book at the beginning to illustrate how nannyism can snowball from a mere annoyance to something far more corrosive.

Mandated seat-belt laws are the bellwether of the modern nanny state. Obligatory buckling up wasn't the first time government regulated personal safety to defend us from our own dangerous penchants, but it was the most public and wide-ranging, and, consequentially, has had the longest gestation period.

Two decades ago wearing a seat belt was a choice and the now-forgotten distinction between personal and public safety was still well defined. After seat-belt laws passed, the debate surrounding similar regulations veered from concerns about whether laws kept us free, to whether they kept us safe.

The Highway Safety Act and the National Traffic and Motor Vehicle Safety Act, passed in 1966, began the earnest regulation of automotive industry and highway standards. It also created the National Highway Safety Bureau, which later became the National Highway Traffic Safety Administration (NHTSA).

As far back as 1970, federal government proposed that all vehicles manufactured after January 1, 1973, be equipped with air bags or automatic belts. In 1984, NHTSA proposed that automatic restraint systems be required in new vehicles unless two-thirds of the U.S. population was covered by local mandatory seat-belt laws by the end of 1989.

To make the dream a reality, in the mid-to-late '80s, states were blackmailed to meet federal criteria for front-seat passenger seat belts or face cuts in highway funding. Initially, the tack was rejected by more than thirty state legislatures, but after some prodding (and a little more arm-twisting) most states jumped aboard. Today, most Americans believe not only that forcing drivers to buckle up is a good idea but that questioning the value of mandatory seat-belt laws, unless you live in New Hampshire, lands you somewhere between the Flat Earth Society and the Klu Klux Klan.

In mandatory seat-belt laws, nannies had discovered not only a way to save citizens from their own self-destructive stupidity but the perfect pitch for their proselytizing rhetoric. When the soft sell was unsuccessful, nannies began attacking anyone opposing government's good-intentioned protection by calling them radical, selfish, coldhearted miscreants who had turned their backs on society.

A wonderful example of this came when in 1985 New York governor Mario Cuomo said that those opposing the mandatory seat-belt law were "N.R.A. hunters who drink beer, don't vote and lie to their wives about where they were all weekend."

Incredibly, my wife is virtually always privy to my whereabouts on weekends. And no, I am not a member of the NRA, nor have I ever shot an animal. And two decades after such laws were codified I bitterly protest mandatory seat-belt laws as an inexcusable intrusion on my personal liberty. Whether I want to protect myself in such a manner is no one's business but my own.

While that manner of thinking puts me in the distinct minority nowadays, it wasn't always the case. In 1977, a Gallup Poll claimed that "a huge majority" of 78 percent opposed a law that would fine a person $25 for failure to use a seat belt. This represents an *increased* resistance to similar laws from 1973. At that time 71 percent opposed a seat-belt law.

★ ★ ★

Today, New Hampshire is the only state that does not coerce those older than seventeen to buckle up. And in my research for this book, I could only unearth a single example in the past decade of an American challenging seat-belt laws on principle.

In 2005, fifty-three-year-old libertarian activist Kenneth Prazak contested the Illinois village of Algonquin over his long-lost right to drive around unbuckled. In court he shouted slogans like "Say yes to choice" and "Say yes to freedom." Prazak backed up his rallying call by spending two years and more than $2,000 of his own money fighting the injustice of a $25 ticket. Why would he do that? "Well, the principle is, first of all, we're losing our freedoms day by day in this country . . . where the government is the nanny state, controlling every aspect of our lives. I'm doing my little part to try to restore individual freedom and self-responsibility in this country."

No one was surprised when it took a jury a meager seven minutes of deliberation to convict Prazak of his crime. Algonquin police officer Nicholas Corso, the lone witness to the incident, testified that he pulled over an unbelted Prazak, who explained to him that "he didn't believe in seat belts." Corso told the jury that Prazak told him he would never wear a seat belt and the "government has no right to tell him to wear one."

It did, of course. Not only did Prazak waste his time and money and lose his case, but local authorities concluded that arguing over the legality of seat-belt laws was so frivolous that he should reimburse them. "It's going to be punishment for him and his attorney," the prosecutor explained. "It will hopefully deter people from filing frivolous claims in the future and relieve citizens and taxpayers of the burden of paying for them."

THE REAL COST

Let's take a closer look at the numbers to see just how frivolous challenging seat-belts laws really is. These days, the NHTSA authorities claim that seat-belt legislation has reduced the number of casualties in road accidents by more than 10,000 lives every year. But as is often the case, quantifying the fantastic numbers used by government agencies can be complicated. After all, automobile fatality rates have been declining progressively since 1925.

They have decreased by 50 percent every twenty years, with seat-belts laws and without them. In truth, we have no idea how many people would be saved by seat-belt laws—because most citizens would voluntarily wear seat belts. Many other facts, including safer car designs and better road conditions, also play a part.

It's curious, then, that according to the Insurance Institute for Highway Safety in Maine, a state with more or less the identical population as New Hampshire, the number of auto fatalities is also nearly identical (Maine's 169 to New Hampshire's 166 in 2005). Other states with comparable populations, like Hawaii (140) and Idaho (275), have similar rates of auto-related death percentages according to miles driven. Actually, when the group broke down the "Number and percent of fatally-injured passenger vehicle occupants by belt use and state" they found that New Hampshire (107) had done better than Maine (135).

A fairer way to contrast the value of seat-belt laws is by comparing fatalities per every 100 million miles traveled rather than by pure numbers. And here too, New Hampshire's improvement since the mid-'80s ranks slightly above average for the nation.

There's a very simple answer to why laws make little difference. The majority of American citizens buckle up for reasons of self-preservation and the safety of their children. They purchase top-of-the-line baby and booster seats. They drive safely and slowly. They buy Volvos, Volkswagens, and SUVs because they deem those cars safer than others. How many of you have ever overheard anyone buckling up their kids while saying, "Geez, we wouldn't want to get a ticket"?

Admittedly, there is always a minority who engage in risky, careless, crassly uncaring or even willfully neglectful behavior. Those people, we should also concede, will probably ignore seat-belt laws, anyway. Naturally we should do our best to convince them to wear seat belts, and that's where government involvement should end.

Let's assume for the sake of argument that 10,000 lives are saved because of the threat of a $50 ticket. If safety belts are indeed so significant a lifesaver, why not mandate fines that actually dissuade criminal behavior? After all, if we can save 10,000 lives, why not 25,000? If it's a matter of life and death, isn't it the moral obligation of government to charge $1,000 per ticket? That's the argument nannies give for all their impositions. If it is so vital to saving lives, why not raise the fine to $7,000 or $20,000? Or arrest people who ignore the law?

This is the danger of many nanny laws. The most obvious and immediate consequence of coerced seat-belt laws (or any nanny law) has been the swiftness in which government has gone from tender cajoling to rigid insistence. The "Click It or Ticket" campaign, sponsored by the NHTSA, is an example of this overreach. The operation's function is to convince young people that buckling up will save their lives. The price tag for the effort is $30 million on yearly television ads alone.

The crusade consists of more than appealing and insightful commercials. More than ten thousand law enforcement agencies are mobilized around the nation, employing checkpoints, issuing tickets via "primary" seat-belt laws, and practicing zero-tolerance policy. "America should be on notice. Click It or Ticket. No exceptions. No excuses. No warnings," threatened one of the campaign's proponents.

"Primary" seat-belt laws mean that if you fail to buckle up police now have the legal justification not only to pull you over but to demand that you produce ID, answer their questions, and allow them to search your car. The allegedly small-government conservative administration of President Bush proposed a $400 million incentive to reward state governments that adopted "primary" seat-belt laws in 2004, a onetime grant equal to 500 percent of the highway safety money they received in 2003. Even before this none-too-subtle federal enticement, more than twenty states and Washington, D.C., had laws on the books that permit police to pull over drivers not wearing seat belts.

Walter Williams, an economist at George Mason University, has been writing in opposition to coerced seat-belt laws for years. His takedown of the "Click It or Ticket" campaign is a stark reminder of what we're really dealing with:

> Imagine you're having a backyard barbeque. A cop walks in and announces, "This is a random health and safety check to see whether you've removed the skin from the chicken before you served it." Though delicious in taste, we all know that chicken skin contains considerable unhealthy fat. If you're caught serving chicken skin, the cop gets your ID and issues you a $50 ticket.
>
> If something like this were to occur, most Americans—I hope—would see such an action as ludicrous, offensive and a gross violation of our liberties. But not so fast. Let's think about it. Each year, obesity claims the lives of 300,000 Americans and

adds over $100 billion to health-care costs. Doesn't that give government the right to dictate what we eat? If you're the least offended by the notion of government dictating our diets, pray tell me how it differs in principle from seatbelt laws and especially the new federal enforcement program called "Click It or Ticket."

As *Nanny State* has argued, there *is* no difference in principle when you legislate personal behavior. The only variation is degree. The food police may be annoying, undercut choice, and disregard free will, but the "Click It or Ticket" campaign and primary seatbelts laws have already provided us with an erosion of our constitutional rights.

In April of 2001, *Time* relayed the incredible story of Gail Atwater, and the long-term consequences of minor laws, that found its way to the Supreme Court: "You're driving down the road, minding your own business when it suddenly occurs to you that you've forgotten to buckle your seat belt. And then, just as you reach down to fasten the strap, you see flashing red and blue lights in your rearview mirror. Not such a nice surprise. But it gets worse: Instead of getting a ticket, you're arrested and handcuffed. And the U.S. Supreme Court has no complaints."

Atwater, an average Texas mom, was hauling her children home from soccer practice. A journey millions of other moms and dads embark on each day. Somewhere along Atwater's route a toy fell—or was thrown—out of the vehicle. And for those of you who have children, you empathize. A favorite lost toy will not do. Thus, Atwater allowed a child to stand on the front seat while she, only two blocks from her house, and moving at a snail's pace, retraced her route so that the kids could catch sight of their lost plaything. En route, a local policeman observed Atwater's car crawling along at a meager fifteen miles per hour with unbuckled passengers.

Driving around without seat belts is a violation of Texas's primary seat-belt laws. The indignant officer not only ticketed the mom but gave her a demeaning lecture. Atwater didn't take kindly to a sermon over an inconsequential misdemeanor and when she retorted, the officer snapped on the bracelets and placed her in a cruiser. A neighbor was forced to arrive to take custody of—what we assume must have been—some horrified children. Atwater was taken to the local jail to be processed and her vehicle was towed away.

Atwater didn't contest the seat-belt violation, which amounted to $50, but her distaste for the abusive police officer was a different story. After discussing the incident with her husband, and coming to the realization that the mundane crime of failing to fasten a seat belt did not merit jail, Atwater decided to file a lawsuit against the patrolman, his employer, and the city of Lago Vista.

Atwater's lawyers argued that her arrest was unconstitutional and undermined common-law rules pertaining to arrests and searches. The police, her lawyers contended, needed an arrest warrant for misdemeanors that did not involve a breach of the peace. And the Fourth Amendment, as any layman can read, states that the "right of the people to be secure in their persons, houses, papers, and effects, against unreasonable searches and seizures, shall not be violated." Basically, police can only arrest citizens if the arrest is "reasonable," a legal term that essentially balances the individual's privacy interests against the government's interests in keeping a safe and orderly society.

How many run-of-the-mill Americans would deem an unbuckled seat belt a "reasonable" cause for police apprehension? Implausibly (to many legal experts) the Supreme Court majority threw aside her complaint. They admitted that Atwater was subjected to "gratuitous humiliations" and "pointless indignity," but, as it turns out, wearing a seat belt was more important.

Justice Sandra Day O'Connor, in the minority, warned of the consequences of granting "such unbounded discretion" to authorities. In O'Connor's words, "As the recent debate over racial profiling demonstrates all too clearly, a relatively minor traffic infraction may often serve as an excuse for stopping and harassing an individual." Ira Glasser, retired director of the American Civil Liberties Union, claimed it was one of "the scariest decisions to come down in a long time, a horrendous decision." Glasser's views on the situation were echoed by critics from every side of the ideological spectrum.

What began as nudging toward self-preservation has led to one of the "scariest" Supreme Court decisions in a long time. So next time a nanny claims that you're overreacting to a small, good-intentioned intrusion on liberty, tell them to wait fifteen or twenty years to get full effect—because as with seat belts, nannies are rarely satisfied with a minimal first step.

They'll typically answer with the platitude: "It saves lives!" If saving lives trumps self-determination, then why do we allow people to drive fifty-five miles per hour and not force them to travel at five miles per hour? If it is constitutional to ban trans fats, why not ban excessive sugar, artificial flavors, or all unhealthy additives?

If saving lives is the only reason we have laws, then we'll never have enough.

WE PAY AND WE PAY

Seat-belt laws are the most fully realized of nanny laws, thus the most instructive. There are significant costs inherent even in a law most Americans would consider a no-brainer. Throughout *Nanny State,* we've reviewed the unintended consequences of dictating personal behavior: the unnecessary inhibiting of the free market, the undermining of incentive, the inexcusable practice of snatching away choices, and the inexcusable practice of ignoring free will. But nannyism has other expenditures, many of them often hidden.

People act more recklessly when (purported) risk is removed. Professor John Adams, a risk expert and professor emeritus of geography at University College London, has been skeptical regarding the benefits of seat-belt laws for twenty-five years. Adams began studying safety data and discovered that mandated safety belts resulted in virtually no change (and in certain cases a slight increase) in road-accident deaths in the eighteen countries he surveyed that had imposed such laws on their citizens.

Adams isn't alone. Sam Peltzman, a University of Chicago Graduate School of Business economics professor, also claims that people have a tendency to react to safety regulations by increasing risky behavior. This, he posits, offsets many of the benefits of the regulation. Adams and Peltzman hypothesized that risk compensation makes individuals behave more cautiously when the perception of risk rises. They contend that drivers feel safer wearing seat belts and thus increase the risk they pose to other drivers and pedestrians by driving more recklessly when they're buckled up.

When citizens believe even minor menaces are removed and no longer their responsibility, it erodes self-sufficiency. When we believe government is our babysitter, we have a tendency to disengage from the process. Risk compensation is a theory that applied to all areas of life.

The rigidity of nanny regulations does not allow consumers to practice common sense and protect themselves. More than a decade ago critics accused the NHTSA of covering up air-bag deaths that may have taken the lives of at least fifty-two Americans—thirty-two of them children who were smothered by the force of the bag.

Walter Williams, the outspoken critic of seat-belt laws, penned a letter in 1997 to the acting chief counsel of the U.S. Department of Transportation requesting permission to dismantle the air bags in his own car. Williams had no children. He owned the vehicle. He was putting no one other than himself in potential danger. And in this situation, he was trying to put himself in a safer position.

"Acting under the assumption of being an emancipated adult, living in a free country," Williams wrote, "I am very concerned for my safety in light of a number of recent reports about air bags going off and killing people. I herein request permission to have the air bag in my car deactivated. Thank you for your assistance."

More than a month later, James R. Hackney, director of the Office of Crashworthiness Standards, wrote Williams back with the bad news: "In your letter, you request approval to disconnect one or both of the air bags in your vehicle. I regret to inform you that, at this time, we cannot grant your request to authorize your auto dealer or repair shop to disconnect your air bags."

Digest that information. Your own car. Your own safety. Not your choice. Later on, air bags were produced that were safer for small children and on/off buttons were installed.

Nannies deliberately—and quite deftly—smear the lines between public and private interests, between life-or-death vices and innocuous habits, between their business and yours. Aside from the important topics of free will and liberty, nannies, in their drive to save us from Coca-Cola and pornography, employ emotive arguments and alarmism over reasoned discussion. But in their righteousness they've become liars. *Nanny State* has documented scores of unreliable statistics used by nannies to forge public policy. When we add up some of the fantastical numbers they use, we begin to understand the improbability of their claims.

Obesity, we're expected to believe, kills 400,000 Americans

each year. Add in trans fats, and you have another 30,000 casualties a year, according to Michael Jacobson. The Center for Science in the Public Interest also tells us that the "Forgotten Killer"—otherwise known as salt—knocks off another 150,000 Americans a year. Drunk driving kills 17,000. Mothers Against Drunk Driving claims that college drinking kills 1,700 people a year. Smoking kills 400,000 and secondhand smoke puts another 50,000 on the nanny-state death roll.

That's already more than a million people. Does anyone die of old age anymore?

These numbers are manipulated. But perhaps one of the answers is multiple inclusion of thousands of people. A person can die at the ripe age of eighty-five from heart disease after smoking for fifty years. He may be lucky to have escaped that long, but certainly he has no place on nanny-state statistics. Or he could have been obese and a smoker. Nanny groups make no such distinction when they're busy frightening soccer moms on *Oprah* and *Fox News*.

The consequences of these bolstered numbers are clear. If the NHTSA claims that seat-belts *laws* save 10,000 people a year, how could we not allow an officer to arrest you for failing to buckle up? If the surgeon general of the United States declares passive smoke an extraordinarily hazardous toxin that causes disease on contact, then all of a sudden outdoor smoking bans seem reasonable. If, as a Mothers Against Drunk Driving spokesperson has asserted, drinking is analogous to heroin addiction, then the question becomes, Why aren't we instituting zero-tolerance policies and police stings at local pubs across the nation?

This obfuscation is eroding the public's ability to recognize the difference between desirable policy and ineffective, intrusive policy. It undermines the public's ability to decide the appropriate amount of attention an issue deserves.

As both political parties now habitually take advantage of nannyism to further their own special interests, neither feels that it's essential to guard citizens from the increasing overreach of the state. This way everyone loses. Democrats will protest the Patriot Act and government's invasion of the bedroom, yet they see little hypocrisy in advocating draconian regulations that infringe on personal property rights in the name of safety. Conservatives, on the other hand, will grouse about the economic intrusions of government, yet see no hypocrisy in promoting their own moral sensibilities as law. Big-government Republican George W. Bush has given perfunctory speeches extolling the virtues of limited government, yet, just like President Clinton before him, his administration has allotted hundreds of millions of taxpayer dollars to strengthen and inflate the nanny state's power. Neither political party maintains a consistent ideological position that works to keep government out of our lives. And they won't until Americans begin applying the type of pressure that moves politicians to act.

There are already too many regulations. "America started out with three federal laws—treason, counterfeiting and piracy. In 1998, the American Bar Association counted more than 3,300 separate federal criminal offenses on the books—more than 40 percent of which had been enacted in just the past 30 years. These new laws cover more than 50 titles of the U.S. Code and encompass more than 27,000 pages," wrote Rebecca Hagelin, vice president of the conservative Heritage Foundation in 2003.

Obviously, as the world evolves, so does the call for new regulations, but the Congressional Research Service, according to Hagelin, can't even tell us how many federal crimes exist: "Are we that much more evil than we were 200 years ago that we need this many laws to keep us off of each other? Or has the nanny state veered completely out of control—creating crimes where no evil existed, pinning blame where no harm was intended?"

The explosion of laws is certainly one of the contributing factors to American's lack of confidence in government. (I realize numerous other dynamics are in play as well, namely corruption, poor governance, and failed policies.) There are those who are concerned with the sheer number of regulations and a growing feeling that they are no longer in control of even the most commonplace aspects of their lives. Then there are those who believe in an energetic and involved government, but who are soon confronted with the fact that it is impossible for government to live up to its promises.

A 2002 ABC News poll—taken when the nation was still split evenly on Iraq—showed that only 38 percent trusted government "when it comes to handling social issues like the economy, health care, Social Security, and education." This is especially pronounced among the young. In 2004, a poll of one thousand Americans ages fifteen to twenty-five found that those who say they trust the government to do the right thing (this included foreign affairs) a lot or some of the time fell from 62 percent in January 2002 to 50 percent in November 2003.

If we don't trust government to handle social security or foreign entanglements, then why on Earth do we trust them to dictate what we put into our mouths, what toys our children play with, or what we watch on television? A suspicion of government—or of those in power—is healthy for a democracy. It's the very reason the founders designed checks and balances and God created talk radio and bloggers. But the fact that we don't trust them yet we allow them to reach into the most personal aspects of our lives is bewildering.

Micromanaging our lives won't make us safer, healthier, and more decent. Only self-control will. But the overbearing and unrelenting crush of regulations does lead Americans to discard their individual ingenuity, resourcefulness, and belief systems. What's more, nanny laws are uncharacteristic of the American temperament. They breed political correctness and gratuitous coddling. They undercut risk and incentive. They make life staid and unappealing by eliminating choices perfectly reasonable adults should be able to make on their own. Most important, they weaken our freedom, our most valuable resource.

THIS IS STILL A FREE COUNTRY, RIGHT?

Or at least, it should be. There are more regulations each year that focus on our habits and predilections. The least we can ask is that lawmakers ask the question: Is this infringing on the self-reliance, free will, and liberty of the average citizen? Because as classical-liberal thinker Wilhelm von Humboldt once said, "A society in which the citizens were compelled to obey even the best behaviors might be a tranquil, peaceable, and prosperous one. But it would always seem to me a multitude of well-cared-for slaves, rather than a nation of free and independent men."

First it was safety, then health, and now nurturing the minds and souls of Americans. In effect, every facet of American life is fair game: cigarettes, liquor, G-strings, french fries, jungle gyms, baggy pants, Truman Capote novels, and your livelihood. Bureaucrats of every ideological variety can be heard shouting, "Something needs to be done."

For many politicians and activists, nannyism has trumped self-determination and liberty, resulting in an avalanche of intrusions on our lives. This low-grade, feel-good tyranny—dictating where we smoke, what we eat, what we watch—has exacted a substantial toll in both obvious and obscure ways.

We've built the freest and most dynamic society the world has ever seen. To let these lightweight babysitters take over would be absurd, self-destructive, and categorically un-American.

ACKNOWLEDGMENTS

My good fortune began when I connected with my agent, Sloan Harris, and it continued apace when I began working with my editor, Becky Cole. A rookie author couldn't ask for a better pair. Thanks to both for their counsel, professionalism, and support. Thanks also to Brianne Ramagosa and everyone at Broadway Books, and to Katharine Cluverius at ICM.

My alarm over the growing nanny state first materialized in my *Denver Post* columns. For the chance to spout off in the pages of a magnificent newspaper, I'm indebted to Greg Moore and Gary Clark. Many thanks also to my editor, Chuck Murphy, who habitually challenges worn-out ideas with irritating facts and ironclad logic. Glenn Asakawa was a lifesaver for snapping the pictures.

Harris Vederman is a comrade in the cause. I am grateful for his advice, passion, and friendship. Thanks also to friends Brad Cohan, John Ealy, Andy Matthews, Chuck Plunkett, and Angela Clemmons for their assistance and patience. Jeff Goldstein, the man who runs the first-class ProteinWisdom.com, read the manuscript and offered numerous needed upgrades. I'm also grateful to Matthew Abbott, Catherine Amble, and Melissa Rudd at Dartmouth for chipping in with research. Also, thanks to Mary Elkins for her work on the Web site.

Mom and Dad drilled the importance of liberty and personal responsibility into my head early and often. I'm still humbled by their story and forever grateful. My appreciation also goes out to their significant others. My brothers Oren (his family: Anne, Hannah, and Noah) and Boaz are always there for me. Thank you to both Pauls for allowing me to bounce ideas off them—as a matter of fact, thanks to the entire Pietrofeso clan for their encouragement and support.

Leah and Adira lost Dad for many nights and weekends—though I can promise them it was harder on me. I am always grateful to them. But to my wife, Carla, I owe the greatest debt. Not only does she patiently listen to endless iterations of every silly idea that pops into my head, she somehow keeps me focused on what's important. She makes it all worthwhile.

NOTES

Introduction: Tyranny of the Busybody

2 *New York City Council was working overtime* Editorial, "Whatever It Is, They're Against It," *New York Post,* December 29, 2006.
2 *San Francisco decreed that cookie-scented strips* "Cookie-Scented Milk Ads Dunked," *Monterey County Herald,* December 6, 2006.
2 *"backyard laws"* Cinnamon Stillwell, "San Francisco Is Nanny State U.S.A.," SFGate.com, February 8, 2005.
2 *"pet guardian"* R. Scott Nolen, "Pet Owners in San Francisco Become 'Pet Guardians,' " *Journal of the American Veterinary Medical Association* Online, March 1, 2003.
3 *implant an identifying microchip* Lee J. DiVita, "Chicago Ordinance Passes: 'It's the Deed, Not the Breed,' " *Journal of the American Veterinary Medical Association* Online, January 1, 2002.
3 For Chicago's bans, see Fran Spielman, "Alderman Wants to Limit Fatty, Fried Fast Food," *Chicago Sun-Times;* and Jonathan Hoenig, "Chicago's Mob Rule," *Smart Money,* May 1, 2006.
3 *"threatened to use their legislative might"* Josh Noel and Mickey Ciokajlo, "Fido, Beware. You're Next," *Chicago Tribune,* July 25, 2006.
3 *banned sledding* "Fear of Lawsuits Prompts Sledding Ban," TheOmaha Channel.com, January 3, 2007.
3 *In the California towns* See Chapter Three.
4 *assemblyman Felix Ortiz* Radley Balko, "In the Reign of Cotton Mather," *Forbes,* May 9, 2005.

5 *Senator Carl Kruger explained* "Ban Proposed on Cell Phones, iPods in Crosswalk," MSNBC.com/NBC NY, February 7, 2007.

6 For *Vanity Fair*'s takedown of Mayor Bloomberg, see Christopher Hitchens, "I Fought the Law in Bloomberg's New York," *Vanity Fair*, February 2004 (the essay is also featured in Christopher Hitchens, *Love, Poverty, and War: Journeys and Essays*, Nation Books, 2005); and Jennifer Steinhauer, "Mayor and Editor, Fussing over Fuming," *The New York Times*, January 18, 2004.

9 *"We have a responsibility"* President George W. Bush, remarks on Labor Day in Richfield, Ohio, September 1, 2003, www.whitehouse.gov/news/releases/2003/09/20030901.html.

9 *"like grandparents"* David Henderson, "History and Culture: The Joy of Freedom," *Hoover Digest* 2 (2002).

9 *"as we think about a ten-year-old child"* Sarah Schweitzer, "Card Says President Sees America as a Child Needing a Parent," *The Boston Globe*, September 2, 2004.

9 *"trying to do too many things"* "Poll: Majority Believes Government Doing Too Much," CNN.com, October 27, 2006.

10 *In the United Kingdom* Shannon McKenzie, "Survey Debunks 'Nanny State' Myth," *Public Health News*, July 2, 2004.

11 *"We would have been a grosser"* Lee Kuan Yew, *From Third World to First: The Singapore Story: 1965–2000* (HarperCollins, 2000), 183.

11 *"Freedom of the press"* Han Fooket Kwang, "Lee Kuan Yew: The Man Behind His Ideas," Singapore Press Holdings & Times editions, 1998, quoted from International Press Institute's assembly, 1971.

12 For more on Stewart, see Judith Silver, "Movie Day at the Supreme Court or 'I Know It When I See It': A History of the Definition of Obscenity," FindLaw.com, January 2003.

13 *"Mind your own business. Keep your hands to yourself."* P. J. O'Rourke, "The Liberty Manifesto," speech to Cato Institute, Washington, D.C., May 6, 1993.

Chapter One: Twinkie Fascists

17 *Mulligan's is perhaps best known* John Kessler, "It's a Deep-Fried Train Wreck, but I Can Die Happy," *Atlanta Journal-Constitution,* April 21, 2005; and Editorial, "In praise of the Luther Burger," *Chicago Tribune,* February 21, 2005.

18 *During a* Tonight Show *monologue* Richard L. Eldredge, "Buckhead Restaurant Learns Tough Lesson," *Atlanta Journal-Constitution,* April 28, 2005.

18 *Gateway Grizzlies to create* Heather McPherson, "Burger Has Us All Glazed 'n' Amused," *Orlando Sentinel,* August 23, 2006.

19 *"you choke that [Hamdog] down"* Daniel Yee, "Health Officials Wage Tough Fight Against Tasty, Southern-Fried Staples," Associated Press, February 9, 2005.

20 *"Americans need to understand"* Rob Stein, "Obesity Passing Smoking as Top Avoidable Cause of Death," *The Washington Post,* March 10, 2004.

21 *The first salvo came* Eliot Marshall, "Public Enemy Number One: Tobacco or Obesity?," *Science,* May 7, 2004.

21 *"inflated the impact of obesity"* Betsy McKay, "CDC Study Overstated Obesity as a Cause of Death," *The Wall Street Journal,* November 23, 2004.

22 *In April 2005* Katherine M. Flegal, Ph.D., and Edward W. Gregg, Ph.D., "Being Obese, Underweight, Associated with Increased Risk of Death," *The Journal of the American Medical Association* (April 2005); and Patricia Neighmond, "Study Revises Death Rate from Obesity," National Public Radio, *All Things Considered,* April 20, 2005.

23 *"have the sense to realize"* Dahleen Glanton, "The South's Deep-Fried Dilemma: Can Culture Survive a Low-fat Diet?," *Chicago Tribune,* May 16, 2006.

23 *According to a 2006 Associated Press poll* Libby Quaid, "Poll: Ameri-

cans Are Overweight but Read Food Labels," Associated Press, July 2, 2006.

23 *"got to move beyond personal responsibility"* Gary Andres, "The Waistline Wars," *The Washington Times*, April 20, 2005.

23 *"is not merely a matter of individual responsibility"* Bruce Silverglade, "Conference Report: Generation Excess," www.tacd.org/events/meeting6/generation_report.htm.

24 *"blaming the victim"* Kelly Brownell and Marion Nestle, "Are You Responsible for Your Own Weight?," *Time*, June 7, 2004.

24 *"The combination of poor diet"* Marion Nestle, *Food Politics: How the Food Industry Influences Nutrition and Health* (University of California Press, 2003), 7.

24 *"who bears the greatest responsibility"* Andres, "The Waistline Wars."

25 *In June 2006, a 136-page report* The Keystone Forum on Away-From-Home Foods: Opportunities for Preventing Overweight and Obesity, www.keystone.org/Public_Policy/Obesity.html.

25 *Cutting portions in fast-food places* Francine Palma-Long, M.D., "Cut Portion Sizes in Half to Fight Obesity," *Chicago Tribune*, July 20, 2005.

26 *"are notorious for serving too much food"* Editorial, "Lighten Up, America!; Obesity Epidemic Threatens Nation's Well-Being," *The Dallas Morning News*, June 7, 1998.

26 *"I'm getting ready"* Fran Spielman, "Daley Has a Beef with Calorie Counts," *Chicago-Sun Times*, December 20, 2006.

28 *"monument to decadence"* Phil Vettel, "At 1,420 calories, Hardee's New Monster Thickburger Is Actually Pretty Darn Tasty," *Chicago Tribune*, December 14, 2004.

28 *"if the old Thickburger was Food Porn"* Michael F. Jacobson, "Hardee's Monster Thickburger More Porno Than Ever," http://cspinet.org/new/200411162.html.

28 *"not a burger for tree-huggers"* Andrew Puzder, CNBC interview, CEOWire, November 16, 2004.

29 "*There is profit in poisoning*" Nicholas Von Hoffman, "Eating Ourselves to Death," *Nation,* January 23, 2006.

29 "*borderline lethal dose of sodium*" Center for Science in the Public Interest *Nutrition Action Healthletter* (October 2000).

29 *Michael Jacobson claims that trans fats* "Prisoner Abuse Scandal; Gaza Incursion; Time to Travel; Trans Fat Dangers," CNN *Live at Daybreak,* May 19, 2004.

30 "*I call it the panic du jour*" Gina Kolata, "The Panic Du Jour: Trans Fats in Foods," *The New York Times,* August 14, 2005.

30 "*Trans fat is not a liberty*" Claudia Zapata, "Trans Fat Not a 'Freedom' to Protect," *San Antonio Express-News,* November 20, 2006.

31 "*represents bold, courageous action*" Nanci Hellmich and Bruce Horovitz, "NYC Proposes Ban on Trans Fats in Restaurant Food; Supporters Say Other Cities, States Could Follow," *USA Today,* September 27, 2006.

31 *The American Heart Association, for one* Carl Campanile, "Heart 'Attack' on Ban Group Rips Fat Plan," *New York Post,* November 14, 2006.

33 Eric Schlosser, *Fast Food Nation: The Dark Side of the All-American Meal* (Harper Perennial, 2002); and *Fast Food Nation* (2006), directed by Richard Linklater.

33 Morgan Spurlock, *Don't Eat This Book: Fast Food and the Supersizing of America* (Putnam Adult, 2005); and *Super Size Me* (2004), directed by Morgan Spurlock.

33–34 For the Soso Whaley story, see Dr. Ruth Kava, Ph.D., "30 Day McDiet: Results Are In," www.techcentralstation.com/090804G.html, September 8, 2004. For Whaley's diary, see Competitive Enterprise Institute's series "Debunk the Junk," www.cei.org/pages/debunk/debunk_the_junk.cfm. See also Andrew Stuttaford, "Crushing Mr. Creosote," *National Review* Online, April 29, 2004.

35 For the fictional story of Irwin Leba, see Joshua Foer, "The More You Weigh, the More You Pay," *Esquire* (April 2006).

36 *It took nearly three weeks* Peter Carlson, "Of Flab and Flimflammery;

Veteran Prankster Behind Esquire's 'Fat Tax' Spoof," *The Washington Post*, March 25, 2006.

37 *If society had the right* David Shaw, *The Pleasure Police: How Bluenose Busybodies and Lily-Livered Alarmists Are Taking All the Fun Out of Life* (Doubleday, 1996), 137.

37 *"smart ideas to fix the world"* "16 Smart Ideas to Fix the World," *U.S. World & News Report*, December 29, 1997.

37 *promoted by medical writers* Suzanne Leigh, "Twinkie Tax Worth a Try in Fight Against Obesity," *USA Today*, December 2, 2004.

37 *the powerful American Medical Association's* Barry Wigmore, "Doctors Call for 'Fat Tax' on Coca-Cola and Pepsi," *The Daily Guardian*, June 12, 2006.

37 *"We could envision taxes on butter"* Editorial, "Nanny-State Nonsense," *New York Post*, July 5, 2006.

38 *"Congress and state legislatures could shift"* Fred Sampson, "Here's the Skinny on 'Fat Taxes': Knowing What to Eat Is More Healthful Alternative," *Nation's Restaurant News*, December 16, 2002.

39 *the nation's worst big-city mayor* Jyoti Thottam, "Kwame Kilpatrick/Detroit," *Time*, April 17, 2005.

39 For Detroit mayor Kwame Kilpatrick and fat tax, see Sarah Karush, "Hungry for Revenue, Detroit Ponders Fast-Food Tax—a Nickel Extra for That Big Mac," Associated Press, May 8, 2005; and "Detroit Mayor Kwame Kilpatrick Discusses the Need for a Fast-Food Tax in His City," NBC News transcript, May 10, 2005.

39 *Felix Ortiz had already proposed* "New York Assemblyman Felix Ortiz and Dr. Elizabeth Whelan Discuss a Proposed Tax on Junk Food as a Way to Control the Obesity Crisis," NBC News transcript, June 12, 2003.

40 For the story of Jazlyn Bradley, see Ed Vulliamy, "Super-Sized Teenagers Sue McDonald's," *The Observer*, November 24, 2002; Bruce Bartlett, "Grease Job," *National Review*, November 27, 2002; and John Cloud, "A Food Fight Against McDonald's," *Time*, December 2, 2002.

41 *"I always believed McDonald's"* Jonathan Wald, "McDonald's Obesity Suit Tossed," CNNMoney.com, January 22, 2003.

42 *"You don't need nicotine"* On Point, *Rocky Mountain News,* July 26, 2002.

42 *"singularly responsible for making attorneys"* Linda Stasi, "Try Having a Salad, Kids," *New York Post*, February 23, 2003.

42 *"Americans as the most pathetic"* Libby Copeland, "Snack Attack; After Taking on Big Tobacco, Social Reformer Jabs at a New Target: Big Fat," *The Washington Post*, November 3, 2002.

42 *"Do you realize the whole world"* Neil Buckley, "Have Fat Will Sue," *Financial Times*, December 12, 2003.

42 For the Caesar Barber story, see Robert Fulford, "Save Me from Myself—or I'll Sue You," *National Post*, December 7, 2002; Editorial, "Finger-lickin' Dumb," *The Washington Times*, December 12, 2002; and Karen Crummy, "Fast-Food Junkies Sue Eateries over Fatty Food," *Boston Herald*, July 26, 2002.

43 Kelly D. Brownell, Ph.D., and Katherine Battle Horgen, Ph.D., *Food Fight: The Inside Story of the Food Industry, America's Obesity Crisis, and What We Can Do About It* (McGraw-Hill, 2003).

43 *"an attractive element"* Marguerite Higgins, "Obesity Suits Eye Children as Props," *The Washington Times*, August 7, 2003.

44 *Banzhaf's vanity license plate* Michael Crowley, "He's All Over 'Em Like a Cheap Suit," *National Journal*, December 17, 1994.

44 *"we're going to sue them"* Interview with Charles Osgood, CBS News transcript, August 11, 2002.

45 *"Why should I be forced"* Steven Martinovich, "Snack Attack: Public Health Activists, Flush with Victory over 'Evil' Tobacco, Have Turned Their Sights on the Fast-Food Industry," *Ottawa Citizen*, February 21, 2002.

45 *"What we are seeing"* Andrew Gumbel, "The Man Who Would Sue America's Junk-Food Industry," *The New Zealand Herald,* June 8, 2002.

45 *didn't buy Samuel Hirsch's argument* Michael I. Krauss, "My 'Big Fat'

Update: Courts Disserve Rule of Law and Food Lawsuits Decisions; and Legal Backgrounder," Washington Legal Foundation, May 6, 2005; see also *Pelman v. McDonald's,* 396 F.3d 508 (2nd Cir. 2005).

46 *California attorney general Bill Lockyer* Lisa Jennings, "Calif. Filings Portend More Prop. 65 Lawsuits," *Nation's Restaurant News*, September 18, 2006.

46 *Jacobson wondered why* Ian Miller, "Wendy's Sued for Toxic French Fries," *Los Angeles Sentinel,* November 13, 2002.

46 *"a person of average weight"* Center for Consumer Freedom, "The Dose Makes the Poison Someone Should Tell California's Attorney General," May 15, 2006.

46 *the sugar substitute saccharin* Sheryl Gay Stolberg, "Bid to Absolve Saccharin Is Rebuffed by U.S. Panel," *The New York Times*, November 1, 1997.

47 *"Cookie Controversy"* Peter Jennings, *World News Tonight,* ABC News transcript, March 18, 2005.

48 *fanned the fire of the Girl Scout Cookie controversy* Kim Severson, "So Much for Squeaky Clean Cookies," *The New York Times,* March 9, 2005.

48 *"Weighing In: Helping Girls Be Healthy Today, Healthy Tomorrow,"* Girl Scout Research Institute, www.girlscouts.org/research/pdf/weighing_in.pdf.

48 *"balanced, healthy living is not about denial"* Jennings, *World News Tonight.*

49 *"just know that you're going to"* "How Unhealthy Is Ice Cream? Results of a New Study," *Good Morning America,* ABC News transcript, July 24, 2003.

49 *"list the calorie (and, ideally, saturated fat)"* Michael F. Jacobson, Ph.D., and John F. Banzhaf III, "Coronary in Cone: Companies Threatened with Law Suits for Failing to Warn About Artery-Clogging Fats and Calories," banzhaf.net/docs/icecreamltr.html.

49 *"We know consumers don't assume"* Marguerite Higgins, "Lawyers

Scream About Ice Cream; Chains Warned to Add Labels or Face Litigation," *The Washington Times*, July 25, 2003.

50 *"Kids don't want to buy carrots"* "State Representative Seeks to Curb School Cookie Sales," Associated Press, April 29, 2005.

50 *"peanut butter and Marshmallow Fluff"* Steve LeBlanc, "Fluffernutter Sandwich Angers Mass. Senator," Associated Press, June 21, 2006; and Elizabeth Mehren, "The Nation; Marshmallow Fluff Is the Stuff Legislation Is Made Of," *Los Angeles Times*, June 26, 2006.

51 For more on Fluffernutter, see www.marshmallowfluff.com/pages/fluffernutter.html.

51 *"I've been eating Fluff"* Philip McKenna, "Can This Spread Be Stopped; Lawmaker Wants Schools to Put a Lid on Fluff," *The Boston Globe*, June 19, 2006.

51 *"There is no need to call out specific foods"* Ibid.

52 *"Teaching kids to make good choices"* Nikole Hannah-Jones, "Schools to Widen Bans on Goodies," *The News & Observer* (Raleigh), May 10, 2006.

52 *would ban high-fructose corn syrup* Bill sponsored by Juan Zapata (Republican, Miami) of the Florida State Legislature (HB 629) 2005.

52 *"Stop. Step away from the junk food"* Susan Combs, "Growing Pains: In American Children, Bigger Is Not Always Better," Agriculture Commissioner press release, May 8, 2002.

52 *"We have an opportunity"* Kelley Shannon, "Texas Lawmakers Allow Cupcakes in Schools," Associated Press, March 10, 2005.

53 *more than $8,000 for failing* Kim Breen, "Junk Food at School Still Reigns: New Rules' 1st Year Sees More Fruits and Veggies, but Old Habits Bite Back," *The Dallas Morning News*, June 7, 2005.

53 *spoke to Leo Lesh* David Harsanyi, "Attack on Snacks Lacks Teeth," *The Denver Post,* April 17, 2006.

54 *"did not offer support for the hypothesis"* Roger Dobson, "Snacks Not the Cause of Obesity in Children," *The Independent,* September 19, 2004; and "Study Paints Good Picture of Life for American Kids Except

When It Comes to Childhood Obesity," NBC News transcript, July 18, 2003.
54 *"in 2002, there were 31"* Maggie Fox, "U.S. Children Healthier, Except Minorities," *Reuters Health*, July 20, 2005.
54 Stephen Moore and Julian Simon, *It's Getting Better All the Time: 100 Greatest Trends of the Last 100 Years* (Cato Institute, 2000).

Chapter Two: Days of Whine

56 *"You can't seriously want to ban alcohol"* Mayor Joe Quimby, or Joseph Fitzpatrick Fitzgerald Fitzhenry Quimby Jr., aka "Diamond Joe" Quimby, is the fictional, corrupt mayor of Springfield on *The Simpsons*. In one episode, Springfield's nannies discover a long-forgotten municipal law banning alcohol. Helen Lovejoy, the local do-gooder, reasons, as nannies often do, "Oh, won't somebody *please* think of the children?" Soon enough, Springfield is thrown back into the era of Prohibition.
57 *mayor John Hickenlooper* Nanny Gibbs, "The 5 Best Big-City Mayors," *Time*, April 25, 2005.
57 *The Coors family* Joseph Coors was one of the initial donors to the Heritage Foundation, founded in 1973. For more, see "Heritage Foundation President Edwin Feulner on the death of Joseph Coors," www.heritage.org/About/coors_tribute.cfm.
58 *most "intoxicated" city list* "America's Drunkest City," *Men's Health* (September 2004).
58 *Modern Drunkard Magazine* can be found at www.moderndrunkard magazine.com. Some of the better bits are featured in Frank Kelly Rich, *The Modern Drunkard: A Handbook for Drinking in the 21st* Century (Riverhead Trade, 2005).
58 *The 2005 convention held in Denver* Megan McCloskey, "Drink Up! Boozeheads Gather to Get Soused," Associated Press, June 3, 2005.
59 *"The government [is] getting deeper"* Sean Higgins, "In Vino Veritas: Or Something Like That . . . ," *National Review* Online, March 17, 2006.

60 *Thomas Jefferson, some historians suggest* Andrew Barr, *Drink: A Social History of America* (Carroll & Graf, 1999), 370.

60 For more on Benjamin Rush, see David Barton, *Benjamin Rush: Signer of the Declaration of Independence* (Wallbuilders Press, 1999).

60 For more on the Whiskey Rebellion, see William Hogeland, *The Whiskey Rebellion: George Washington, Alexander Hamilton, and the Frontier Rebels Who Challenged America's Newfound Sovereignty* (Scribner, 2006); and Thomas P. Slaughter, *The Whiskey Rebellion: Frontier Epilogue to the American Revolution* (Oxford University Press, 1988).

61 For a quick introduction to Carry Nation, see the Kansas State Historical Society Web site at www.kshs.org/exhibits/carry/carry1.htm.

61 For more on Anthony Comstock, see www.pbs.org/wgbh/amex/pill/peopleevents/e_comstock.html.

61 There are many meticulous and fascinating books available on Prohibition. I found John Kobler, *Ardent Spirits: The Rise and Fall of Prohibition* (Da Capo Press, reprint 1993) was the most useful.

62 Paul M. Johnson, *A History of the American People* (HarperCollins, 1998).

63 *"For me," Califano once declared* Joseph Califano Jr., *Inside: A Public and Private Life* (Public Affairs, 2004), 464.

63 *"Availability is the mother of abuse"* Mary Pat Flaherty, "Study Describes Quiet 'Epidemic' of Teenage Prescription Drug Abuse," *The New York Sun*, July 8, 2005.

63 *"Using Mr. Califano's false logic"* Arthur Sobey, "Reefer Madness Logic," *The Wall Street Journal*, March 31, 1999.

63 *One such hard-hitting study* National Institute on Alcohol Abuse and Alcoholism, www.niaaa.nih.gov/NewsEvents/NewsReleases/welfare.htm. Health and Human Services secretary Donna Shalala alleged that Califano had misstated the evidence.

63 *statistics that were "not credible"* Kathy McNamara-Meis, "Burned," *Forbes MediaCritic* (Winter 1995). McNamara-Meis found that many of the "statistics" CASA cited were originally only *conjecture*. One number

Califano used came from a student handout that was explicitly labeled "not intended to reflect any kind of original research."

64 *One of the more egregious of these reports* "Teen Tipplers: America's Underage Drinking Epidemic," Columbia University, Center on Addiction and Substance Abuse, February 26, 2002.

64 *the percentage of alcohol consumed* Tamar Lewin, "Teenage Drinking a Problem but Not in Way Study Found," *The New York Times*, February 27, 2002.

64 *Discussing his memoir* Tim Russert, "Joseph A. Califano Jr. Discusses His New Book, *Inside: A Public and Private Life*," CNBC News transcript, April 10, 2004.

64 According to Activist Cash, an industry trade group, by the end of 2000, CASA had $44.9 million in the bank and was paying six-figure salaries to at least ten people. Califano's salary was around $375,000. For more specific information about CASA's finances, see www.casacolumbia.org/absolutenm/templates/AboutCASA.aspx?articleid=448&zoneid=1.

64 *"Califano is essentially a reincarnation"* Christopher Shea, "In Drug-Policy Debates, a Center at Columbia U. Takes a Hard Line," *The Chronicle of Higher Education*, October 3, 1997.

65 *"set the historical record straight"* Joseph A. Califano Jr., "Don't Stop This War," *The Washington Post*, May 26, 1996.

65 *this editorial were a rehash* Mark H. Moore, "Actually, Prohibition Was a Success," *The New York Times*, October 16, 1989.

66 *In South Dakota a couple of years ago* In 1998, HB 1257 was "to provide for the protection of children from prenatal exposure to alcohol and drugs . . . (9) Who was subject to prenatal exposure to alcohol or any controlled drug or substance not lawfully prescribed by a practitioner." The bill failed. Exposure to any alcohol is quite ambiguous. So the following day, the South Dakota Senate amended the bill and passed it 31 to 3 and the House voted 56 to 12 to approve the Senate's changes, which adds a person who is "pregnant and *abusing* alcohol or drugs" (italics mine).

67 *"Maybe the answer is lowering"* Melanie Wells, "Coors Chief: Consider Lower Drinking Age," *USA Today,* September 10, 1997.
67 *Soon enough, the opposition began* Mark P. Couch, "Coors Ripped for '97 Proposal to Lower Drinking Age," *The Denver Post,* June 25, 2004; and Mark P. Couch, "Drinking-Age Query Keeps Bubbling Up," *The Denver Post,* October 29, 2004.
68 *In 1984, transportation secretary* "Even Higher Drinking Age Possible," United Press International, July 2, 1984.
69 According to the National Institute on Alcohol Abuse and Alcoholism, binge drinking is defined as a pattern of alcohol consumption that brings the blood alcohol content level to 0.08 percent or above. This pattern of drinking usually corresponds to more than four drinks on a single occasion for men or more than three drinks on a single occasion for women, generally within about two hours.
69 *A Harvard School of Public Health study* Julie Sevrens Lyons and Kim Vo, "Study: College Drinking More Deadly Than Ever," *The Mercury News* (San Jose), April 10, 2002.
69 *"We want people to be free"* Randy Dotinga, "Quandary for Colleges: How to Battle Binge Drinking," *The Christian Science Monitor,* January 18, 2005.
69 For more on Glynn Birch and drinking games, see Christopher Leonard, "Anheuser-Busch Pulls Drinking Game from Market," Associated Press, October 19, 2005.
69 *"When you play drinking games"* Jeffrey Gettleman, "As Young Adults Drink to Win, Marketers Join In," *The New York Times,* October 16, 2005.
70 *"drinking by college students"* Glynn R. Birch, "Drinking Contests: Not Fun and Games," letter to *The New York Times,* October 18, 2005.
70 *In Madison, Wisconsin, legislators* WISC-TV/Channel 3000 report and *Women in Higher Education,* "Now Alcohol Is Date-Rape Drug in Wisconsin," both August 2006.
70 *The local district attorney Brian Blanchard* Brian Blanchard, "Rape Law Change a Strong Reminder," *Wisconsin State Journal,* July 10, 2006.

71 *In 2006, North Carolina governor* Elliot West, "It's Now Easier to Buy a Shotgun in NC Than a Keg of Beer," *The Raleigh Chronicle,* August 23, 2006.

71 *In Austin, Texas, it was reported* Mark Lisheron, "Beer Kegs Would Be Registered Under New Bill," *The Austin American-Statesman*, January 20, 2005.

71 *New York governor George Pataki* Alison Bert, "Pataki Signs Keg Law to Curb Teen Drinking," *The Journal News,* July 26, 2003.

72 *"There is a ritual every university"* Hara Estroff Marano, "Wimp Nation," *Psychology Today,* www.psychologytoday.com/articles/pto-20041112-000010 .html. Well worth reading to better understand consequences of the nanny state on children.

72 *In a* New York Times *op-ed piece* John M. McCardell Jr., "What Your College President Didn't Tell You," *The New York Times*, September 13, 2004.

72 Morris E. Chafetz, *Big Fat Liars: How Politicians, Corporations, and the Media Use Science and Statistics to Manipulate the Public* (Nelson Current, 2005), 89–103.

73 *Gregg Anderson was resolute* Vanessa O'Connell, "Uneasy Compromise: To Keep Teens Safe, Some Parents Allow Drinking at Home," *The Wall Street Journal*, September 14, 2004.

74 *"We want parents to understand"* Ibid.

74 *To improve the life in parks* David Harsanyi, "Limits on Park Tippling Irrelevant," *The Denver Post,* August 11, 2005.

75 *How can the author defend getting drunk* Coleman Andrews, "In Defense of Getting Drunk," *Los Angeles Times,* January 2, 1994.

77 For the Debra Bolton story, see Brigid Schulte, "Single Glass of Wine Immerses D.C. Driver in Legal Battle," *The Washington Post,* October 12, 2005; and Editorial, "Hold the Wine," *The Washington Post,* October 13, 2005.

77 For a breakdown of blood alcohol content, see www.csus.edu/indiv/l/limb/calculators/alcohol.htm.

77 *If you get behind the wheel* Brigid Schulte, "D.C. Chief Defends Officers' Judgments in DUI Arrests," *The Washington Post*, October 14, 2005.
78 *Police arrested 321 people* Schulte, "Single Glass of Wine."
78 *In 1998, the U.S. House approved a measure* Robin Lee Allen, "Operators Vow to Keep on Fighting BAC Bill," *Nation's Restaurant News*, October 16, 2000.
79 *"may wind up in this country"* "Surface Transportation Act Reauthorization," hearing of the Transportation and Infrastructure Subcommittee of the Senate Environment and Public Works Committee, May 7, 1997.
79 *"There is no safe blood alcohol"* Katherine P. Prescott, "MADD's Mission Is to Save Lives," *Chicago Tribune*, February 18, 1997.
79 For more on Candace Lightner and blood alcohol content, see Ralph Vartabedian, "The Nation; A Spirited Debate Over DUI Laws," *Los Angeles Times*, December 30, 2002.
80 For more about MADD's history, see www.madd.org/aboutus/1122. For specific membership numbers when Lightner was replaced, see Tom Gorman, "MADD Chief Replaced by S.D. Chapter Head," *Los Angeles Times*, October 12, 1985.
80 *"I worry that the movement I helped create"* Kristen Lopez Eastlick, "MADD Agenda Goes Mad with Neo-Prohibitionism," *Atlanta Journal-Constitution*, March 25, 2002; and Eric Peters, "MADD House; Is Mothers Against Drunk Driving Out of Control?," *National Review*, September 28, 1998.
81 *According to the National Highway Traffic* Motor Vehicle Traffic Crash Fatality Counts and Estimates of Fatality Counts and Estimates of People Injured for 2005, www.nrd.nhtsa.dot.gov/pdf/nrd-30/ncsa/ppt/2006/810639.pdf.
81 *Back in 1982, a shocking 60 percent* According to the CDC Research and Evaluation Actions there has been a decrease in alcohol-related fatal crashes involving young drivers over the past twenty years. Alcohol-related fatal crash rates have decreased by 60 percent for drivers ages sixteen to seventeen and 55 percent for drivers ages eighteen to twenty,

according to a study from the Centers for Disease Control and Prevention, www.cdc.gov/ncipc/factsheets/driving.htm.

82 *"Honestly, I put forward this bill"* Jason Silverman, "Locking Out Drunks Ignites Debate," *Wired News,* February 21, 2004.

83 *"If the public wants it and the data support it"* Jayne O'Donnell, "Will All Autos Some Day Have Breathalyzers?," *USA Today,* April 25, 2006.

83 *a bill was introduced* "Proposal Mandates Ignition Interlocks for All Cars," *The Newspaper,* March 27, 2007, www.thenewspaper.com/news/16/1672.asp.

83 For the story of Keith Emerich, see Peter Jackson, "Beer Drinker Loses Appeal over Lost Driver's License," Associated Press, July 8, 2005.

84 On sobriety checkpoints, see Radley Balko, "When Drunk Driving Deterrence Becomes Neo-Prohibition," FoxNews.com, October 6, 2005; and Karina Ioffee, "Statistics Spark Debate on Whether DUI Checkpoints Work," *The Record,* September 18, 2005.

85 For more on the Herndon, Virginia, bar busts, see Paul Bradley, "Police Ruffle Some Feathers Posing as Revelers in Bar Sting," *Richmond Times-Dispatch,* January 19, 2003; and Carol Morello, "Arrests Inside Bars Leave Bitter Hangover in Fairfax," *The Washington Post,* January 16, 2003.

85 *"They tapped one lady on the shoulder"* "Cops Go to Bars to Arrest Drunks," *WorldNetDaily,* January 6, 2003.

86 For more on Virginia's definition of public places, see www.abc.state.va.us.

87 *"sales to intoxicated person stings"* Texas Alcoholic Beverage Commission press release, "TABC Cracks Down on Public Intoxication in an Effort to Reduce DWI's," August 26, 2005.

87 *"We believe responsible adults"* Matt Phinney, "State to Keep Tabs on Bars," *San Angelo Standard-Times,* September 16, 2005.

87 KXAN-TV in Austin reported that one of the hardest-hit clubs in Austin is Dallas Nightclub, which has seen its business drop off by more than 80 percent since "Operation Last Call."

87 *"It's killed our business"* "Alcohol Commission Puts Hold on Public Intoxication Program," KTEN Television, April 24, 2006.

87 *liable if a customer becomes intoxicated* See www.madd.org/aboutus/1621: "MADD strongly supports by means of legislation or case law the right of victims of alcohol related traffic crashes to seek financial recovery from establishments and servers who have irresponsibly provided alcohol to those who are intoxicated or to underage persons, or who serve past the point of intoxication individuals who then cause fatal or injurious crashes."

87 The liability of bars discussed here is also often referred to as "dram laws." In eighteenth-century England, gin shops sold homemade liquor by the dram—which amounts to about a spoonful of the good stuff. When the King of England decided to tax these dram shops, they quickly dug in underground.

88 For more on the Massachusetts happy-hour ban, see George R. McCarthy, "There Seems to Be Wide Support for the Ban," *The Washington Post*, November 3, 1985; and Leo C. Wolinsky, "Part of Crackdown on Drunk Driving; Measure Takes Sober Aim at 'Happy Hours,' " *Los Angeles Times*, March 7, 1985.

89 For more on the Illinois happy-hour ban, see Robert Davis, "Happy Hour Gone, Happy Days Here," *Chicago Tribune*, January 30, 1990.

90 For more on the end of ladies' night, see Tatsha Robertson, "Last Call for Ladies' Night," *The Boston Globe*, June 17, 2004.

90 *I was in a bar in Kentucky* "Tobacco at the Crossroads: A Debate on the Ethics of Reduced Harm Products," speech given at Southern Methodist University, October 23, 2004, hitchensweb.com/SMUspeech.htm.

91 For more on New York bar crawling, see Fredric U. Dicker, "Party's Over for All-You-Can-Drink Bar-Hoppers," *New York Post*, July 31, 1999.

92 *"hawking America's costliest"* Steve Piachente, "Thurmond Fights Wine Labels Hinting of Health Benefits," *The Post and Courier* (Charleston), April 26, 2000.

92 For George Hacker on sports fans, see Joe Holley, "Beer, Boorishness

in Stands Spoil Games for Some Fans," *The Washington Post*, November 21, 2005; and Mike McAllister, "Beer Muscles," SportsIllustrated.com, November 23, 2004.

93 For a contemporary take on the self-imposed ban on radio advertising, see the editorial, "Regulation of Liquor Ads Necessary but Ban Exceeds Government's Role, *South Florida Sun-Sentinel*, June 21, 1996.

93 The Clinton/Bronfman meeting was widely reported. For the best take, see David Brooks, "William Jefferson Comstock," *The Weekly Standard*, November 25, 1996.

94 *The Federal Communications Commission* Cristina Merrill and Judy Warner, "Spirited Debate: Liquor Ads on Air," *Adweek*, November 4, 1996.

95 For Kennedy interview, see Mark McEwen, "Representative Joseph Kennedy Discusses Legislation to Keep Hard Liquor Ads Off Television and Radio," *CBS This Morning* transcript, September 3, 1996.

96 "*research has yet to document*" Jeffrey T. Haley, "Liquor Sales—Studies Indicate Advertising of Alcohol Has Almost No Effect on Consumption," letter to *The Seattle Times*, August 28, 1994; and "Banning Liquor Ads Futile Attempt to Protect Kids," *USA Today*, December 31, 1996.

96 The first time the term "malternative" was used on record was Sara Bongiorni, "Malt-Based Lemonade Tested in San Diego with Some Success," *San Diego Daily Transcript*, March 8, 1996: "The makers of Hooper's Hooch are hoping it will be a British invasion all over again. And San Diego is one of two landing points in the nation for this latest British import. Billed as a 'malternative' to beer and other alcoholic beverages, Hooper's Hooch is a malt-based lemonade that proved a runaway hit last summer when it was introduced in the United Kingdom."

97 For George Hacker on ads, see Ameet Sachdev, "Brewers Tasting Sweet Success," *Chicago Tribune*, July 5, 2001.

97 *A Federal Trade Commission investigation* Melissa B. Robinson, "Fruity Alcohol Ads Criticized," Associated Press Online, July 16, 2002.

97 For more on Bad Frog Beer, see Gail Appleson, "U.S.: Finger-Giving Frog Can Stay on US Beer Labels," Reuters, January 17, 1998; and for the

legal aspects, see Grace H. Yang, "Courts Re-examining First Amendment Issues in Beer Label Advertising," *The Metropolitan Corporate Counsel* (August 1998).

98 *The gesture, also sometimes Bad Frog Brewery, Inc. v. New York State Liquor Authority*, 134 F.3d 87 (1998).

98 For more on Manneken Pis White Ale, see "Belgians Can't Understand Manneken Pis Controversy," *Modern Brewery Age*, April 17, 2000.

100 *"We've been looking for something"* Rob Stein, "A Compound in Red Wine Makes Fat Mice Healthy," *The Washington Post,* November 2, 2006.

101 *mice that were given resveratrol* Nicholas Wade, "Red Wine Ingredient Increases Endurance, Study Shows," *The New York Times*, November 17, 2006.

101 *"equivalent of a potent cholesterol medicine"* Abigail Zuger, "How a Tonic Keeps the Parts Well Oiled," *The New York Times,* December 31, 2002.

Chapter Three: The Smokists

104 *"I really want to see the presence"* Kristan Trugman, "Focus on Controversy; Some Find Hill Cop-Camera Idea Invasive," *The Washington Times,* January 27, 1998.

105 For the story of the Washington, D.C., smoking ban, see Brooke Oberwetter and Michael Tacelosky, "D.C. Council Passes Smoking Ban," *The Washington Post,* December 7, 2005.

105 *was "invalid" and "improper"* Henri E. Cauvin Bar, "Restaurant Smoking Ban Set Back in D.C.; Judge Tells Election Board to Reject Ballot Measure," *The Washington Post,* May 22, 2004.

106 *All my life I've been around people* Carol Schwartz, Press release, "Schwartz Statement on Alcohol Ban," Office of D.C. Council, June 21, 2005.

106 *"a very thought-provoking piece"* Brett Zongker, "Councilwoman One Ups Smoking Ban Supporters by Calling for a Booze Ban," Associated Press, June 21, 2005.

107 For more on history of smoking in America, see John C. Burnham, editor, *Bad Habits: Drinking, Smoking, Taking Drugs, Gambling, Sexual Misbehavior and Swearing in American History* (American Social Experience, No. 28), (New York University Press, 1994).
108 *"First they cleaned up Times Square"* Timothy Williams, "New York City Ushers in Smoke-Free Era," Associated Press, March 29, 2003.
109 *"There are roughly 5 million people"* Michael Saul, "Fumin' Mike Has Got an Ash to Grind," *Daily News* (New York), August 16, 2006.
110 *"It's not a revenue source"* Jacob Gershman, "Bloomberg Wants to Go Deeper into the Cigarette Tax Business," *The New York Sun*, January 24, 2006.
110 *"If someone is going to drive"* David Herszenhorn, "Nassau May Follow City's Lead on Antismoking Proposal," *The New York Times*, August 24, 2002.
110 *"Free will is not within the power"* William Foege, "The Growing Brown Plague," *The Journal of the American Medical Association* 264, 12 (September 26, 1990), 1,580.
111 *"Tobacco's opponents believe"* Jacob Sullum, "The Tyranny of Public Health," *Reason*, October 1, 1998 (Presented at the Annual Meeting of the Association of American Physicians and Surgeons, Raleigh, NC).
112 *"I understand, of course"* Fran Lebowitz, *The Fran Lebowitz Reader* (Vintage, 1994), 290.
112 *absurd, childish, peevish* "Fran Fans Flame for Smokers," *New York Post*, August 16, 2002.
112 *"Putting aside my overall disdain"* Ibid.
113 *"Under current New York City law"* Graydon Carter, editor's letter, *Vanity Fair*, February 2004; see also Rebecca Louie, Suzanne Rozdeba, Zoe Alexander, and Ben Widdcombe, "Vanity Fair Kicks Bloomberg's Butt" *Daily News* (New York), January 6, 2004.
113 *"Fundamentally, people just don't want"* David Gray, "Smoke Gets in Your Eyes," *The Scotsman*, April 24, 2003.
114 *"No employee should be forced to choose"* Liz Szabo, "Secondhand

Smoke Debate 'Over'; Surgeon General Says New Report Clears the Air," *USA Today*, June 28, 2006.

115 *When Wernimont took a closer* According to Wernimont, the American Cancer Society conducted an air-quality study on secondhand smoke concentrations indoors in 2002 and found it 532–25,000 times safer than OSHA regulations for the same components as secondhand smoke. Source: cleanairquality.blogspot.com/2004/04/american-cancer-society-test-results.html.

115 *This crusade came to a crescendo* See www.surgeongeneral.gov/library/secondhandsmoke.

116 "*The debate is over*" Szabo, "Secondhand Smoke Debate 'Over.' "

116 *50,000 people die each year* Scores of smoking-prevention groups have used this number as of early 2007. Americans for Nonsmokers' Rights, for instance, claim that "We now know that 53,800 people die every year from secondhand smoke exposure." Source: www.no-smoke.org/getthefacts.php?id=13.

116 *Lung cancer and cardiovascular diseases* Gio Batta Gori, "The Bogus 'Science' of Secondhand smoke," *The Washington Post*, January 30, 2007.

118 *So how could it possibly be* Michael Siegel, "Surgeon General's Communications Misrepresent Findings of Report," The Rest of the Story, June 28, 2006, www.tobaccoanalysis.blogspot.com/2006/06/surgeon-generals-communications.html.

118 For the EPA study on secondhand smoke, see "Fact Sheet: Respiratory Health Effects of Passive Smoking," www.epa.gov/smokefree/pubs/etsfs.html.

118–19 "*standard scientific methodology*" Gio Batta Gori and John C. Luik, *Passive Smoke: The EPA's Betrayal of Science and Policy* (Fraser Institute, 1999); and Alan Charles Raul and Stephen F. Smith, "Judicial Oversight Can Restrain Regulators' Use of Junk Science," *Legal Backgrounder*, January 8, 1999.

119 "*probably much less than you took to get*" Ronald A. Taylor, "EPA Panel Reports Non-smokers at Risk," *The Washington Times*, April 19, 1991.

119 *In May of 2003, Dr. James Enstrom* Sabin Russell, "Study Disputes Fears About Secondhand Smoke; but Critics Say Data Is Dated," *San Francisco Chronicle*, May 16, 2003; Dennis Constant, "Case Against Secondhand Smoke Vanishes into Thin Air," *Chicago Sun-Times*, October 22, 2005; and Rosie Mestel, "Study Downplays the Health Risks from Secondhand Smoke," *Los Angeles Times*, May 16, 2003.

119 *A long-term study released* Dominic Lawson, "MPS Should Have Banned Drinking in Smoking Clubs Rather than the Other Way Around," *The Independent*, February 17, 2006; and Robert A. Levy, "Smoke-Free or Free to Smoke?," *Reason*, August 23, 2001.

120 *"there's a good chance"* John Berlau, "The Data That Went up in Smoke," *Investor's Business Daily*, April 8, 1998.

120 *The most notable example* Curt Woodward, "Smoking Ban in Helena, Mont., Cuts Number of Heart Attacks in Half, Study Finds," Associated Press, April 2, 2003.

121 *Its sample was tiny* Richard P. Sargent, Robert M. Shepard, and Stanton A. Glantz, "Reduced Incidence of Admissions for Myocardial Infarction Associated with Public Smoking Ban: Before and After Study," *British Medical Journal*, April 5, 2004.

121 *Later, Missouri chemist* Bill Scanlon, "Almost Time to Put Out Smokes," *Rocky Mountain News*, June 24, 2006.

121 *To illustrate the damage* Editorial, "Miracle in Helena," *The New York Times*, October 15, 2003.

121 *When panic, junk science, and paternalism* Mary Vallis, "California Suburb Bans Outdoor Smoking: Even on Apartment Patios," *National Post*, February 22, 2006.

122 *"We salute Calabasas"* Dana Bartholomew, "Come Friday, Cigarettes in Calabasas, Calif., Go up in Smoke," *Daily News* (Los Angeles), March 14, 2006.

124 *"Every court which has ever addressed"* News release, "City Bans Smoking on Sidewalks and Streets—Smokers Relegated to 'Outposts,' " U.S. Newswire, February 2, 2006.

124 "*OK, but let us briefly adopt*" John Harris, "The Question: Has the War on Smoking Gone Too Far?," *The Guardian*, March 20, 2006.
125 "*We have to legislate civility*" Lisa Leff, "Bay Area City Says Secondhand Smoke Makes Bad Neighbor," Associated Press, August 21, 2006; and Sophia Kazmi "Dublin Wants Smokers Indoors," *Contra Costa Times*, June 8, 2006.
125 "*We have a tremendous opportunity*" Dana Yates, "Belmont to Be First U.S. City to Ban All Smoking," *The Daily Journal*, November 17, 2006.
126 *In late 2006, a Colorado district judge* Charley Able, "Condo Owners Lose Right to Smoke in Own Home," *Rocky Mountain News*, November 17, 2006.
126 "*We looked around at other categories*" Charles Sheehan, "Smoking Lounge Rolling to Future," *Chicago Tribune*, January 19, 2006.
127 "*It's a rebellion on the part of*" Charles Osgood, Cynthia Bowers, "Tobacco Company Finds Loophole in Chicago Smoking Ban," CBS News transcripts, August 10, 2006.
127 "*The sleek, dimly lit bar*" Carl Campanile, "Cig Ban Scofflaws Light Up Ash-Toria," *New York Post*, May 8, 2006.
128 "*a swearing of secrecy*" Kery Murakami, "Smokers Find Refuge in Secret Nicotine Dens," *Seattle Post-Intelligencer*, May 31, 2006.
128 "*Nobody likes taxes*" Jacob Gershman, "Bloomberg Wants to Go Deeper into the Cigarette Tax Business," *The New York Sun*, January 24, 2006.
128 *The fact is, even according to* Patrick Fleenor, "Cigarette Taxes, Black Markets, and Crime: Lessons from New York's 50-Year Losing Battle," Cato Institute, February 6, 2003.
129 A *New York Health Department* Carolyn Thompson, "Study: Most N.Y. Smokers Buy at Least Some Cigarettes Tax-Free," Associated Press, November 2, 2005.
129 "*While investigators have not found*" Fleenor, "Cigarette Taxes, Black Markets, and Crime."
130 "*We note that in 'Tom and Jerry'* " Shan Ross, "Smoking Ban Hits Tom 'n' Jerry," *The Scotsman*, August 22, 2006.

130 *One of the more notorious* Edward Wyatt, "Goodnight Moon," *The New York Times*, November 17, 2005.

131 *"Excellent start, HarperCollins"* Karen Karbo, "Goodbye, Moon," *The New York Times*, December 4, 2005.

132 *The Beatles, for instance* Liz Kelly, "Beatles: The White-Washed Album," *The Washington Post* Online, March 30, 2006.

132 *"We have never agreed"* Terry Ott, "Paul Butts out on New Abbey Road," *Toronto Star*, February 1, 2003.

133 For the Thornton Wilder story, see Ben Macintyre, "Last Word: The Literary Smoker Is Dying, *The Times* (London), April 1, 2006.

133 *Attorney generals of thirty-two states* Valerie Kuklenski and Brent Hopkins, "Movie Smoking Has State Officials Fuming" *Daily News* (Los Angeles), November 19, 2005.

133 *"This is consistent"* Ibid.

134 *"We should treat smoking"* Stanton Glantz, "Give Movies with Smoking Scenes an R, Witness Says," US Fed News, May 11, 2004.

135 *"I think the day will come"* Andrew DeMillo, "Ark. Governor: Day Will Come When Cigarettes No Longer Sold," Associated Press, August 2, 2006.

136 For more on Ron Teck's plan, see Editorial, "Health Bigotry," *Investor's Business Daily*, February 8, 2006.

136 *"A misanthrope is someone"* Florence King, "I'd Rather Smoke Than Kiss," *National Review*, July, 9, 1990.

136 *"Americans think they have a lot of rights"* Philip Dawdy, "Big Nanny Is Watching You," *Seattle Weekly*, January 18, 2006.

Chapter Four: The Playground Despots

139 *approximately seventeen American children die* "1994 Survey Finds Public Playgrounds Pose Hidden Perils," U.S. Public Interest Research Groups and Consumer Federation of America, www.pirg.org/consumer/products/playgrnd.htm#report.

140 *One morning, parents and children* Kim Breen, "Going Back and Forth on Schoolyard Safety District Bans Swings, Citing Legal Liability; Parent Ridicules Action," *The Dallas Morning News*, February 25, 2005.
140 *When local pools opened* Tim Rogers, "The End of the Cannonball," *D Magazine* (June 2006).
140 *"The rationale behind it is ludicrous"* Breen, "Going Back and Forth."
141 *In Broward County, Florida* "Rules of the Playground," www.broward.k12.fl.us/safetydept/PDFFiles/05-06PlaygrdManualPTII-EquipPics.pdf.
141 *"Suppose that a regulation"* Charles Murray, *What It Means to Be a Libertarian* (Broadway Books, 1997), 74.
143 For more on the Daisy Powerline Airgun ban, see Andrew Ferguson, "Government Overbearing in Its Impulse to Be Motherly—Consumer Product Safety Commission's Lawsuit Against Daisy Powerline Airguns," *Bloomberg News*, November 12, 2001.
143 *This story had a happy ending* Editorial, "A Red Ryder Christmas: The Government Decides Not to Ban BB Guns. Hooray!," *The Wall Street Journal*, November 28, 2003.
143 *The vagaries of modern living* Consumer Product Safety Commission, "Backyard Pool: Always Supervise Children, Safety Commission Warns," CPSC Document #5097, www.cpsc.gov/cpscpub/pubs/5097.html. For updated numbers on choking and other accidental death totals, check out the CPSC library, www.cpsc.gov.
143 *As one of the commissioners* Press release, "CPSC Files Lawsuit Against Daisy Manufacturing Co. to Recall Two Models of Daisy's Powerline Airguns Due to Defects," U.S. Consumer Product Safety Commission, October 30, 2001, www.cpsc.gov/cpscpub/prerel/prhtml02/02029/html.
144 *"the procession of proclamations"* David Ho, "Safety Agency Nominee Defends Record," Associated Press, July 25, 2001.
144 For the baby bath seat story, see "A Full Court Press to Ban Baby Bath Seats—Reactions to Consumer Product Safety Commission's Failure to Ban Baby Bath Seats," Consumer Product Safety Commission, *CPSC Monitor*, November 2000.

144 *It was such a serious threat* Editorial, "Time to Get Serious About Safety," *The Plain Dealer* (Cleveland), December 27, 2005.

145 "*Imagine a parent holding a soapy*" Jeff Taylor, "Ring of Power," *Reason* (March 2001).

145 "*It should not be too much to ask*" Leo Morris, "The Nanny State War," *The News-Sentinel* (Fort Wayne), August 3, 2001.

146 *The columnist Debra Saunders* Debra J. Saunders, "Supersized Nanny State," TownHall.com., August 31, 2005.

147 For more on Common Good, see www.cgood.org.

147 *Like when Illinois became* Leah Hope, "State to Ban Sale of Yo-yo Waterball," ABC7Chicago.com, June 7, 2005.

147 "*If we know a toy like the yo-yo*" Press release, "Governor Rod R. Blagojevich Signed Legislation Today Making Illinois the First State in the Nation to Ban a Dangerous Child Toy—'Yo-yo Water Balls,' " Illinois Department of Public Health, June 8, 2005, www.illinois.gov/PressReleases/ShowPressRelease.cfm?subjectID=3&RecNum=4021.

148 For more information on and quotes by W.A.T.C.H., see www.toysafety.org.

149 "*dangerously sized candy*" Frankie Edozien, "Candy 'Ban' Plan—Sweets Eyed," *New York Post*, May 26, 2005.

149 "*Remind students that no costumes*" Elizabeth Hays and Kathleen Lucadamo, "It's Frankenllien! Please, Mr. Chancellor, Don't Spoil Halloween," *Daily News* (New York), October 29, 2004.

150 "*What if the gum had been given*" L. Burrell, "Student Suspended for Sharing Caffeine Gum," Associated Press, May 27, 2006.

150 For the Heather Lindaman story, see Eric Vance, "Dodgeball Story Exemplifies Political Correctness," *The Patriot Ledger*, November 25, 2004; and Michael Gormley, "N.Y. Lawsuit Kicks Dodgeball into Court," Associated Press, November 20, 2004.

151 *Complaints by parents* Wendy Leung, "Girl, 12, Charged with Battery in School Game," *Inland Valley Daily Bulletin*, Los Angeles Newspaper Group, February 15, 2006.

151 *"Any time you throw an object"* Robert Lipsyte, "BackTalk; Dodgeball, in Adult Hands," *The New York Times,* March 3, 2002.

151 *To properly understand* Neil Seeman, "Dodge This," *National Review,* May 4, 2001.

152 *"A person trying to record"* Ibid.

152 *"physical fighting"* "Violence-Related Behaviors Among High School Students—United States, 1991–2003," Centers for Disease Control and Prevention, www.cdc.gov/mmwr/preview/mmwrhtml/mm5329a1.htm.

152 *In Beaverton, Oregon* Susan Harding, "Is Litigation Taking the 'Play' Out of Kids' Playgrounds?," KATU television transcript, May 8, 2006.

152 *The principal of Willett Elementary School* "Massachusetts School Bans Tag Amid Fears of Injuries, Lawsuits," Associated Press, October 18, 2006.

153 *"little kids were coming in and saying"* Op-ed, "Obsessiveness Worse for Children Than Sweets, Tag," *San Gabriel Valley Tribune,* October 26, 2006.

153 *"The idea of loosely running around"* Zay N. Smith, "Life Can Be Better at the Top," *Chicago Sun-Times,* June 28, 2006.

153 *"Tag may look OK socially"* "More N.J. Schools Banning Playground Games," Associated Press, November 18, 2002.

153 *"Tag games, when structured correctly"* Neil F. Williams, "The Physical Education Hall of Shame," *Journal of Physical Education, Recreation & Dance* (February 1994).

153 For more on Olivia Lichterman's story, see "Madison Students Fight for Right to Play 'Tag,' " New3 transcript, Madison, Wisconsin, September 2005.

154 *"They've been told by their coaches"* Hara Estroff Marano, "A Nation of Wimps," *Psychology Today* (November/December 2004).

154 *In some Massachusetts municipalities* Russell Nichols and Raja Mishra, "Measure Calls for Soccer Helmets; Value of Headgear Is Much Debated," *The Boston Globe,* December 14, 2000.

155 *"the best thing since sliced bread"* Jere Longman, "Soccer Headgear: Does It Do Any Good?," *The New York Times,* November 27, 2004.

156 *"Basically, we have been practicing"* Julia Glick, "Cheerleaders Face Limit on Stunts, Dispirited by Changes," Associated Press, March 11, 2006.
156 *"It's just too sexually oriented"* Op-ed, "Legislating Morality; Houston Legislator's Proposed Cheerleader Law Part of Misguided Trend to Let Government Play Taste Police," *Houston Chronicle*, March 20, 2005.
157 *"It's not an attack on baggy pants"* Mary Vallis, "Virginia Poised to Be Pull-Up-Your-Pants State," *National Post,* February 10, 2005.
157 *At Pope John XXIII Regional High School* "Catholic School Principal to Students: Thou Shalt Not Blog," MTV News transcript, October 25, 2005.
157 For ratings of Web sites, see www.nielsen-netratings.com.
158 *"Social networking is not a fad"* "Bill Would Bar Social Networks in Bid to Guard Kids," Washington Internet Daily, May 12, 2006.
158 For the Deleting Online Predators Act of 2006, see thomas.loc.gov/cgi-bin/query/z?c109:H.R.5319:.
159 *"I touch Sophie because she touch me"* "Girl, 5, Forced to Apologize for Hugging Classmate, Parents Looking for New School for Girl," TheBoston Channel.com, April 5, 2006.
160 For the story of Cazz Altomare, see Meghan Daum, "Here and Now; Unbearable Hugs; Let's Say Adieu to the Tentative Embrace as Social Convention," *Los Angeles Times*, July 28, 2005.
160 *North Carolina boy named Jonathan Prevette* Katy Kelly and David J. Lynch, "The Kiss that Shook the Nation," *USA Today,* September 26, 1996.
161 *"The connotation is you're getting"* Jay Lindsay, "Experts Say Sexual Harassment Not Possible for Most 6-year-olds," Associated Press, February 8, 2006.
161 *When a ten-year-old girl* John Derbyshire, "The Problem with 'Zero': On Tolerance and Common Sense in the Schools," *National Review,* May 28, 2001.
162 *"End the War—on Errorism"* Parvas and Kathy George, "Boy Questioned over Sketches," *Seattle Post-Intelligencer,* April 28, 2004.

162 For the story of Bretton Barber, see Jim Irwin, "ACLU Leader Highlights Questions About Patriot Act," Associated Press, November 8, 2003.
162 For the story of James Lord, see Alexa Aguilar, "He's Back, but Teen's Blessing Is on Hold, He Says," *St. Louis Post-Dispatch*, January 29, 2004.
163 *I went through four years* Nat Hentoff, "When Schools Silence God Talk," *USA Today*, August 28, 2006.
163 *"Abortion is Homicide"* Loredana Vuoto, "Pro-lifers Suited to a T; Teens' Views Often Result in School Hassle," *The Washington Times*, April 27, 2004.
163 *"Be Ashamed"* Editorial, "When Students Speak; Does the First Amendment Protect Public School Students Who Want to Bait Gays?" *The Washington Post*, August 7, 2006.
164 *Not long ago, two professors* David L. Hudson, Jr., "Silencing Student Speech—and Even Artwork—in the Post-Columbine Era," FindLaw.com, March 4, 2004.
164 *When a ten-year-old* Valerie Hoff, "Student Suspended for Gun Gesture," Channel 11 Atlanta transcript, March, 4, 2004.
165 *Is violence presented when* Hudson, "Silencing Student Speech."
165 *"It's about an inch long"* Hannah Wolfson, " 'Inch Long' Toy Gun Causes Big Trouble," *The Birmingham News*, February 26, 2004.
165 *What have school officials* Jonathan Rauch, "The Rise of Antisocial Law," American Enterprise Institute, Bradley Lecture Series, December 11, 2000.

Chapter Five: Yahweh (or the Highway)

168 *"It is a ridiculous notion"* Matt Curry, "Texas Governor Mobilizes Evangelicals," Associated Press, June 12, 2005.
168 *"I think* all *we should legislate"* Laurie Goodstein, "Ashcroft's Life and Judgments Are Steeped in Faith," *The New York Times*, January 14, 2001.
169 *"government exists"* Douglas E. Kneeland, "A Summary of Reagan's Positions on the Major Issues," *The New York Times*, July 16, 1980.

169 *"values are important"* President George Bush, Address to Joint Session of Congress, February 27, 2001, www.presidency.ucsb.edu/ws/print.php?pid=29643.

170 *This whole idea of personal autonomy* Rick Santorum, *Morning Edition,* National Public Radio, August 4, 2006.

171 *. . . as an Evangelical who refrains* John Micklethwait and Adrian Wooldridge, *The Right Nation: Conservative Power in America* (Penguin Press, 2004), 262.

171 A *nanny-state hat trick* Carlos Guerra, "Perry's Promises About Robin Hood, Tax Relief and Ideology," *San Antonio Express-News,* April 13, 2004.

172 *The CBS network* John Dunbar, "CBS Defends 'Wardrobe Malfunction' in Court," Associated Press, November 21, 2006.

172 *"nothing this Commission has done"* Kyle Stock, "Broadcasters Say Indecency Rules Changing," *The Post and Courier* (Charleston), June 25, 2004.

172 *"I'd prefer using the criminal process"* Brooks Boliek, "Lawmaker Calls for Criminalizing TV Indecency," *The Hollywood Reporter*, April 7, 2005.

173 *"her voice cracked"* Betsy Rothstein, "Rep. Heather Wilson: A Buzz Kill, or a Mom Who Wants Kids to Grow Up with Some Decency?," *The Hill,* March 30, 2004.

173 *Texas Republican congressman Ron Paul* Ibid.

174 *From a meager $4,000* Joel Achenbach, "Dropping the F-Bomb," *The Washington Post,* June 25, 2006.

174 For more on the Broadcast Decency Enforcement Act, see thomas.loc.gov/cgi-bin/bdquery/z?d109:s.00193:.

174 A Time *magazine poll* James Poniewozik, "The Decency Police," *Time,* March 28, 2005.

174 For Pew Research Center poll information, see www.people-press.org.

175 *For example, when the* FCC Jeff Jarvis, "The Shocking Truth About the FCC: Censorship by the Tyranny of the Few," BuzzMachine.com, November 15, 2004.

175 *One of the largest fines imposed* Todd Shields, "CBS Stations: Indecency Complaints Invalid," *Mediaweek*, June 13, 2006.
175 *The FCC has also taken* Brooks Boliek, "FCC Checks Live TV Tapes for Dirty Words," *The Hollywood Reporter*, July 12, 2006.
175 *Legendary director Martin Scorsese* "Scorsese Upset with FCC Criticism," WENN Entertainment News Wire Service, May 8, 2006.
176 *"in rare contexts"* Editorial, "Fining the Blues," *The Washington Post*, March 20, 2006.
176 Harry G. Frankfurt, *On Bullshit* (Princeton University Press, 2005).
177 *"I believe that the FCC"* Jeff Jarvis, "In Defense of Bullshit," Buzz Machine.com, March 28, 2006.
177 *"This is really, really, fucking brilliant"* Brooks Boliek, "No FCC Action vs. Bono over Globes F-word," *The Hollywood Reporter*, October 7, 2003.
177 *"I don't want to be sitting there"* David Whitney, "Obscenity Bill Creates Controversy for California Congressman," Scripps Howard News Service, April 12, 2004.
178 For the entire bill describing profanity, see thomas.loc.gov/cgi-bin/query/z?c108:H.R.3687:.
179 *"We believe Congress should authorize"* Jonathan Curiel, "Decency Gets Some Heavy Opposition," *San Francisco Chronicle*, May, 16, 2004.
180 *"If I can see it on my TV"* Ibid.
180–181 *The bipartisan Indecent and Gratuitous* Dimitri Vassilaros, "Subscribing to Nanny State TV," *Pittsburgh Tribune-Review*, March 18, 2005.
181 *"dangerous thing"* Jube Shiver Jr., "FCC Chief Turns Up Heat on Broadcasters," *Los Angeles Times*, April 21, 2004.
181 *"continuing to try to exert"* Joanna Weiss, "Cooling Down of 'Bedford Diaries' Makes FCC Policy a Hot-Button Issue," *The Boston Globe*, March 25, 2006.
182 *"invades our homes persistently"* Laura Sullivan, "Administration Wages War on Pornography," *The Baltimore Sun*, April 6, 2004.
182 *jaw-dropping $13 billion a year* Alex Chadwick, "Tech and Porn Conventions Collide in Las Vegas," NPR News, January 11, 2007.

183 *"The simple fact is"* Dawn C. Chmielewski and Claire Hoffman, "Porn Industry Again at the Tech Forefront," *Los Angeles Times*, April 19, 2006.

183 For *Stanley v. Georgia,* see caselaw.lp.findlaw.com/cgi-bin/getcase.pl?court=US&vol=394&invol=557.

183 William B. Lockhard, Chairman, *The Report of the Commission on Obscenity and Pornography* (Bantam Books, 1970).

184 *"morally repugnant and offensive"* Michael Scherer, "Debbie Does Washington," Salon.com, November 11, 2005.

184 *"most perfect addictive substance"* Jack Hitt, "The Diddly Award; Outfront; Sam Brownback," *Mother Jones,* May 1, 2005.

184 For more statistics on masturbation, see WebMD, "Your Guide to Masturbation," www.webmd.com/content/article/45/2953_487.htm.

185 *"Pornography really does"* Hitt, "The Diddly Award."

185 *Jill Manning, a sociologist* Scherer, "Debbie Does Washington."

185 *Judith Reisman, of the California Protective* Ryan Singel, "Internet Porn: Worse Than Crack?," *Wired News,* November 19, 2004.

186 *"The campaign should combat the messages"* Ibid.

186 *Rapes per capita* David A. Fahrenthold, "Statistics Show Drop in U.S. Rape Cases; Many Say Crime Is Still Often Unreported," *The Washington Post,* June 19, 2006.

187 *"Compared to terrorism"* Julie Kay, "U.S. Attorney's Porn Fight Gets Bad Reviews," *Daily Business Review,* August 30, 2005.

187 *That same month, the FBI posted* Barton Gellman, "Recruits Sought for Porn Squad," *The Washington Post,* September 20, 2005.

188 *"We concur with the message"* Interview with author, September 22, 2005.

189 For the 1996 Communications Decency Act, see www.fcc.gov/Reports/tcom1996.txt.

189 For the Children's Online Protection Act of 1998 and all related information, see www.copacommission.org.

189 *"billions of URLs"* Nicole Wong, "Judge Tells DoJ 'No' on Search Queries," posted on Google corporate blog, March, 17, 2006, http://

googleblog.blogspot.com/2006/03/judge-tells-doj-no-on-search-queries.html.

190 *"Young people are experiencing"* Declan McCullagh and Elinor Mills, "Feds Take Porn Fight to Google," CNET News.com, January 19, 2006.

190 For more on .xxx domain issues, see Declan McCullagh, "Bush Administration Objects to .xxx Domains," CNET News.com, August 15, 2005; and Declan McCullagh, "Senators Question .com Price Increases," CNET News.com, September 20, 2006.

190 *"has been a plague on our society"* Patrick Trueman, "FRC Praises Bush Administration Effort to Block '.XXX' Domain," Family Research Council, August 17, 2005, www.frc.org/get.cfm?i=pr05H14.

191 *"You cannot have that [porn] tax"* Randy Dotinga, "Love the Sinner, Hate the Sin Tax," *Wired News,* August 8, 2005.

191 *"We'd not necessarily be pleased"* Ibid.

192 *"As soon as we get a universal"* Ibid.

192 *"This bill is way off base"* Ed Vogel, "Tax for Strip Clubs Draws Challenge, ACLU Says Plan Unconstitutional," *Las Vegas Review-Journal,* April 13, 2005.

192 *"I don't know why the Constitution"* Ibid.

194 *"Everybody should pay"* Adam Goldman, "Nevada Considers Taxing Prostitutes," Associated Press, February 27, 2003.

194 *"When you talk about paying taxes"* Ibid.

194 *"lewd dress"* Mobile, Alabama, Sec. 39–112. Same—Indecent dress, etc. It shall be unlawful for any person to appear in any public place in a state of nudity or lewd dress, or make an indecent exposure of his person, or to perform or commit any indecent act (Code 1965, § 41–21.1).

194 *for a massage* Mobile, Alabama, Sec. 8–48. It shall be unlawful for any establishment, regardless of whether it is a public or private facility, to operate a massage parlor, bath parlor, or any similar type business, where any physical contact with the recipient of such service is provided by a person of the opposite sex. Any person violating the provisions of this section shall, upon conviction, be punished as provided in chapter 1, ar-

ticle II, City Code (1991) and in addition to such penalty, it shall be grounds for revocation of the license of the owner or manager of the establishment as provided by section 8–63 (Ord. No. 27–049, § 12, 6–1–76).
194 *sunbathe nude* Mobile, Alabama, Sec. 39–113. Any person who, while naked or insufficiently clothed to prevent indecent exposure of his person, shall bathe, wade, wash or swim in the Mobile River or in Mobile Bay or in any watercourse, pond, pool or ditch within the city or its police jurisdiction shall be punished as provided in chapter 1, article II, City Code (1991) (Code 1965, § 41–39; Ord. No. 65–004, 1–17–89).
195 *"have many recognized beneficial uses"* Philip Rawls, "Supreme Court Declines Review of Alabama Sex Toy Ban," Associated Press, February 22, 2005.
195 *One of the rowdy perps* Glenna Whitley, "You Can't Buy a Vibrator in Burleson, but There Are Plenty of Dildos," *Dallas Observer*, April 8, 2004.
196 *"what we do is not obscene"* Steve Rubenstein, "Vibrator Case Dismissed in Texas," *San Francisco Chronicle,* July 30, 2004.
196 *"One of the things that was so outraging"* Lara Loewenstein, "Sex-Toy Sales Bans Absurd, Invasion of Privacy," *University Wire,* April 11, 2005.
196 *In June of 2003* "Supreme Court Strikes Down Texas Sodomy Law: Ruling Establishes New Legal Ground in Privacy, Experts Say," CNN.com, November 18, 2003.
197 *Representative Gerald Allen called for* Mark Strassmann, "Alabama Bill Targets Gay Authors," CBS.com, April 27, 2005.

Chapter Six: Mission Creep

200 For the story on Louisiana florists, see Jacob Sullum, "Flower Power: Free the Florists!," *Reason* (April 2004).
200 *In August of 2006, the Fifth U.S. Circuit Court* Press release, "Louisiana Florist Case Moot Decision Upholding Licensing Regime Vacated," Institute for Justice, August 2006, www.ij.org/economic_liberty/la_florists/8_1_06pr.html.

201 *One of their clients* Virginia Postrel, "Hair-Raising Laws," *Reason* (April 1997); and "Litigation Backgrounder: Challenging Barriers: To Economic Opportunity," Institute for Justice, www.ij.org/economic_liberty/ca_hairbraiding/backgrounder.html.

201 *Take the case of Mike Fisher* Editorial, "Danger! Unlicensed Manicurist on the Loose!," *New Hampshire Union Leader,* May 11, 2005.

202 *"makes food taste more intensely"* Gabrielle Hamilton, "Good Enough to Fine," *The New York Times,* April 27, 2006.

203 *In 2006, members of the Chicago City Council* Gary Washburn and Mickey Ciokajlo, "Foie Gras Ban May Be Next; Daley's People Set to Push for Repeal, Natarus Reveals," *Chicago Tribune,* September 15, 2006.

203 *"barbaric practice"* "NJ Legislator to Propose Foie Gras Ban," AFX International Focus, September 28, 2006

204 *"We have children getting killed"* Fran Spielman, "Phooey! Mayor Scoffs at Council Ban on Foie Gras: Alderman Defends Vote on 'Inhumane' Delicacy," *Chicago Sun-Times,* April 27, 2006.

204 *"The ways that lobsters"* Liz Austin, "Whole Foods Market Bans Sale of Live Lobsters," Associated Press, June 15, 2006.

204 *"We place as great an emphasis"* Karen von Hahn, "Noticed: Killing with Kindness," *The Globe and Mail,* October 7, 2006.

205 *$4 million to $5 million worth of fresh lobsters* Kim-Mai and Joe Yonan, "Seller Scoffs at Lobster Ban," *The Boston Globe,* June 17, 2006.

205 *"Last year, we had to dump"* Laura Parker, "It's a Fight in Florida, and It's Ugly," *USA Today,* December 9, 2004.

206 *The committee appears to be technically* Editorial, "Let Them Eat (Ugly) Tomatoes," *The Christian Science Monitor,* December 23, 2004.

207 *"This is like* Footloose *coming to New York"* Mary Vallis, "Dancing Without a Licence Still Illegal in N.Y.: Lawsuit Dismissed," *National Post,* April 8, 2006.

207 *New York takes this variety of reckless* Tricia Romano, "The Safety Dance; You Can't Dance if You Want To," *The Village Voice,* November 27–December 3, 2002.

208 *"There are inherent dangers"* David Eggert, "Michigan May Require Online Dating Checks," Associated Press Financial Wire, March 28, 2005.

208 For the Dating Service Consumer Bill of Rights, see www.oag.state.ny.us/consumer/tips/dating_service.pdf.

209 *"Maybe there are people"* Jose Martinez, "Can't Buy Her Love: B'klyn Woman Sues Dating Service for Overcharging & Underdelivering," *Daily News* (New York), August 5, 2006.

210 *International Marriage Broker Regulation Act* Eduardo Porter, "U.S. Men and Foreign Women Face Roadblock in Walk Down the Aisle," *International Herald Tribune,* October 18, 2006.

210 *"failed to establish"* "INS 'Mail-Order Bride' Report, AILA InfoNet Doc. No. 99030999," International Matchmaking Organizations: A Report to Congress, March 9, 1999.

210 *"For more than 20 years"* John F. Banzhaf III, "Final Frontier for the Law?," *National Law Journal,* April 18, 1990, http://banzhaf.net/pottyparity.html.

211 *"We're talking about the quality of life"* Lisa L. Colangelo, "Mayor Signs Bill on 'Potty Parity' Function," *Daily News* (New York), June 7, 2005.

212 *"We don't consider cats and dogs"* "West Hollywood Makes Cat Declawing Against the Law," *CBS News* transcripts, *The Osgood File,* August 20, 2003.

213 *"What it really does"* Kim Curtis, "San Francisco Officials Pass Law Mandating Humane Treatment for Backyard Dogs," Associated Press, January 11, 2005.

213 *"I was reading this"* Suzanne Herel, "S.F. Planning to Unleash Dog-Care Rules; Ordinance Would Define Adequate Pooch Amenities," *San Francisco Chronicle,* January 6, 2005.

214 *"Owning a dog can be"* Press release, "Governor Schwarzenegger Signs Legislation to Outlaw Inhumane Dog Tethering," Office of the Governor, September 27, 2006.

214 *Scooby's Law* Michael Coleman, "Scooby Law Lacks Support in House," *Albuquerque Journal,* May 26, 2006.
215 For more on Jay Cohen and online gambling, see "Busted Flush—Online Gambling," *The Economist*, October 7, 2006.
216 *"It is extraordinary how many"* Andy Vuong, "Battle Brewing for Web Betting Bill Would Ban U.S. Transactions," *The Denver Post,* October 3, 2006.
217 *"It's glamorized on TV"* Martha Irvine, "Poker's Popularity Grows Among Teens," Associated Press, November 30, 2004.
217 *One of the most infamous* Felisa Cardona and Erin Emery, "24 Arrested as Cops Raid Poker Game in Palmer Lake," *The Denver Post,* April 28, 2005.

Chapter Seven: How We Pay

221 *"N.R.A. hunters who drink beer"* American Notes, "Hunting for Trouble," *Time,* May 27, 1985.
222 For the Kenneth Prazak story and quotes, see *The Situation with Tucker Carlson,* MSNBC transcript, December 14, 2005; and Charles Keeshan, "Village Gives up Seat Belt Battle," *Daily Herald* (Chicago), March 14, 2006.
223 *These days, the NHTSA authorities* Donna Glassbrenner, "Estimating the Lives Saved by Safety Belts and Air Bags," National Center for Statistics and Analysis, National Highway Traffic Safety Administration, Paper No. 500, 2003, www.fcsm.gov/03papers/Glassbrenner.pdf.
223 For Insurance Institute for Highway Safety study, see www.iihs.org/research/fatality_facts/statebystate.html#sec3.
223 For NHTSA fatality numbers, see www.nrd.nhtsa.dot.gov/pdf/nrd-30/NCSA/TSFAnn/TSF2005.pdf.
225 *The allegedly small-government conservative* Editorial, "A 'Tough Love' Seat Belt Law," *The Virginian-Pilot*, January 6, 2004.
225 *Imagine you're having a backyard barbeque* Walter Williams, "Click It or Ticket," *Jewish World Review,* September 10, 2003.

226 *In April of 2001* Jessica Reaves, "Feel Confined by Your Seat Belt? How About Handcuffs?," *Time*, April 24, 2001.

228 *"As the recent debate over racial profiling"* Bill Mears, "Justice O'Connor, a 'Sensible' Jurist," CNN.com, January 18, 2006.

229 *Professor John Adams* David Bjerklie, "The Hidden Danger of Seat Belts," *Time*, November 30, 2006.

229 Sam Peltzman, "Regulation and the Natural Progress of Opulence," a lecture given at the American Enterprise Institute in 2004, www.aei.org/publications/pubID.21216,filter.all/pub_detail.asp.

229 For more on the air-bag controversy, see Walter Williams, "It Ain't Necessarily So," *Jewish World Review*, September 12, 2001.

230 *requesting permission to dismantle* Walter Williams, "Air Bag Safety Coverup," *Capitalism Magazine*, April 28, 1997.

232 *"America started out with three federal laws"* Rebecca Hagelin, "Criminal?," Townhall.com, October 8, 2003; and for a closer look at the expansion of laws, see Candice E. Jackson and William Anderson, "Washington's Biggest Crime Problem: The Federal Government's Ever-Expanding Criminal Code Is an Affront to Justice and the Constitution," *Reason* (April 2004).

234 *"A society in which"* Wilhelm Von Humboldt, "The Limits of State Action," 1792, http://oll.libertyfund.org/Home3/html.php?recordID=0053.

BIBLIOGRAPHY

Arnold, Andrea. *Fear of Food: Environmentalist Scams, Media Mendacity, and the Law of Disparagement.* Free Enterprise Press, 1998.

Baird, Robert M. (editor), and Rosenbaum, Stuart E. *Pornography: Private Right or Public Menace?* Prometheus Books, 1998.

Barone, Michael. *Hard America, Soft America: Competition vs. Coddling and the Battle for the Nation's Future.* Crown Forum, 2004.

Bartlett, Bruce. *Impostor: How George W. Bush Bankrupted America and Betrayed the Reagan Legacy.* Doubleday, 2006.

Barton, David. *Benjamin Rush: Signer of the Declaration of Independence.* Wallbuilders Press, 1999.

Bennett, James, and DiLorenzo, Thomas. *From Pathology to Politics: Public Health in America.* Transaction Publishers, 2000.

Boaz, David. *Libertarianism: A Primer.* Free Press, 1998

———. *The Libertarian Reader: Classic and Contemporary Writings from Lao Tzu to Milton Friedman.* Free Press, 1998.

Bovard, James. *Lost Rights: The Destruction of American Liberty.* Palgrave Macmillan, 1995.

Brownell, Kelly D., and Horgen, Katherine Battle. *Food Fight: The Inside Story of the Food Industry, America's Obesity Crisis, and What We Can Do About It.* McGraw-Hill, 2003.

Burnham, John C. (editor). *Bad Habits: Drinking, Smoking, Taking Drugs, Gambling, Sexual Misbehavior and Swearing in American History.* (American Social Experience, No. 28). New York University Press, 1994.

Burns, Eric. *The Smoke of the Gods: A Social History of Tobacco.* Temple University Press, 2006.

———. *The Spirits of America: A Social History of Alcohol.* Temple University Press, 2004.

Califano, Joseph A. *Inside: A Public and Private Life.* Public Affairs, 2004.

Campos, Paul. *The Obesity Myth: Why America's Obsession with Weight Is Hazardous to Your Health.* Gotham, 2004.

Carey, George W. *Freedom and Virtue: The Conservative/Libertarian Debate.* Intercollegiate Studies Institute, 1984.

Chafetz, Morris E. *Big Fat Liars: How Politicians, Corporations, and the Media Use Science and Statistics to Manipulate the Public.* Nelson Current, 2005.

Charen, Mona. *Do-Gooders: How Liberals Hurt Those They Claim to Help (and the Rest of Us).* Sentinel, 2004.

Cowen, Tyler. *In Praise of Commercial Culture.* Harvard University Press, 1998.

Critser, Greg. *Fat Land: How Americans Became the Fattest People in the World.* Mariner Books, 2004.

Dilorenzo, Thomas. *How Capitalism Saved America: The Untold History of Our Country, from the Pilgrims to the Present.* Three Rivers Press, 2005.

Easterbrook, Gregg. *The Progress Paradox: How Life Gets Better While People Feel Worse.* Random House, 2003.

Edwards, Chris. *Downsizing the Federal Government.* Cato Institute, 2005.

Edwards, Griffith. *Alcohol: The World's Favorite Drug.* St. Martin's Griffin, 2003.

Fischer, David Hackett. *Albion's Seed: Four British Folkways in America.* Oxford University Press, 1989.

Frankfurt, Harry G. *On Bullshit.* Princeton University Press, 2005.

Friedman, Milton, and Friedman, Rose. *Free to Choose: A Personal Statement.* Harcourt, 1990.

Fumento, Michael. *The Fat of the Land: The Obesity Epidemic and How Overweight Americans Can Help Themselves.* Penguin, 1998.

Gori, Gio Batta, and Luik, John C. *Passive Smoke: The EPA's Betrayal of Science and Policy.* Fraser Institute, 1999.

Hayek, F. A. *The Road to Serfdom: Fiftieth Anniversary Edition.* University of Chicago Press, 1994.

Healy, Gene. *Go Directly to Jail: The Criminalization of Almost Everything.* Cato Institute, 2004.

Henderson, David R. *The Joys of Freedom: An Economist's Odyssey.* Prentice Hall, 2002.

Higgs, Robert. *Against Leviathan: Government Power and a Free Society.* Independent Institute, 2004.

Hitchens, Christopher. *Love, Poverty, and War: Journeys and Essays.* Nation Books, 2005.

Hogeland, William. *The Whiskey Rebellion: George Washington, Alexander Hamilton, and the Frontier Rebels Who Challenged America's Newfound Sovereignty.* Scribner, 2006.

Howard, Phillip K. *The Death of Common Sense: How Law Is Suffocating America.* Warner Books, 1996.

Johnson, Paul M. *A History of the American People.* HarperCollins, 1998.

Kekes, John. *A Case for Conservatism.* Cornell University Press, 2001.

Kimball, Roger. *Experiments Against Reality: The Fate of Culture in the Postmodern Age.* Ivan R. Dee, 2002.

Kobler, John. *Ardent Spirits: The Rise and Fall of Prohibition.* Da Capo Press, reprint 1993.

Kramer, Hilton. *The Betrayal of Liberalism: How the Disciples of Freedom and Equality Helped Foster the Illiberal Politics of Coercion and Control.* Ivan R. Dee, 1999.

Layard, Richard. *Happiness: Lessons from a New Science.* Penguin Press HG, 2005.

Lebowitz, Fran. *The Fran Lebowitz Reader.* Vintage, 1994.

Lender, Mark Edward, and Martin, James Kirby. *Drinking in America: A History*. Free Press, 1987.

Levy, Ariel. *Female Chauvinist Pigs: Women and the Rise of Raunch Culture*. Free Press, 2005.

Lightner, Candy, and Hathaway, Nancy. *Giving Sorrow Words: How to Cope with Grief and Get on with Your Life*. Warner Books, 1991.

Lockhard, William B., Chairman. *The Report of the Commission on Obscenity and Pornography*. Bantam Books, 1970.

MacDonald, Heather. *The Burden of Bad Ideas: How Modern Intellectuals Misshape Our Society*. Ivan R. Dee, 2001.

Micklethwait, John, and Wooldridge, Adrian. *The Right Nation: Conservative Power in America*. Penguin Press, 2004.

Miller, Joel. *Size Matters: How Big Government Puts the Squeeze on America's Families, Finances, and Freedom*. Nelson Current, 2006.

Milloy, Steven J. *Junk Science Judo: Self-Defense Against Health Scares and Scams*. Cato Institute, 2001.

Moore, Stephen, and Simon, Julian. *It's Getting Better All the Time: 100 Greatest Trends of the Last 100 Years*. Cato Institute, 2000.

Murray, Charles. *In Pursuit: Of Happiness and Good Government*. ICS Press, 1994.

———. *What It Means to Be a Libertarian*. Broadway Books, 1997.

Nestle, Marion. *Food Politics: How the Food Industry Influences Nutrition and Health*. University of California Press, 2003.

Paul, Pamela. *Pornified: How Pornography Is Transforming Our Lives, Our Relationships, and Our Families*. Times Books, 2005.

Reavill, Gil. *Smut: A Sex-Industry Insider (and Concerned Father) Says Enough Is Enough*. Penguin Group, 2005.

Rich, Frank Kelly. *The Modern Drunkard: A Handbook for Drinking in the 21st Century*. Riverhead Trade, 2005.

Roberts, Paul Craig, and Stratton, Lawrence M. *The Tyranny of Good Intentions: How Prosecutors and Bureaucrats Are Trampling the Constitution in the Name of Justice*. Prima Lifestyles, 2000.

Safire, William. *Lend Me Your Ears: Great Speeches in History.* W. W. Norton, 2004.

Sager, Ryan. *The Elephant in the Room: Evangelicals, Libertarians and the Battle to Control the Republican Party.* Wiley, 2006.

Schlosser, Eric. *Fast Food Nation.* Harper Perennial, 2002.

Shapiro, Ben. *Porn Generation: How Social Liberalism Is Corrupting our Future.* Regnery, 2005.

Shaw, David. *The Pleasure Police: How Bluenose Busybodies and Lily-Livered Alarmists Are Taking All the Fun Out of Life.* Doubleday, 1996.

Slivinski, Stephen A. *Buck Wild: How Republicans Broke the Bank and Became the Party of Big Government.* Nelson Current, 2006.

Sowell, Thomas. *Basic Economics: A Citizen's Guide to the Economy, Revised and Expanded.* Basic Books, 2003.

———. *The Vision of the Anointed: Self-Congratulation as a Basis for Social Policy.* Basic Books, 1996.

Spurlock, Morgan. *Don't Eat This Book: Fast Food and the Supersizing of America.* Putnam Adult, 2005.

Stacey, Michelle. *Consumed: Why Americans Love, Hate, and Fear Food.* Touchstone, 1995.

Stossel, John. *Give Me a Break: How I Exposed Hucksters, Cheats, and Scam Artists and Became the Scourge of the Liberal Media.* Harper Paperbacks, 2005.

Strossen, Nadine. *Defending Pornography: Free Speech, Sex, and the Fight for Women's Rights.* New York University Press, 2000.

Sullum, Jacob. *For Your Own Good: The Anti-Smoking Crusade and the Tyranny of Public Health.* Free Press, 1998.

———. *Saying Yes.* Tarcher, 2004.

Surowiecki, James. *The Wisdom of Crowds.* Anchor, 2005.

Yew, Lee Kuan. *From Third World to First: The Singapore Story: 1965–2000.* HarperCollins, 2000.

INDEX

ABOUT THE AUTHOR

David Harsanyi is a staff columnist at the *Denver Post*. In addition to a thrice-weekly column, his writings on politics and culture have appeared in the *Wall Street Journal*, the *Weekly Standard*, *National Review*, the *Christian Science Monitor*, and other publications. He has appeared on Fox News (*The O'Reilly Factor*, *The Big Story*), PBS, NPR, and dozens of radio talk shows across the country. He lives in Denver, Colorado.